Harry Potter's World

Pedagogy and Popular Culture

Shirley Steinberg and Joe Kincheloe, Series Editors

Harry Potter's World

Multidisciplinary Critical Perspectives

**Edited by
Elizabeth E. Heilman**

RoutledgeFalmer   New York and London

Published in 2003 by
RoutledgeFalmer
29 West 35th Street
New York, New York 10001
www.routledge-ny.com

Published in Great Britain by
RoutledgeFalmer
11 New Fetter Lane
London EC4P 4EE
www.routledgefalmer.com

Copyright © 2003 by Taylor & Francis Books, Inc.
RoutledgeFalmer is an imprint of the Taylor & Francis Group.

Printed in the United States of America on acid-free paper.

10 9 8 7 6 5 4 3 2 1

Library of Congress Cataloging-in-Publication Data

Harry Potter's World : multidisciplinary critical perspectives / edited by Elizabeth E. Heilman.
    p. cm.
Includes bibliographical references and index.
ISBN 0–415–93373–0—ISBN 0–415–93374–9 (pbk.)
    1. Rowling, J. K.—Criticism and interpretation. 2. Children's stories, English—History and criticism. 3. Fantasy fiction, English—History and criticism. 4. Rowling, J. K.—Characters—Harry Potter. 5. Potter, Harry (Fictitious character) 6. Wizards in literature. 7. Magic in literature. I. Heilman, Elizabeth.

PR6068.O93 Z73 2002
823'.914—dc21   2002021966

To Alex, my amazing son

To my spirit-filled daughters,
Anneliese, Kathleen, and MaryRose

To book-reading sons and daughters everywhere
and the parents and teachers who guide them.

Contents

Acknowledgments

I would like to express my appreciation for the talented cast of scholars who have contributed to this book. I am grateful for their wisdom and insight as they often worked through several drafts and read and commented on other chapters in the collection. This was a collective effort. I also appreciate the critical feedback I received from colleagues JoAnn Phillion, Jill May, and George Font at various stages of this work. I thank my research assistant, Samantha Hopper, for her critical reading and eye for detail, and my dear husband, David Stattelman, for reading and editing my portions of the manuscript.

Heather Day, Barbara Bobbit, and Laurel Bobbit provided valuable editorial assistance and I thank them for their careful work. I am also grateful to Barbara Bobbitt for fourteen years of friendship and our many conversations about gender, race, media, capitalism, power, and culture. I would also like to thank Joanne Braxton and Robert Fehrenbach of the Department of English, and Roger Smith of the Department of Government at the College of William and Mary for the inspiration they provided when I first began the academic study of literature, democracy, and culture; and Jesse Goodman and Robert Arnove of Indiana University, for honoring and helping to hone my critical perspectives. I owe you all my sincerest thanks.

Fostering Critical Insight through Multidisciplinary Perspectives

Elizabeth E. Heilman

I bought my first *Harry Potter* book and read it with my son, Alex, then eleven, because I kept hearing about the books. What I heard was mostly good. I heard that they were exciting and fun—so much so that adults were reading them behind false grown-up covers. Already, in 1998, *Harry Potter* was an unavoidable cultural phenomenon.

Though I was initially put off by the sheer popularity of the books I was intrigued by the idea of transgressive adults wrapping the book in plain paper so they could read it on the subway. This phenomenon has since grown into the biggest children's publishing and merchandising phenomenon of modern times. In 1998, there were no spin-off products, but by the Christmas season of 2001, I was able to find an entire aisle of toys in a major department store devoted to a mind-boggling array of *Harry Potter* paraphernalia.

With more than 100 million copies of Rowling's books in print worldwide in some thirty-five languages, Harry Potter is present in most of the public and cultural spaces in which we live. The narrative story, images, and lessons of the books are infiltrating the lives and imaginations of readers and consumers of related products. I encounter Harry Potter in all sorts of places that I go to regularly—the bookstore, the software dealer, the library, the card shop, and the local schools. I hear *Harry Potter* discussed in coffee shops and on National Public Radio. I see the face of the Harry Potter actor peering out from prosaic magazines such as *TV Guide*, *Ladies Home Journal*, and *Vanity Fair*, and I find references to Harry Potter in the more cerebral offerings of *The New Yorker*, *Atlantic Monthly*, and *Salon*.

When narrative text and images become such a pervasive part of the cultural environment they also become part of the identity of people who read and consume the images and narratives. *Harry Potter* then is not just books we read or movies we see or things we buy. The text and images of *Harry Potter* become part of who we are. This is true of individuals and it is true of "us" as a global culture. *Harry Potter* books have been read, discussed, celebrated, and vilified in Taiwan, Mexico, Mozambique, and Russia. They are read by children in Harlem, children on Indian reservations, and children in Siberia. To a large degree (as Jorge Luis Borges has famously suggested) we are what we read. So, what does the popularity of *Harry Potter* suggest about who we are? What do the books themselves have to say and how do they say it? This book examines *Harry Potter* from some of the major theoretical and critical vantage points for the study of literature and culture. It is my hope that these essays will provide new perspectives on the various themes, literary devices, and ideological viewpoints of the *Harry Potter* books as well as an appreciation for the complexity of meanings literature offers for individuals and for culture more broadly. Yet, there are "only" fourteen chapters in this book. Literature and culture can be examined from multiple theoretical and critical vantage points and each tradition offers extensive points of analysis and implications. There are many other ways in which these books could be analyzed.

Cultural Studies Perspectives

In the first section of this book, Tammy Turner-Vorbeck, Peter Appelbaum, and Deborah J. Taub and Heather L. Servaty explore *Harry Potter* as a cultural phenomenon. Their work is a form of "cultural studies," a critical tradition that draws from the fields of anthropology, communications, history, literary criticism, political theory, sociology, and psychoanalysis in order to critique both texts and cultural practices. The cultural studies movement has redirected literary criticism more broadly into cultural criticism that considers texts in terms of their social, political, economic, and cultural influence rather than their literariness alone, and encourages the study of mass culture and popular forms in addition to elite genres and canonical works. These chapters are not focused so much on looking inside of the books. Instead, they focus on looking at the ways in which the books and the *Harry Potter* phenomenon fit into contemporary culture.

Turner-Vorbeck's chapter, "Pottermania: Good, Clean Fun or Cultural Hegemony?," critically examines the intensive marketing efforts related to the *Harry Potter* books, and product spin-offs, and considers issues of imagination, power, and control. Reading, along with other aspects of child culture, is increasingly becoming an opportunity for marketing and consumerism instead of a private, relatively low-cost, pleasure. Turner-Vorbeck's concerns are supported by Alex Wang whose appendix describes problems with authenticity in the books and movies. But, as Appelbaum argues in chapter 2, "to 'blame' the successes of *Harry Potter* on corporate marketing alone begs the question. After all, some potential product hypes don't make it, while others do. And few of them start out as a quiet book from an unknown author. . . . Do we want to say that children are passive, naive recipients of greedy corporate cultural products?" Appelbaum, in "Harry Potter's World: Magic, Technoculture, and Becoming Human," argues that "the books and associated 'fanware' are key sites for the cultural construction of science and technology, and that in speaking to issues of magic and science, technology and culture, *Harry Potter* is emblematic of the kinds of cultural practices that lead to its popularity."

While Appelbaum sees the books as characteristic of technoculture, Christian censors around the world see the books as diabolic stories encouraging occult practices, magic, and witchcraft. Some parents, who may not be concerned about magic and witchcraft, see the books as yet another example of overly scary and violent media that children should not be exposed to. These matters are important not only for cultural theorists to ponder but also for psychologists and teachers to consider. Exactly how are children influenced (or not) by what they read? In chapter 3, "Controversial Content in Children's Literature: Is *Harry Potter* Harmful to Children," Taub and Servaty explore these issues. They explain that children's responses to literature vary a great deal according to the developmental and psychological contexts in which they are reading.

Reader Response and Interpretive Perspectives

The psychoanalytic view that responses to literature are highly variable and that meaning is a product of individual psychic response to a work is consistent with a broad body of literary theory in which literature is understood as that which is received by the reader rather than that which is created by the author. According to Stanley Fish (1980), reader response theory focuses on "an analysis of the developing responses of the reader in relation to the words as they succeed one another in time" (p. 27). At its most extreme, this theory suggests that the reader is really the author. This idea is consistent with philosophical postmodernism, which emphasizes "local knowledge" and questions the truth of any collective authoritative interpretation or "meta narrative." Chapters 4, 5, and 6 highlight the ways in which readers supply important textual content by projecting their identity, past experiences, preoccupations, and cultural orientations onto the text.

In chapter 4, Kathleen F. Malu observes, "when individuals read texts, they search for different narrative themes. Inevitably readers are drawn to texts because these themes resonate with them or captivate them." Her chapter, "Ways of Reading *Harry Potter*: Multiple Stories for Multiple Reader Identities," explores interpretation. Another example of the ways in which reader identity is related to interpretation is provided by Native American author Hollie Anderson in her chapter 5, "Reading *Harry Potter* with Navajo Eyes." One of the dilemmas with interpretive theory is that it doesn't envision a text as being able to alter, expand, or enrich readers' ideas about themselves or the world. Yet Anderson and Malu suggest that this can occur, particularly when texts are discussed with peers, parents, and teachers.

Some readers take the act of individual response a step further into active creation. Though reading can be understood as a kind of authoring because readers bring so much of themselves to their interpretations, some readers actually write their own episodes or rewrite parts of Rowling's stories. They use the "original" characters, settings, and themes as the basis for the creation of their own stories. Often the new characters and plot twists begin to strongly reflect the identity, life situations, and preoccupations of the author. In chapter 6, Ernest Bond and Nancy Michelson "explore the theoretical underpinnings for the participatory authoring of literary worlds" and then they examine examples of student writing in response to the *Harry Potter* series—particularly writing on the World Wide Web.

Reader response theories suggest that each reader creates a text as they read. Yet, certainly the texts seem to exist on their own. Readers cannot read in a void. Readers' and authors' interpretations are intimately tied up with all previous experiences, including experience of other texts. It may be equally plausible to suggest that, instead of understanding each reading as the creation of a new text, we should think of texts and interpretation as primarily derivative. Anytime we understand something, it is because we relate it to an idea, text, or category we have already seen. Thus, each text and each reading of text is actually intertextual. A book, and even a paragraph, is chock-full of direct and indirect references to these other texts, media, and experiences. There is nothing new under the sun. The debts of texts to other texts seem endless. As Barthes (1977) describes this:

> The text is a tissue of quotations drawn from the innumerable centers of culture . . . the writer can only imitate a gesture that is always interior, never original. His only power is to mix writings, to counter the ones with the others, in such a way as never to rest on any one of them. (pp. 146–47)

From this point of view, a literary work is no longer the product of an author's original thoughts. Instead, the author is a recycler who is limited by the availability of a preexisting language system with words, signs, and symbols, and a preexisting literary system with conventions for things like plot, genre, characterization, images, and narrative voice.

These ideas about literature fall within the broad category labelled "poststructural," which is not a single theory but a group of theories that share similar ideas and a rejection of earlier "structural" approaches to literature. In its most narrow sense, structuralism assumes that a work has intrinsic meaning that preexists the realization of any meaning. If nobody is around to hear a tree falling in a forest, a structuralist would say that there is still a sound, but a poststructuralist would not. Furthermore, a structuralist believes that the individual, the unconscious, and the social and cultural world are all composed of the same signs, codes, and conventions, all working according to similar principles. Literary texts are also structured according to these same signs, codes, and conventions. Literature, consequently, is best understood as a complete system of reference. Individual works can be studied according to the ways in which they both participate in this complete system and possess identifiable literary conventions of language, plot, genre, characterization, images, and narrative voice.

Literary Perspectives: The Hero, Myth, and Genre

Structuralist literary critics believe that they can dissect, evaluate, and describe a text's literariness and importance. What seems tricky here is that this often requires an analysis of the ways in which the text is intertextual or related to other texts. Chapters 7, 8, and 9 constitute critiques that fall, to some extent, within the structuralist tradition. As Genette (1988) describes in *Structuralism and Literary Criticism*, the structuralist critic analyzes the themes, motifs, and key words that create the text.

In chapter 7, "Harry Potter—A Return to the Romantic Hero," Maria Nikolajeva explores the *Harry Potter* novels in terms of "displacement of myth" and genre eclecticism and suggests that Harry "appears as a reaction to a long chain of ironic characters, showing ambiguity in their concepts of good and evil, gender transgression and other tokens of the postmodern aesthetics." In chapter 8, "Generic Fusion and the Mosaic of *Harry Potter,*" Anne Hiebert Alton states that "Rowling's incorporation of a vast number of genres in the books in the tradition of genre criticism. She explains that genres often dismissed as 'despised' genres—including pulp fiction, mystery, gothic and horror stories, detective fiction, the school story and the closely related sports story, and series books—appear throughout the *Harry Potter* books, along with more 'mainstream' genres (at least in children's literature) such as fantasy, adventure, quest romance, and myth" and she concludes that ultimately, "Rowling has fused a number of genres to create something new: a generic mosaic which is a composite, made up of numerous smaller pieces combined in a way that allows them to keep their original shape and structure and yet changes their individual significance, and thus the meaning of the whole." In chapter 9, "Wizardly Challenges to and Affirmations of the Initiation Paradigm in *Harry Potter,*" Deborah De Rosa scrutinizes the ways in which the *Harry Potter* novels conform to and depart from the heroic literary patterns of initiation. In addition to employing genre criticism, these chapters provide examples of archetypal myth criticism. In this type of criticism, writers consider the idea that literature, myths, religion, dreams, and imagination all reflect a "collective unconscious" of archetypal human character types, heroes, and situations.

Critical and Sociological Perspectives

Chapters 10 through 14 of this book examine the treatment of particular themes: home and family (10); learning, knowing, and schooling (11); gender (12); insiders and outsiders (13); and civic leadership (14). These chapters are written in ways that combine elements of both structuralism and cultural studies. Structuralism tends to be a comparative methodology in that a close reading of the text reveals the use of literary themes, patterns, systems, and structures. A critic then compares the use of these elements in one text with other texts. Cultural studies, however, also considers texts in terms of their social, political, economic, and cultural influence rather than their literariness or comparative use of theme alone.

Texts inevitably contain ideological messages about who has power and why and what is of value, and they include commentary on normalcy and success. Ideological critique aims to show how ideology functions both within texts and around texts, since texts are also produced in the midst of certain social, economic, and political contexts. What is allowed to be in print and what is collectively considered to be literature at any given historical point is related to these ideological and power-driven contexts.

Ideological critique encourages critical reading, which enables the reader to understand the subtle and overt ideologies of the text. Ideology can be hard to see because the most compelling ideology comes in the form of the more subtly suggestive and pleasurable reading. Readers can be ideologically influenced without being aware of it. As Foucault affirms, power in modern society can be hard to recognize because "a relationship of power is that mode of action which does not act directly and immediately on others. Instead it acts upon their actions" (Foucault, 1983, p. 229). Yet, readers also respond to ideological messages in different ways. Ideological texts, like other texts, are multivalent. They can be read in multiple ways and in multiple contexts. Also, there are multiple ideologies, not just one ideology.

A postmodern critique of ideology aims to reveal systems of thinking that legitimate particular worldviews and enable oppression, but, at the same time, acknowledges that there is no ideologically free reality to compare it to. In addition, post-Marxist cultural studies of literature attempt to recognize that literature and cultural products can simultaneously represent, reproduce, and transform cultural, political, and institutional norms. They can be both literary and ideological and text can promote both liberation and oppression.

In chapter 10, "Comedy, Conflict, and Community: Home and Family in *Harry Potter*," John Kornfeld and Laurie Prothro examine the ways in which home and family are represented and how these representations compare with other examples in children's literature. They show how "the home and family that Harry finds at Hogwarts gives him the strength to stray and separate as he undertakes his ultimate quest: to find his parents and thereby find his place in the world." In chapter 11, "The Seeker of Secrets: Images of Learning, Knowing, and Schooling," Charles Elster shows how "on the surface, the *Harry Potter* books depict a traditionally dichotomous view of learning: school learning, which is stodgy and bookish, and 'real learning,' which involves solving the big problems

of life. But on second look, this dichotomy is less than adequate in defining the world of Harry Potter. Harry is depicted as an active seeker after
knowledge, a participant in 'inquiry based learning.' And his school learning does contribute to the solution of the mysteries he works hard to solve.
Furthermore, the world of Hogwarts School is one in which learning is
more than the mastery of classroom subjects; it also involves the mastery
of a complex social order of loyalty and competition, and of problematic
teacher-student relationships."

In chapter 12, I examine gender identity conventions and hierarchies
in the *Harry Potter* books and reveal that the *Harry Potter* books often feature females in secondary positions of power and authority and replicate
some of the most demeaning, yet familiar, cultural stereotypes. The girls
often giggle, cry, and gossip. Physically unattractive girls are shunned. Yet
boys are also stereotypically portrayed with the strong, adventurous, independent boy serving as a heroic expression of masculinity, while the weak,
nonsuccessful male is mocked and sometimes despised. In chapter 13,
"Images of the Privileged Insider and Outcast Outsider," I write with
Anne E. Gregory that, "because text helps to form our perspectives of the
world, it is important to consider what types of cultural information is
being transmitted to us about social class, peer group affiliations, abil-
ity/disability, culture, and nationality through the characters and their
positioning in these books."

Finally, in chapter 14, "The Civic Leadership of *Harry Potter*: Agency,
Ritual, and Schooling," Rebecca Skulnick and Jesse Goodman analyze
how J. K. Rowling positions Harry Potter as a civic leader. This chapter
ultimately brings us full circle by ending with a narrative vignette of a fifth
grade classroom in which censorship and popular culture collide. They
observe that "*Harry Potter* tells us that the institution is a place of goodness; if you only trust in the institution, or act as Harry and perform rites
of heroism in favor of the institution, the institution will support the interests of the children." They question what happens "when principals make
decisions based on the politics of their constituents, when teachers do not
act out of fear of losing their jobs; when students rip up books because
they cannot read."

Conclusion

I have assembled this collection as a curriculum theorist dedicated to the
notion that democracy and social justice must rely on the critical intellec-

tual insights, civic courage, and imaginative power of communities, rather than the best ideas of any authority. The critical study of literature and culture is essential to such a vision. In the postmodern context in which we live, cultural products promoted by multinational corporations can serve as a powerful form of authority promoting unequal relations of power and a dreary aesthetic. Yet, literature and culture can be read in many ways, particularly with assistance from critical works such as this. We can talk back to *Harry Potter*. In order to have rich conversations and develop critical insight and imagination, I contend that the engagement of popular and literary texts should draw from multiple paradigms and employ multiple theoretical lenses.

In this collection, I have tried to provide a multidisciplinary framework that can bring interesting and potent theories to students of literature, children, their parents, and their teachers. I hope this text helps to bridge the gap between critical theory and critical pedagogy. Though literary theory has moved away from structuralism and New Criticism to include poststructuralist and cultural studies analyses, these approaches have had little effect on the ways in which literature in taught in undergraduate studies and even less in K–12. Similarly, though there is an increasing body of scholarship on critical pedagogy, critical literacy, multiculturalism, and critical and reflective social studies, things have changed very little across the curriculum.

Thus, in addition to the significance of this collection for literary and cultural studies, this book is important because it can help parents and teachers to make school curriculum and conversations about books more meaningful. Exploring critical and liberating ways of reading is certainly a valuable goal, but it is hard to do, even with support.

Chapters providing "Reader Response and Interpretive Perspectives" can help teachers think about the complexity of reader's motivations and responses. Chapters on "The Hero, Myth, and Genre" can help children understand literary structures. The "Critical and Sociological" chapters can help parents and teachers stimulate powerful discussions and integrate powerful curricular themes considering who has power in society. These chapters can give support for discussions about the construction of identity, the meaning of home, the difference between schooling and learning, and what it means to be a leader.

Curriculum—especially Social Studies and English—can potentially serve as a vehicle for deconstructing these complex issues. Without support, teachers developing curriculum around these books sometimes focus on trivia, for example, having students create models of Hogwarts School or invent their own flavor of Every Flavor Bean. Much critical scholarship asks teachers to use powerful critical themes, address popular culture, and make meaningful connections to students' interests. This book gives teachers a tool to do so on a range of levels, examining the relationship among cultural products and power at the macro level of political and economic structures—but also at the micro level, considering cultural and aesthetic nuances in language, texts, and personal responses.

References

Barthes, R. (1977). *Image, Music, Text.* New York: Hill and Wang, 1977.

———. "The Death of the Author." In *Image, Music, Text.* Trans. S. Heath. New York: Hill and Wang; 1977. 142–48.

Fish, S. *Is There a Text in this Class?: The Authority of Interpretive Communities.* Cambridge: Harvard UP, 1980.

Foucault, M. "The Subject and Power." In *Michel Foucault: Beyond Hermeneutics and Structuralism.* Chicago: U of Chicago P, 1983. 208–26.

Genette, G. "Structuralism and Literary Criticism." In *Modern Criticism and Theory.* Ed. David Lodge. New York: Longman, 1988.

Part I

Cultural Studies Perspectives

Chapter One

Pottermania: Good, Clean Fun or Cultural Hegemony?

Tammy Turner-Vorbeck

Pottermania has become a cultural phenomenon. The *Harry Potter* books, the *Harry Potter* movie, the related media publicity, and an expanding selection of heavily marketed paraphernalia permeate our popular culture and have significant societal implications for children and for child culture. This cultural phenomenon reaches far beyond its seductive surface appearance of good, clean, fantastical childhood fun (Monk, 2000; Papinchak, 2000) into a darker place where the psyche of American children, both collectively and individually, is made vulnerable and their process of identity construction, their beliefs, and their childhoods are for sale.

The purposeful infringement on and manipulation of children and child culture by corporate interests is both serious and alarming and it deserves critical examination. This chapter seeks to frame such a critical examination through both sociological and cultural studies perspectives. The cultural commercialization of childhood and the Neo-Marxist view of the role of media in creating cultural hegemony will be discussed. The *Harry Potter* books participate in cultural hegemony by featuring social normative messages and middle-class cultural hierarchies. Finally, human agency and the possibility for resistance to the preponderance of commodity fetishism, of which *Harry Potter* is an example, is considered.

The Cultural Commercialization of Childhood

Corporate consumerism is increasingly targeting child culture. Contemporary elements of child culture, such as television, movies, and computer games, were created in the age of late capitalism and have always been closely associated with marketing tactics, such as print advertising and commercials in the electronic media. Recently, however, the traditional icons of child culture, such as children's literature, toys, art, and music, have been and continue to be increasingly infiltrated and manipulated through the skillfully crafted images of marketing and media giants such as the Disney Corporation. "Disney's all-encompassing reach into the spheres of economics, consumption, and culture suggests that we analyze Disney within a range of relations of power" (Giroux, 1998, p. 63). Pottermania has reached the level of cultural phenomenon that deserves similar consideration. Like Disney's before (and probably after) the *Harry Potter* phenomenon, one need only stroll through the aisles of any large, American department store to find evidence of Pottermania's impending legacy on the images of childhood.

In their book *Kinderculture: The Corporate Construction of Childhood*, Steinberg and Kincheloe (1998) critique the corporate construction of childhood and state:

> Using fantasy and desire, corporate functionaries have created a perspective on late-twentieth-century culture that melds with business ideologies and free-market values. The worldviews produced by corporate advertisers to some degree always let children know that the most exciting things life can provide are produced by your friends in corporate America. The economics lesson is powerful when it is repeated hundreds of thousands of times. (p. 4)

Should it be alarming that a fundamental element of childhood, such as the pleasure of reading a good book, is now targeted by those who seek to shape the collective imagination of an identifiable demographic buying unit en masse? The *Harry Potter* phenomenon, or Pottermania, presents a focal point through which to consider this and related questions. The fact that the *Harry Potter* books and their associated paraphernalia are cultural products created and produced by adults for consumption by children is clear. These cultural products and elements of child culture contain powerful messages of what constitutes social and cultural normalcy and they, therefore, call for continuing critique.

When children's identities and child culture are used as the means to the end of creating the consummate future consumer, one must seriously question the proclaimed innocuousness of Pottermania. Henry Giroux warns in his book *Stealing Innocence* that "as culture becomes increasingly commercialized, the only type of citizenship that adult society offers to children is that of consumerism" (2000, p. 19). This notion holds significant implications for not only relationships between adults and children but also for the future of our society as a whole.

The fact that children today are living in a postmodern world facilitates corporate consumerism's full frontal attack on child culture. Strinati (1993) describes postmodernism as the breakdown of the distinction between culture and society. The idea is that popular cultural signs and media images increasingly dominate our sense of reality and the way we define ourselves and the world around us (p. 360). Kellner (1998) argues that child culture's traditional artifacts are being replaced and manipulated by media culture artifacts. He is concerned that

> a commercially produced and dominated youth culture has replaced traditional artifacts of children's culture. In this media youth culture, popular music, television, film, and video and computer games create new idols, aspirations, and artifacts that profoundly influence the thought and behavior of contemporary youth. (p. 85)

Our postmodern children are living in a state that Baudrillard (1983) calls *hyperreality* in which simulation and appearance come to be more "real" and meaningful to children than substance and reality. Children are continually bombarded with information and supersaturated by the media. Disney is a classic representation of corporate consumerism meets the postmodern world. Giroux writes that Baudrillard "has captured the scope and power of Disney's influence by arguing that Disneyland is more 'real' than fantasy because it now provides an image upon which America constructs itself" (1998, p. 55). But what *is* the significance of corporate consumerism's targeting of child culture when children today are living in a postmodern hyperreality? The answer to this inquiry lies in the interrelationship of our culture and societal institutions and the divergent individual ways these are mediated by children.

A Neo-Marxist Perspective on the Media

Although long criticized for its overly deterministic and reductionist emphasis, Marxism is nonetheless able to lend its central tenets for a useful critical examination of societal and cultural phenomenon. Marxist critical theory can be used to examine Pottermania and explore the questions concerning the significance of its impact upon our culture and our society. "Marxist critical theory draws our attention to the issue of political and economic interests in the mass media and highlight social inequalities in media representations" (Chandler, 2001, p. 14).

A central tenet of Neo-Marxism affirms "Cultures are structured in ways that enable the dominant group holding power to have the maximum control with the minimum of conflict" (Lye, 1997, p. 1). In this light, ideas of the way things are and how the world should and does work are taught for legitimization of the current order of society. Cultural values and practices are constructed to appear normal and natural, rendering them beyond question. Thus, when Pottermania features corporations imprinting upon and manipulating children and child culture, it is not viewed as anything unusual or threatening. The books and related products are seen as good, clean, capitalist fun rather than something sinister in need of perlustration.

Childhood and child culture represent prime opportunities for exercising such ideological control.[1] Woodson (1999) states:

> Children are a prerequisite for cultural reproduction over time and childhood literally exists as the site of enculturation. Adults and social institutions are invested in ascribing meaning onto and into childhood in order to maintain social order and the socialization of children negotiates not only behavior patterns but also identity formation. (p. 3)

Inasmuch as diligent awareness and governance over what takes place at this "site of enculturation" seems paramount, yet, these approaches simply do not occur when cultural phenomena such as Pottermania are uncritically received and viewed as part of the natural landscape of American childhood.

According to Chandler (2001), Neo-Marxist Louis Althusser:

> Introduced the concept of a mechanism of interpellation, whereby subjects (produced by culture) are constituted as the effects of pre-given structures. Ideology functions to constitute individuals (produced by nature) as subjects. Individuals are interpellated (have social identities conferred on them) primarily through "ideological state apparatuses (ISAs), including the family, schooling, and the mass media. It is through ISAs that people gain both a sense of identity and an understanding of reality. (p. 7)

Pottermania can and should be examined through this sort of Neo-Marxist lens to consider the political and social functions of these mass media texts. As Chandler (2001) describes, "The subject (viewer, listener, reader) is constituted by the text and the power of the mass media resides in its ability to 'position' the subject in such a way that their representation are taken to be reflections of everyday reality" (p. 7).

Most scholars of child culture believe that children are *participants* in their own cultural production and expression. Similarly, they contend that the ways in which children interpret media are subject to their daily life experiences and environment. This notion is synchronous with the per-spective of Cultural Marxism whose primary figure is a contemporary, Stuart Hall. Using Althusser's premises, Hall (1982) argues that the media *appear* to reflect reality when, in fact, they *construct* it. Hall supports Althusser's idea that the mass media do reproduce interpretations (from ideas that are embedded in symbols and cultural practices) that serve the interests of the ruling class, but he also supports the idea that the mass media are a field of ideological struggle. However, how much struggle is really possible when confronted with a capitalist marketing machine that seduces its public through normative messages consisting of comfortable, familiar images and the appearance of "good, clean fun"? Is it realistic to believe that child culture can be a place of ideological struggle in the face of commodity fetishism?

Commodity Fetishism

The infringement of consumerism on child culture is particularly evident in the mass marketing of the *Harry Potter* products. Far beyond the *Harry Potter* books currently published by Scholastic, Inc., we now have the *Harry Potter* movies from Warner Brothers (of AOL Time Warner), which are also to be available on DVD for private use and ownership. This first, wildly successful movie is scheduled to be followed by other *Harry Potter* movie sequels. Available for sale is a movie poster book, a movie soundtrack, a wall calendar, postcard books, sticker books, a guidebook to the world of Harry Potter, a *Harry Potter* UNO card game, carrying cases, glow-in-the-dark puzzles, board games, video games, magic sets, books of spells, Hogwarts House Watches, a Golden Snitch puzzle, Harry Potter boxer shorts, Harry Potter action figures, Bertie Bott's Every Flavor Beans, the textbooks that the character of Harry Potter used in the *Harry Potter* books, and even a Harry Potter leather embossed trunk to "store books, clothes, and more."

The proliferation of these items constitute a blatant exploitation of the genuine excitement for children's literature that stems from children's true interests. In the effort to create more profits for its shareholders, con-glomerates, such as AOL Time Warner, which holds distribution rights to *Harry Potter* products, supersaturate the marketplace with every conceiv-able spin-off product. In addition to the products themselves, these media giants use their distribution channels, which they also own and operate, to supersaturate the media with advertisements and news stories for their products. For example, when Warner Brother's studios makes an investment, as it did by purchasing the movie rights for *Harry Potter*, it can then turn to its sister companies within the same organization to help ensure the movie's profitability. They can make a short story run in the widely respected periodical *Time* magazine describing the "phenomenon" of Harry Potter and how children in the United Kingdom are wildly enthusiastic about the books. Then, AOL's CNN news subsidiary begins making headlines about the "phenomenon." Shortly after the "phenomenon" makes headlines, Pottermania is scheduled for a special interest segment in primetime news on CNN and also on CNN Classroom, bringing the "phenomenon" directly to the children in schools. Perhaps AOL's *People* magazine also concurrently runs a biography on J. K. Rowling. *Fortune* and *Money* magazines could also be called upon for support as they are all controlled by the same megacorporation, AOL Time Warner. Once the "phenomenon" takes root, AOL Time Warner has vast advertising capabilities within its own reach. Commercial advertising begins on its own TBS Superstation, TNT, and The Cartoon Network. In all, AOL Time Warner boasts access in one form or another to over 100 million U.S. households. It creates and then supports the phenomenon of Pottermania.

This is an example of the business model concept of vertical integration in which megacorporations control the entire process of distribution. By using its vast enterprise to *infuse* popular culture with Pottermania, the conglomerate then controls every commercial aspect of Pottermania and they, therefore, "own" a significant segment of popular culture. The insidious nature of all of this is that these corporations not only own a segment of popular culture through their control of the commodity but also they *created the fetishism*—the need, the desire, and the very market—for that commodity! Such commodity fetishism is even modeled in the *Harry Potter* books themselves as the children among the characters long to purchase particular kinds of brooms and trading cards.

The fundamental implication at work here is that there need be nothing aesthetically valuable or unique about that upon which an imposed phenomenon is generated. Is it something special about the *Harry Potter* books that has caused such a sensation or is the sensation artificially manufactured and simply centered around them? An understanding of commodity fetishism supports the latter position. If the *Harry Potter* books were, indeed, worthy of such widespread adulation, then the support for them would have naturally risen up from the people rather than being pushed down upon them by mass media marketing.

Corporate consumerism's mass marketing of manufactured cultural products does not simply represent its infringement upon and control over the articles of child culture; it also involves exercising control over the imaginations of children. When children are no longer able to sit with a book and create its images, sounds, voices, smells, and sensations from their own act of reading, they have been robbed of the free use of their own minds. Take the example of a third grader who has seen all of the media hype for the *Harry Potter* movie on television and in print advertisements along with the related products brought to school by her classmates. She considers herself deprived as she is one of the last students in her class who has still not seen the *Harry Potter* movie. She pleads with her parents to go and see the movie and, after doing so, she decides to buy the first *Harry Potter* book in the series. She sits down to read the book with the images from the advertising, the commercials, the movie, and the product spin-offs all swirling around in her mind, creating even more anticipation. She then emerges within thirty minutes from her bedroom to announce to her parents that the book is nothing like she expected and she is bored with it. This is the story of my own eight-year-old daughter.

What is the moral of this story? Once a cultural phenomenon such as Pottermania takes hold, the majority of children are destined to find their first exposure not to the authentic items of child culture (in this case, the *Harry Potter* book itself). Rather, their first experience is often with the marketing spin-offs, which represent corporate America's interpretation of the real thing. In this respect, children's imaginations are certainly being severely limited and led through corporate mass marketing. However, as if encroachment upon children's imaginations is not bad enough, what is perhaps even more alarming is that these manufactured images feature embedded social normative messages. What are these messages and what are their implications?

Social Normative Messages

It is no longer safe to assume that children are able to generate purely their own reflections upon items of child culture such as literature for children. The trespassing of manufactured images into the landscape of the imagination of children is limiting children's capacities to freely imagine; yet, these manufactured images also come with both overt and covert embedded messages. Cultural products aimed at children now seem to inspire as much, if not more, cultural authority and legitimacy for teaching children specific roles, values, and ideals as that wielded by the more traditional sites of learning, such as the public schools, religious institutions, and the family (Giroux, 1998). The power that the creators of these messages wield is both enormous and significant. This fact warrants careful and critical consideration of the type of messages that those cultural products are sending to children.

In this book, Heilman and Gregory, Kornfeld and Prothro, Goodman and Skulnick, and Heilman (among others) explore how ideology functions within the *Harry Potter* texts through critical reading and ideological critique. The Gregory and Heilman chapter in this book examines the process of intertextuality in forming world perspectives through the reading of the *Harry Potter* texts. The authors argue that it is necessary to "consider what types of cultural information is being transmitted." Specifically, they explore social normative messages present in the *Harry Potter* texts that involve social class, peer group affiliations, race, culture, and nationality. Kornfeld and Prothro use their chapter to discuss the treatment of home and family in the *Harry Potter* texts. They uncover stereotypical roles of dominant, head-of the-household father and stay-at-home mothers who are the primary caretakers of house and family, along with messages about the importance of conformity in which "the parents' prime directive seems to be to fit in and make no waves."

The Heilman chapter finds that the *Harry Potter* books "feature females in secondary positions of power and authority and replicate some of the most demeaning, yet familiar, cultural stereotypes for both males and females."

The *Harry Potter* books feature images of nuclear families without the inclusion of representations of the divorced, step, single, gay or lesbian, or adoptive or foster families of our contemporary society. The books also reinforce cultural stereotypes of power and gender, consistently portraying women as secondary characters. In addition, there is little cultural diversity represented and, when it is presented, it is in the form of tokenism and colonialism. Racialized groups of wizards, giants, and other creatures are presented in a hierarchical order in which racial difference creates one's social place. Such social normative messages about families, community, race, and gender exemplify who is *not* a part of the conversation by the exclusion of their representation in the texts. What appears to be represented in the *Harry Potter* books, then, is an aggregation of quintessential, hegemonic, hierarchical middle-class social and cultural values.

The fact that the social normative messages in the Harry Potter texts are ones of exclusivity is bothersome and warrants critical attention, but there are additional inherent implications here. When voices are excluded from the conversation, or in this case, from the text, there is another, subtle message being transmitted. As Giroux (2000) explains, "When adults cling to the idea that a thriving free market economy, with its insidious consumer-based appropriation of freedom and choice, provides the greatest good for the greatest number . . . it is easier for adults to claim that social problems are individual problems" (p. 6). Therefore, those not represented in the texts, those not living the good life, those being oppressed, persecuted, abused, neglected, or simply left behind by mainstream society must be somehow to blame. It is made inconceivable, from this perspective, that society itself might be to blame. Reinforced by these dominant messages it is easier and more comfortable to believe that such societal ills are the result of the problems and deficiencies of individuals themselves. Giroux (2000) writes:

> Little is mentioned about the violence perpetuated by those middle-class values and social formations—such as conspicuous consumption, conformity, snobbery, and ostracism—that reproduce racial, class, and gender exclusions. Nor is much said about how middle-class values legitimate and regulate the cultural hierarchies that demean marginalized groups and reinforce racial and economic inequalities. (p. 17)

If these social problems are viewed as incidental (outside of the middle-class world) and a result of individual deficiencies and errors, there is no reason to be alarmed, to try to change it or to resist cultural hegemony found in unexamined places such as Pottermania. Where can one turn in order to begin to find hope that the process of cultural hegemony can be interrupted?

Human Agency and Resistance

Structural Neo-Marxist and Cultural Marxist theories provide useful theoretical tenets with which to view the cultural phenomenon of Pottermania. Using Neo-Marxism as a lens, attention is drawn to political and economic interests in corporate consumerism and the mass media and the resultant social inequalities constructed and reinforced in media and text representations. However, strictly examining the ways in which humans are acted upon by such cultural hegemonic structures leaves out a vital element of the equation, namely, human agency. Expanding these tenets of structural Neo-Marxism to poststructuralist concerns with power and knowledge and adding notions of human agency and resistance magnifies their power. One of the major representatives for poststructuralist thought is Michel Foucault (sometimes also labeled as a postmodernist, along with Baudrillard) who initially focused upon structures but moved beyond that focus to examine power and the linkage between power and knowledge. Power, in the form of cultural hegemony through corporate consumerism's creation and manufacture of Pottermania, is difficult to identify because "A relationship of power is that mode of action which does not act directly and immediately on others. Instead it acts upon their actions" (Foucault, 1983, p. 229). Despite Foucault's notion of the insidious way in which power is enacted upon people, critical theorists such as Pierre Bourdieu have continued to attempt to link agency and structure in a meaningful way. Bourdieu (1990), who considers the question of the opposition between objectivism and subjectivism, states that such a strictly structuralist view creates an "absurd opposition between individual and society" (p. 31). This shift in perspective helps to bring back the promise of an individual's ability to reflect upon his or her own situation. Crediting resistance theorists with combining ethnographic and European cultural studies to attempt to demonstrate that social and cultural reproduction can and does meet with elements of opposition, Aronowitz and Giroux (1993) state that "resistance theorists have developed a framework and method of inquiry that restores the critical notion of agency" (p. 67). The focus on how power and hegemony create subordinate social classes as seen through a structuralist perspective is tempered through resistance theory to "restore a degree of agency and innovation to the cultures of these groups" (p. 68). These theories of resistance with their emphasis on human agency indicate that there is hope for our ability to talk back to the social normative messages we constantly and consistently receive through corporate consumerism's waging of a war of cultural hegemony. How might this resistance occur? What tools do we have at our disposal? Where do we begin?

Talking Back to Pottermania

A characteristic of late capitalism is that human thinking becomes mechanized as the mind begins to correspond to a machine. In this way, the human mind becomes a segmented and degraded instrument that has lost its capacity for critical thought, "especially its ability to imagine another way of life" (Aronowitz, 1992, p. 80). What, then, are the possibilities for resistance? To create room for resistance, awareness must be raised and critical thought must be allowed to return. In order the achieve this, space must be created in between the imposed phenomena and the people from whom the phenomena allegedly arose. There are obvious fronts on which to fight this battle: literary criticism and media literacy. It is within literary criticism that the true, aesthetic value of children's books can be critically considered and it is within the view of the media as a site for ideological struggle that hope lies for the possibility of resistance to the ravages of Pottermania on child culture.

When considering the huge success of Pottermania, critical questions should come to mind, "What is special about the *Harry Potter* books?" and "Are they deserving of such a heralded place in our culture?" Jack Zipes (2001) uses a Marxist critical theory perspective to examine children's literature. He warns: "Phenomena such as the Harry Potter books are driven by commodity consumption that at the same time sets the parameters of reading and aesthetic taste" (p. 172). Pennington (2002) likewise warns that "the series is fundamentally failed fantasy" (p. 1). Zipes argues that the Harry Potter series is not a reinvention and reinvigoration of the fantasy genre but rather a less than admirable example of what good fantasy writing can be. He also warns, as do authors of chapters in this book, that the *Harry Potter* books contain dangerous themes such as sexism. The fact that the *Harry Potter* books are able to be critically examined and determined to be aesthetically "failed fantasy," containing dangerous social normative messages, supports the argument that perhaps these books are not innocuous, good, clean fun and that the implications of the cultural phenomenon surrounding these books needs to be further scrutinized.

Beyond the inquiry into the aesthetic value of children's literature and the social messages found within books lies the additional promise of the creation of a media literate public, consisting of both adults and children. This aspect of "talking back" to Pottermania is crucial as it represents a chance for resistance against the corporate mass marketing machines that have come to dictate what constitutes popular culture. McLaren et al. (1995) emphasize that developing a critical understanding of the media is crucial for teachers, parents, and children and that it needs to go beyond interpreting the meaning found in media messages. Media literacy, in a broad sense, refers to the ability of individuals both to reflect upon and to analyze their own consumption of media and how they are subtly influenced by media messages. This kind of critical thinking is capable of beginning to create the necessary space between the people and their real artifacts of culture and the artificially manufactured phenomena of Pottermania. The authors of these chapters hope that this book can help readers to do just that.

Notes

1. This is not always a matter of groups deliberately planning to oppress people or alter their consciousness (although this can happen) but rather a matter of how the dominant institutions in society work through values, conceptions of the world, and symbol systems to legitimize the current order (Lye, 1997).

References

Aronowitz, S. *The Politics of Identity*. New York: Routledge, 1992.

Aronowitz, S., and H. Giroux. *Education Still Under Siege*. (2nd ed.) Westport: Bergin and Garvey, 1993.

Baudrillard, J. *Simulations*. Trans. N. Dufresne. New York: Semiotext(e), 1983.

Bourdieu, P. *In Other Words: Essays toward a Reflexive Sociology*. Cambridge: Polity P, 1983.

Chandler, D. *Marxist Media Theory*. 2001.
    <http:www.aber.ac.uk/media/Documents/Marxism/marxism13.html>

Foucault, M. "The Subject and Power." In *Michel Foucault: Beyond Hermeneutics and Structuralism*. Chicago: U of Chicago P, 1983.

Giroux, H. A. "Are Disney movies good for your kids?" In *Kinderculture: The Corporate Construction of Childhood*. Ed. S. R. Steinberg and J. L. Kincheloe. Boulder: Westview Press, 1998.

———. *Stealing Innocence*. New York: St. Martin's P, 2000.

Hall, S. "The Rediscovery of 'Ideology': Return of the Repressed in Media Studies. In *Culture, Society and the Media*. Ed. M. Gurevitch, T. Bennett, J. Curran, and J. Woollacott. London: Methuen, 1982.

Harry Potter and the Sorcerer's Stone. Dir. C. Columbus. Prod. D. Heyman. Warner Brothers, 2001.

Kellner, D. "Beavis and Butt-Head: No Future for Postmodern Youth." In *Kinderculture: The Corporate Construction of Childhood*. Ed. S. R. Steinberg and J. L. Kincheloe. Boulder: Westview P, 1998.

Lye, J. *Ideology: A Brief Guide*. 1997. <http:www.brocku.ca/English/jlye/ideology.html>

McLaren, P., R. Hammer, D. Sholle, and S. Reilly. *Rethinking Media Literacy: A Critical Pedagogy of Representation*. New York: Peter Lang, 1995.

Monk, J. "Harry Potter Books Are the Best Thing to Happen to Kids in Years." *Library Talk* 13.2 (2000): 23.

Papinchak, R. Rev. of *Harry Potter and the Goblet of Fire* by J. K. Rowling. *People* 54.4 (2000): 43.

Pennington, J. "From Elfland to Hogwarts, or the Aesthetic Trouble with Harry Potter." *The Lion and the Unicorn* 26.1 (2002): 78–97.

Rowling, J. K. *Harry Potter and the Sorcerer's Stone*. New York: Scholastic P, 1997.

———. *Harry Potter and the Chamber of Secrets*. New York: Scholastic P, 1998.

———. *Harry Potter and the Prisoner of Azkaban*. New York: Scholastic P, 1999.

———. *Harry Potter and the Goblet of Fire*. New York: Scholastic P, 2000.

Steinberg, S. R., and Kincheloe, J. L. "Introduction: No More Secrets—Kinderculture, Information Saturation, and the Postmodern Childhood." In *Kinderculture: The Corporate Construction of Childhood*. Ed. S. R. Steinberg and J. L. Kincheloe. Boulder: Westview P, 1998.

Strinati, D. "The Big Nothing? Contemporary Culture and the Emergence of Postmodernism." *Innovation: The European Journal of Social Sciences* 6.3 (1993): 359–75.

Woodson, S. E. "Mapping the Cultural Geography of Childhood or, Performing Monstrous Children." *Journal of American Culture* 22.4 (1999): 31–44.

Zipes, J. *Sticks and Stones: The Troublesome Success of Children's Literature from* Slovenly Peter *to* Harry Potter. New York: Routledge, 2001.

Chapter Two

Harry Potter's World: Magic, Technoculture, and Becoming Human

Peter Appelbaum

Engaging audience

It is important to remember that we all have magic inside of us.
—J. K. Rowling (attributed to Rowling at the Harry Potter Lexicon,
2000, Steve Vander Ark http://www.i2k.com/
~svderark/lexicon/w_spells.html)

Some people are still asking, "What is it about J. K. Rowling's *Harry Potter* books that has made them so popular?" I want to ask, "What is it about our culture that embraces the *Harry Potter* books and has turned *Harry Potter* into such a phenomenon?" There are more subtle and interesting things to look at than, say, the general content of the books. Popular works by successful children's authors, such as Jane Yolen (*Wizard's Hall*, 1991), Phillip Pullman (*Golden Compass*, 1996), Lois Lowry (*The Giver*, 1993), and Natalie Babbitt (*Tuck Everlasting*, 1975), for example, have enjoyed excellent marketing of novels that evoke parallel worlds, magic, and folklore. Each has a preadolescent protagonist beginning to negotiate the psychosocial crisis of individual versus group identity. *Harry Potter* hype may also share characteristics with other recent promotional schemes and product tie-ins, such as *Pokemon, Power Puff Girls, Power Rangers, WWF WarZone*, and so on. But to "blame" the successes of *Harry Potter* on corporate marketing alone begs the question. After all, some potential product hypes don't make it, whereas others do. And few of them start out as a quiet book from an unknown author. To interpret the *Harry Potter* successes as one of corporate culture preying on innocent children (Giroux, 2000) would, I suggest, perpetuate inappropriate assumptions. I wish to debunk three of these *pre*-sumptions: Can we say that consumer culture has trumped all other possible manifestations of liberal democracy? Rather, it may be that market dynamics and individual agency are far more complex. Do we want to say that children are passive, naive recipients of greedy corporate cultural products? Surely children and others act as agents of social change even as they behave in certain socially reproductive ways.

Can we understand the cultural meanings of *Harry Potter* stories (or any other popular cultural artifact) as distanced observers? I suggest that distanced interpretations further collapse the cultural story of *Harry Potter* into the world of children's literature, ignoring the wider range of readers (including college students and other adults)[1] and the cultural phenomena of *Harry Potter* beyond the books themselves (e.g., *Harry Potter* toys; diaries, and other bookstore impulse items; towels, mirrors, and other home decorating products; websites, filk,[2] and other fanware). One thing I have learned from cultural studies is that textual analysis is not enough. Nor is it enough to present a well-honed social analysis of popular culture phenomena (Daspit & Weaver, 1998). It is important to understand how children and other *Harry Potter* fans "read" and interpret the books, cultural products, consumer items, and fanware—the details of the *Harry Potter* culture—as cultural resources out of which people make sense of themselves (Fiske, 1990). It is especially important to learn from people how they "use" popular culture resources to make sense of their lives, their culture, and their fears and fantasies, and through such mediation, to construct new modes of meaning (Eco, 1979; de Certeau, 1984; Appelbaum, 1999).

In this chapter, I describe some of what I have learned through talking with young people in informal and formal interviews about the ways that the popularity of *Harry Potter* texts dovetails well with other mass culture phenomena. I focus particularly on those aspects of *Harry Potter* that speak to issues of technology, magic, and the role of science as popular culture resources. I argue that the books and associated "fanware" are key sites for the cultural construction of science and technology; in speaking to issues of magic and science, technology and culture, *Harry Potter* is emblematic of the kinds of cultural practices that lead to its popularity. Within these cultural practices, we can see science and technology mediating our "common sense." At the same time, socially constructed expectations produce what we know as science and what we recognize as technology. This all happens in and out of science as practiced by scientists, and in and out of our popular cultures. All of this is mixed up and interwoven and, together, called "cultural practices." Within these cultural practices, specific images and conventions are identified as icons of science and technology, indeed, the way the world works; other images become icons for magic, mysticism, and other categories of cultural practices that, for most of us, serve to distinguish what we call science from what we call not-science.

These cultural practices, ways of thinking, and icons, along with their use as metaphors, are what I think of as "technoculture." Technoculture is thus the amalgam of our postmodern society, heavily mediated by and productive of science and technology, both as popular cultures, cultural practices, and icons—and as constructed significantly via science and technology itself. When we listen to children and learn about youth culture, magic and technoculture stand out as essential to the project of becoming human (Appelbaum, 1999). Popular culture narratives set up a kind of hero who confronts technoculture through technoculture itself. And when we listen to readers of *Harry Potter*, we see that the books and fanware are not culturally unique. Instead, they are consistent with technocultural themes of morality and identity in a postmodern society. Children experience power and violence differently from adults, and their notions of magic and technology can be different as well. Caught up in magic and technology is the role of wonder: How teachers respond to children's wonderings about the natural world combines with children's own interpretations of that world. The combination constructs powerful forms of cultural dynamics and conceptions of technology. In both the *Harry Potter* books and in children's lives, school functions to accentuate what constitutes technologies, what constitutes magic and wonder, and, finally, through consumer culture, what it means to become a human being. In this way, I find that the books and the culture that embraces them buttress each others' postmodern efforts to fulfill an outdated enlightenment fantasy of utopia through technology.

The Technoculture of Consumer Culture in and out of School

For children growing up in and with technoculture, concepts of cyborg imagery, biological monsters, fantasy characters, power, knowledge, magic, and prosthetic extensions of self are not categorical. Many things that adults see as newfangled or that cause anxieties are accepted by young people as inherent components of the "natural" world. Thus an adult fear of dehumanization through technology might translate into a performance of identity or a social connection for a child. Obversely, a young person's sense of danger may translate into a technological task for an adult. For a child, technology may be magic or science; power may be a fantasy or a monstrous myth. For a number of the children I have spoken with in my research, power can emerge out of a persistence in seeking knowledge; for others it may be understood as a gift bestowed by biological luck. Knowledge for the children I have spoken with may be conflated with power or magically lost. On the other hand, technology may be a prize or a tool of adult power (Appelbaum, 1999). Thus, we find that chemistry sets are surprisingly popular because children want to pretend to be in a potions class at Hogwarts. Also popular are Animal Planet's sound-enhanced animal toys because Hagrid's Care of Magical Creatures class has tapped into children's simultaneous fear of and love for animals.

Technocentric utopianism for many children is really more aptly described as melancholic acceptance of responsibility. Common wisdom describes technocultural popular culture as a working through of adult fears and fantasies (Waught, 1947; Wright, 2001). Early superhero technoculture reenacted the cold war conflicts of good guys and bad guys in a battle for humanity and the universe. Historians of popular culture (Waugh, 1947; Wright, 2001; Appelbaum, 1999; Napier, 2001) suggest distinct evolution through several periods that characterize the nature of the heroes and the narrative structure in particular ways. Following good guy versus bad guy constructs of the cold war, subsequent cultural commodities demonstrate a phase of inner psychological turmoil, splitting the good versus evil battle into a multiplicity of conflicting identities. For example, Batman and Spiderman, two heroes plagued with inner, psychological turmoil and battling villains who suffer from countless psychological disorders, replaced Superman, a strong, almost invincible boy from small town USA. The literature on popular culture (Napier, 2001; Wright, 2001; Poitras, 2000; Levi, 1996; Rushkoff, 1996) suggests that this psychological phase was subsumed more recently by the *anime* hero. This hero is a "gundam"[3] child who inherits the aftermath of technological havoc wreaked by adults; the hero dons prosthetic devices scavenged from an inherited wasteland in a Romantic gesture of faith in the ultimate goodness of humanity. Gundam children are present in television programs, animated films, video games, role-playing games, and other forms of entertainment.

Harry Potter, the young hero of the books that carry his name, is characterized very much in the spirit of the gundam hero. He is thrust into the most serious fights of good and evil, the ultimate outcome of which will determine the fate of the world "as we know it." This fight of good and evil is one that he inherits from the previous generation, a generation in which his own mother and father failed at the task he himself must now undertake. Harry meets his challenges head on, and with glorious enthusiasm, using whatever latest trick of magic he has been able to obtain and control. These magical artifacts, such as spells and potions, wands, invisibility cloaks, a map that divines the locations of people unseen, and so on, play the same role in these books that a prosthetic hand or megaweapon body suit does for the prototypical gundam hero. Magic, in this sense, becomes a technology. Bruce McMillan, senior vice president and group studio general manager at Electronic Arts (the makers of many successful video and computer games), was recently quoted describing the *Harry Potter* books in this way.

> J. K. Rowling wrote her fiction in a way that game mechanics flow out of it [. . .] The first book [. . .] is packed with moments that seem almost designed to appear in a game: the gauntlet of puzzles that Harry faces to rescue the *Sorcerer's Stone*, the character-building that takes place as Harry learns to be a wizard, and much more. (Hendrix, 2001, pp. 37–38)

If we accept such historical interpretations of superheroes, we might ask, "What's next?" If humans have united within themselves extraordinary powers of destruction and creation, will they or can they bring into being a new evolutionary step? Those of us who work with young children should ask ourselves what the implications are for the types of experiences these children might be offered by adults, given that they are "schooled" in the popular culture to savor the gundam role (Appelbaum, 1999). There are indeed ways that gundam popular culture buttresses common sense attitudes about knowledge and curriculum. For example, the common view of technology as prostheses that amplify the potential powers of humans is consistent with the view that knowledge gained in school are cultural capital. By this I mean that prostheses for the body are part of a more global way of understanding our world in which knowledge is recognized as bits of things that are collected and later "spent" in the marketplace of college admissions and careers (Appelbaum, 1995). Gundam heroes are also built upon techno-utopianism. Science and technology are constructed in the school curriculum as well as popular technoculture as techniques of progress. The gundam hero accepts the premise that science and technology are their own antidotes and thus reconstructs technology as self-perpetuating and necessary. But should or can we seriously respond to gundam desires with and through the school curriculum? Can such desires be interrogated and challenged?

Educators' Responses

Teachers tend to feign disinterest in childhood experiences of cyberculture. They see as part of their job the need to further separate popular from high-status culture. School knowledge is part of that high-status culture. Popular and mass media raise the status of school knowledge when teachers keep them outside of school. But children are intimately caught up in popular media, and they use mass media resources in play, in social relationships, and in imagining possibilities. When teachers preserve the in-school versus outside-of-school boundaries, they cut themselves off from relationships with children directly connected with the most pressing issues of self, identity, morality, power, and knowledge. Sometimes a teacher relies on seemingly positive goals when effecting these boundaries. For a teacher who sees his or her job in terms of demystification or enculturation, it is gravely difficult to construct educational practice as migration into a new culture. This kind of teacher wants, instead, to teach the children about the traditions and cultural legacy of the old culture out of which they are entering the new cultures of *anime*. And, for a teacher who sees her or his job as bestowing the gifts of civilization, it is difficult to do so in terms of a cultural practice that celebrates the Romantic hope of childhood as the savior of humanity. Teachers would more likely understand their role as saving humanity from the strange, challenging actions of the *anime* hero. Furthermore, it is absurd for a teacher to imagine a curriculum that dehumanizes even her or himself as a tool for *anime* heroism or post-*anime* evolution: In the obsessively survivalist mode of teacher practice spawned by standards-based accountability bureaucracies, what possible technologies of self could or would we even think credible? Indeed, what is the role of a teacher other than the conserving one of passing on the wisdom of the past? I suggest that our new technoculture requires teaching practices that facilitate an interrogation of this culture and the facilitation of self-understanding necessary to unravel the intricacies of self-identity in a postmodern world. The "new curriculum" should consider alternative visions of technology that move it away from the metaphor of prosthesis. Consider, for example, Sadie Plant's notion that technology is not just an add-on to the human body that amplifies its powers, but instead serves to reengineer the body itself, creating a new and different cyborg body (Plant, 1997). The *Harry Potter* books speak to the reengineering of the body through technology in their examples of magic used as a tool to regrow human limbs, occasionally (or accidentally) removing someone's bones from a part of their body leaving it temporarily rubbery and deformed to cosmetically enhance someone's teeth, and, most directly, in the role of the "animagi," those who change into animal form. Curriculum, then, must speak fully to issues of identity and questions of what it means to be human in the face of reengineering and cultural change.

This challenge to teachers is consistent with the cultural view that the gundam hero must save the world even as the clueless adults sit idly by, paralyzed by the threats that they themselves have unleashed. What the *Harry Potter* books provide, however, is a reassurance that some adults really do know what is happening, and indeed that these adults can be trusted to come through with support when the going gets rough. Albus Dumbledore, Minerva McGonagall, Sirius Black, and Rubeus Hagrid, for example, often turn out to be fully aware of what is happening, or at least adequately conscious of what Harry and his friends are up to so that they can offer assistance at just the right moments. And Harry and his friends always seem to have recently mastered just enough new spells and tricks to accomplish what is necessary. In the end, as with the gundam hero, it is the child who must save the world. Nevertheless, in these books, the bleakness is tempered. It is almost as if the adults know that the "real" curriculum is outside of the classes and is just enticing enough to interest these children in their preparation for leadership. Real-world challenges provide the problem-solving context so necessary for meaningful learning. As a treatise on education, the *Harry Potter* books make an intriguing statement on the boundaries across the school and popular curricula.[4] If we only knew the story of every other child at Hogwarts, could it be that they, too, are having adventures? Maybe the school is set up to trick people into coming together for real-life problem-solving outside of school under the careful guidance of Dumbledore and his friends?

Power, Wonder, and Magic in an Acquisitive Culture

Power and violence are not always what they seem to be. There is a way in which a child who spends three hours a day playing *Smackdown*, *WWF WarZone*, *Timesplitters*, and other violent video games and then watches a *WWF* video for another hour and a half will recoil in horror and fright at scenes from popular films such as *Rules of Engagement*, or even the final scene in *The Secret of Roan Inish*. *Smackdown* and the *World-Wide Wrestling Federation WarZone* are arcade-style fighting games in which characters use gratuitous violence alone or in groups to render their competitors unconscious or devoid of any life energy. While the fanatic interest in *World-Wide Wrestling's* violent wrestling soap operas has waned in the last few years, many boys and young men still rent the videos for their nostalgic entertainment value. Yet most players and viewers will quickly insist they can tell that the violence is "fake," and that their interest in the entertainment has more to do with the complex strategies involved, or in the intricacies of the soap-opera style plots. *Rules of Engagement*, a 2000 film starring Tommy Lee Jones, Mark Feuerstein, and Samuel L. Jackson, and directed by William Friedkin, which involves a team of marines responding to a fictional attack on a U.S. embassy in Yemen, is rated R for graphic violence. However, much of the violence is implicit and artistically developed through techniques of suspense. *The Secret of Roan Inish*, director John Sayles's 1995 rendering of an Irish folktale, is steeped in magic and tradition. While supposedly suitable for family viewing, at least according to many film critics and its PG rating, the final dramatic scene involves a child's mother returning to the sea to live as a seal, leaving many children horrified at the child's loss of its mother.

Similarly, a young girl might try out seemingly sadistic or masochistic choices in a Purple Moon *Rockett* computer game, yet refuse to view *Rugrats* on television because she finds the character, Angelica, so horrific. The *Rockett* computer games incorporate a narrative about a preteen's life choices; the player makes decisions about what the young girl, Rockett, should do in various social situations. While an adult observer might expect the player's choices to be an indication of what the player might choose in a similar situation, many girls playing the game in fact choose a less socially sanctioned option just to see how it affects the plot. In the *Rugrats* television program, the oldest child, Angelica, is not only extremely bossy but also often puts the younger children into terribly awkward or potentially dangerous situations. Even though viewing *Rugrats* could entertain by allowing viewers the chance to see how children might make poor social choices, or reconcile them, many children actually find the character so reprehensible that they choose another form of entertainment. (Nevertheless, this should be understood in the light of the program's continued popularity.) Visibility of gore, as opposed to realism of violence, can be distinguished by many children as they discuss moral issues and scenarios.[5]

There has been much written in the popular press about the violence of the *Harry Potter* books. It is suggested that the books might be unhealthy because of this. However, the violent scenes are not what entice people to the books and are not what the books per se are about. A *Harry Potter* reader can handle the notions of being scarred for life on the forehead by an evil sorcerer or of a child in the school being killed by this same sorcerer a few books later. What readers of these books have suggested in their discussions with me is that they can easily separate these violent events from the moral contexts in which they take place. It is the morality to which they turn in applying "lessons learned" to their own interactions with "real people" in their lives. I admit to adult incredulity when it comes to this violence, and as educators, we are seriously concerned about the violence or threats of violence through mass culture narratives that affect our daily lives in schools. But reader-response theory remains: Some children read the "dark themes" in *Harry Potter* books as a backdrop to the details and contend with the dark themes on another plane of existence independent of their reading of these books. Similarly, some children are so caught up in the strategic details of video games, *Pokemon*, or the *Magic* card game, that they do not see the violence that adults see readily; they contend with issues of violence and control in thoroughly different ways when violence appears to them as part of a life outside of the game. In particular, invisible but possible violence is far more frightening to these children than larger-than-life cartoonish violence, even when the cartoonish violence is extremely graphic. (For example, *Independence Day* or *The Matrix* would be consumed as enjoyable entertainment, but *Contact* is unbearable because the suspenseful unknown is carried for so long in the film. *Independence Day* would initially seem to be terribly frightening as it graphically depicts aliens coming very close to violently taking over the Earth; *The Matrix* depicts the horrific scenario of a future Earth being nothing more than an illusion for people who have been reduced to energy resources for intelligent machines. *Contact*, which describes the tensions between science and religion when contact with aliens becomes possible depicts no violence but keeps the suspense about the aliens hidden throughout the majority of the film.) I suppose the question comes down to whether or not children can tell the difference between the games and the "real world." We seem to have some evidence to the contrary. Eugene Provenzo (1991) and others have amassed a collection of research that suggests reasons to worry about the culture of violence being so prevalent. In the end, as I talk with and work with children, my own evidence is that they are genuinely living an independent trajectory. The enacted violence could in some ways be said to be consistent with the dark imagery of the *Harry Potter* books and the game-like realism of current high-graphics fighting and shooting games; but I find the causation to be in the other direction. If anything, these images and choices of entertainment are a semantic sign of something in our culture rather than an origin of cultural meaning. That is, the images that children play with tell us more about the fears and fantasies of the adults who provide the images and the resources for making meaning that are available in our culture than about what children are becoming or doing to themselves or our culture. This does not mean that violent and sexist images would never be an origin of meaning for any particular child; it certainly is possible that they could be. It just is not such an origin in my research. And I do not see it as the common experience of most children.

Another popular concern that has led to the books being banned in some communities is the attention to the dark arts and magic in general. It may be feared that young people would become interested in pursuing cultish practices. The use of these features makes the books no different from numerous popular television series and video games (see, for example, the television programs *Buffy the Vampire Slayer*, *Charmed*, the *Final Fantasy* video game series, and the computer game, *Black and White*).[6]

Magic is strongly associated with experiences of wonder. There is little distinction between the *Harry Potter* books and the *Magic: The Gathering* card game, or a cyberhero like *Inspector Gadget* and a round of laser tag. Paintball, for a child, can be a variation on Pokemon, or a dramatic fantasy based on the *Power Rangers*, or—if "I" played paintball last weekend and "you" never have—a real-life "play" of power against another child in the acquisitive culture of childhood. In tapping into magic, many forms of youth technoculture reach into the realm of wonder in ways that establish these cultural commodities as educative experiences in the

Deweyan sense that they promote growth (maybe not growth in the school-culture sense, however). When adults set up school as distinct from the world of wonder (even to compete with popular culture for "coolness" or "cleverness" but in the act clarifying the impossibility of this attempt), they fail children and abdicate their responsibility to participate in mass culture and peer interactions. In denying the potential of wonder through magic, educators are also denying students an environment that is educative. Three questions arise: Should we try to create educational encounters that directly mirror the linking of magic, technology, and wonder as in, for example, Botball tournaments (KISS Institute, 2001)? Should teachers hype science into a parallel form of "edutainment," as in television science programs? Or should educators establish science/technology/wonder as a critical examination of the popular (Appelbaum & Clark, in press; Gough, 1993)? I suggest, in contrast, that children gravitate to the wonder where it is. When wonder is not in the curriculum, they will find it elsewhere, outside of school.

An interesting case study is afforded by Hasbro's marketing of the new toy, Pox™ (Tierney, 2001). The new toy was introduced by identifying who the coolest of the cool children are: roaming playgrounds and neighborhoods. Marketers asked, "Who's the coolest kid you know?" When they landed a kid who said, "Me," they invited the "alpha pup" to get paid to learn a new video game. Fighting monsters are created by collecting body parts and powers. Warriors are put together from the collected parts; then you program a battle sequence by strategically balancing the strengths and weaknesses of the various body parts. The coolest kids can boast about what level they have attained, what potential body parts they have collected; the ones who lose are not humiliated publicly since the game is played stealthily. *Pox* depends not on reflexes as with other video games, but on "the collection of arcana." Asked why they like the game, boys say, "because it's, like, battling and fighting," and "we like violence!" Tierney writes that they sound bloodthirsty without a sign of menace. He cites research that suggests that violent entertainment is actually associated with a decrease in violence among young people. The seeming connection between violent entertainment and violence, he suggests, might be better explained by a strong increase in violence in society begun long before the advent of video games.

Things dominate the life of children. For young people in the early twenty-first century, commodification as the final arbiter of identity and acquisition is intimately entwined with self. If knowledge is the sort of knowledge truly conflated with power, then children voraciously grab for it. But if it is ambiguous in its relation to power, then it is ignored in the interest of efficiency. Thus, a young boy will exert whatever it takes to acquire the new Sims (Electronic Arts, 2000) game before others get it, or to learn a trick from *GamePro* magazine before his friend does; yet the same child could care less about the financial mathematics of purchasing the game unless the money actually makes a difference in his life. In the latter case, if school artificially makes this into a world problem–type experience, the conflicting identity politics is a crucial element in self and community. Similarly, the importance of *Pokemon Gameboy* will fluctuate for many girls depending on its competition for importance with current MTV star details, varying makeup items and body gels, and other technologies of the body. For both boys and girls, technology is a fashion; but this fashion is played out in gendered and other ways. In the *Harry Potter* culture, material products include wizard trading cards, Quidditch brooms, the best owl, a magic pet, and magic treats sold on wizard trains. And these commodities serve parallel functions. For *Harry Potter* readers, consumer culture makes early possession of the books and a child's recall of details into an acquired need that works as cultural capital in analogous ways. Indeed, the child who possesses full command of detail, like the player of the new *Pox*™ game immersed in the collection of arcana, is the one most likely to win. In one sense, this consistency in and out of the books serves to make the stories more "believable" for readers. Students at Hogwarts collect trading cards of great wizards and Quidditch heroes much like young people outside the books obsess over sports cards, and this common consumerism makes the children in the books more "realistic." And Harry quickly learns to covet the latest, most expensive gadgets like a typical child outside the books.

In another sense, acquisitive consumer culture dominates popular and *Harry Potter* culture in ways that make the books emblematic of the culture in which they appear as commodities themselves. Early in *Harry Potter and the Chamber of Secrets*, for example, the competing Slytherin team demoralize the Gryffindors by showing off their new "Nimbus Two Thousand and One" broomsticks. "Very latest model. Only came out last month . . . I believe it outstrips the old Two Thousand series by a considerable amount" (Rowling, 1999a, p. 111). Harry's friends are left holding their outmoded "Cleansweep Fives," no longer competitive with the newer

Nimbus models. In *Harry Potter and the Prisoner of Azkaban* (Rowling, 1999b), Harry is mesmerized by an advertisement for an even newer model, the "Firebolt," which is so hyped that it is priced upon request. Harry "didn't like to think how much gold the Firebolt would cost. He had never wanted anything as much in his whole life" (Rowling, 1999b, pp. 51–52). He tries to console himself by noting that he has never lost a Quidditch match on his Nimbus Two Thousand, yet "he returned, almost every day after that, just to look at the Firebolt" (Rowling, 1999b, p. 52). In this way *Potter* and popular consumer culture intertwine consumerism and technoculture by turning new technologies into coveted consumer products.

It was James MacDonald (1995) who wrote:

> It is my personal myth that today's technology is yesterday's magic. Further, it is intuitive feeling that technology is in effect externalization of the hidden consciousness of human potential. Technology, in other words, is a necessary development for human beings in that it is the means of externalizing the potential that lies within. (p. 75)

The *Harry Potter* books portray MacDonald's wisdom in, for example, their juxtaposition of the flying car and the use of tea leaves to divine fortune, but even more directly in the all-important fixation on the best and latest Quidditch broom. Why would a school full of apprentice wizards need to buy the latest innovation in design and technology? To reemphasize class and justice themes? To satisfy a "real boy's" need for toys and desire? It is the same audience finding this believable that runs out to purchase the newest *Magic* deck, or searches the Internet for rare and expensive no-longer-in-print cards, the same audience that shells out $30.00 for a quarter-inch of plastic that can be painted and used in a *Warhammer* game. And it is the same audience that knows all the lyrics to Brittany Spears's latest video, the dance moves to Christina Aguileira's new video, and the place to buy the coolest body gel.

Harry Potter's World

This chapter is an interrogation of the world that embraces the *Harry Potter* phenomenon; it is not an extensive analysis of the books themselves. I claim that the main thrust of Harry Potter's attraction has mostly to do with its treatment of magic as a commodified technology, just as video games, television cyborgs, and fantasy role-playing games in "our world" treat technology as magic. Insofar as morality is constructed in any of these terrains, it has very little to do with specific plot or imagery and more to do with the "kids' culture" Rushkoff (1996) described as "a delightful mixed-up common ground for all of these digital, magical, and biological sorts of development" (p. 109). This is not to say that young readers are more likely to be interested in the magic than the moral lessons of the books; rather, we can find a technology of morality that constructs identity as multiple and fluid. Because "technology" and "humanity" are overlapping and transgressive as categories in "our world," we can no longer talk about technology as a tool that is wielded in accordance with morality. Instead we must understand morality and technology as mutually constitutive.

In Harry Potter's world, surprises might be lurking in any place or thing. The trick is to ride it through and never give up the chance to have fun. This is the fate of the gundam child. Similarly, kids playing video games do not dwell on the plot, the characters, or what things might seem to be if one were to take a particular event or character as a "message" in some adult way. Take race, gender, or nationality, for example: "Kids routinely choose any and all . . . options and don't think twice about it," writes J. C. Herz (1997), "because the only factor in their decision is a given character's repertoire of kick-ass fighting moves. Ironically, all considerations of race, sex, and nationality are shunted aside in the videogame arena, where the only goal is to clobber everyone indiscriminately" (p. 166). Yet, as Herz points out, kids understand on a deeper level that they are "operating in a disembodied environment where your virtual skin doesn't have to match your physical one, and that you can be an Okinawan karate expert, a female Thai kick-boxer, a black street-fighter from the Bronx, or a six-armed alien from outer space, all within the span of a single game" (p. 166).

Herz notes that adults do not generally approach things this way; they might be disturbed by the idea of a cutesy Japanese schoolgirl committing gruesome, bloody maneuvers, or at least be aware in some semiconscious way that they are choosing this character. For children, however, writes Herz, "shuffling videogame bodies and faces is like playing with a remote control" (p. 167). Adults also tend to see the video games as preprogrammed and predetermined so that the limited selection of identity combinations and options suggests a particular story about identity to these adults. Recent video games, however, employ the "create a character" feature, in which it really does seem like any and all combinations are the goal. "The game starts, cycles through a bunch of avatars, and you punch the fire button when you see one you like. It's channel surfing" (p. 167). When children are imitating the moves of these characters, trying out the "cool" moves and identities, some adults become concerned that there is not a clear separation between the fantasy of the game or television program and the dreams of particular children. This is indeed the case for some children; it is also part of working through our cultural ideas about what "identity" is, and so it may be a necessary experience for children.

Harry Potter books reconstruct in analogous detail the pecking order of schoolground one-upmanship. You cannot just know the spell in Harry's world; you have to study it, practice it, and perfect it. And if you can learn a spell that others do not yet know, you are the coolest. What the Potter books do is destabilize the tension between acquisitive coolness and nerdiness because they take magic and turn it into techniques that can be learned. Thus, Hermione is not all that cool in the books even though she studies the most and learns the most spells because, within the context of the books, she is just a studious nerd in school. Yet other kids in the books who do not take on the characteristics of nerds but know more tricks than the others earn recognition and status. It can be cool to know more magic than other kids. It is pretty much the same outside the books; you must show you have incredibly detailed and specific knowledge that others do not yet have to stay ahead. It is not enough to be the first kid to own the *Sims*, a computer game in which one creates a whole simulated world of people and then manipulates how they interact. You have to know how to download the *Sim* guinea pig off the Net and use it to help two *Sim* families come together and start a new household. Herz (1997) emphasizes the importance of both the arcane knowledge and hand-to-eye coordination. And it is the same for Harry; he is always at the center of the fun because he is always looking for a new, esoteric detail. *Harry Potter* books are an education for the information economy in which everyone pays premium rates for narrow expertise and short-lived skills. Just as Harry will grab at the chance to use a secret map, so too will a first grader voraciously read *Nintendo* magazine, or a fourth grader search out the chat room where one can learn the most arcane code for *Tony Hawke's SkatePro* (a skateboarding video game). To the other characters in the books, Harry is cool not because he can talk to snakes—that is something he was born with—he is cool because he has an invisibility cloak and a really good broomstick. (It is the case in these books that Harry Potter is famous; everyone knows the story of how the most powerful evil Voldemort was unable to kill Harry and that trying to kill the young lad caused Voldemort to lose much of his power and disappear. But in general, we see that most kids in the books find him peculiar and do not treat him as special in any particular way. A more subtle reading registers his fluctuating status; he is sometimes a hero, sometimes a suspect, but in either case, always "special." Outside of the books is another story; most readers identify with Harry in particular.)

Technology, in this sense, is nothing more than a trick, spell, or code; it lets you do things other people do not know about yet. And this is pretty much what MacDonald was referring to as the externalization of potential. As Rushkoff (1996) writes:

> When we look carefully at the reaction of younger cyber-denizens to their Sega-environs, we find that they make no distinction between information and matter, mechanics and thought, work and play, or even religion and commerce. In fact, kids on the frontier of the digital terrain have adopted some extraordinarily magical notions about the world we live in. Far from yielding a society of coldhearted rationalists, the ethereal, out-of-body experience of mediating technologies appears to have spawned a generation of pagan spiritualists whose dedication to technology is only matched by their enthusiasm for elemental truth and a neoprimitive, magical worldview. To a screenager, these are not opposing strategies but coordinated agents of change. (p. 109)

This harkens back to the Enlightenment epistemology that created a kind of confidence about a human being's place in the world even as he or she was decentered in that world because one could know all or understand all and harness it to human advantage. In this view, humans even have the role of controlling the world; if we could only realize this, we could fit into the natural world that is scientifically knowable. The irony is that this is the postmodern era, in which we are no longer supposed to be believing this. Supposedly, we no longer believe in the idea of eternal progress and, with the loss of this rudder, we have presumed the destruction of all of the accompanying beliefs, such as human "rationality," unlimited potential for control, and the ability to create a society in which both individual and collective will can be met. At the same time, there seem to be so many reasons to accept that these possibilities *can* be met through, for example, e-mail and other postmodern notions of Web technology.

The practice of control is almost always destructive; the *anime*/gundam heroes are a direct response. Yet this postmodern era is, in many ways, what Enlightenment people could only have imagined!

But life is not just a party of Enlightenment fulfillment. Kids find themselves in the midst of adult conflicts and power games even as they search out the next form of magic. They have to deal with the stupidity of the previous generation and its disturbing legacy of destructive forces. In this respect, the coordinated agents of change Rushkoff mentions must be employed to specific ends. If Harry can use his new Invisibility Cloak in fending off evil, he is no different from an *anime* heroine wearing her new suit, or a *WWF* character wielding her extra-super-finishing move. "And this is what it's about," writes Herz:

> as the cultural stream of East and West swirl into the Tastee-Freez of global enter-
> tainment. Mythic figures resonate, all the more if they're engaged in some kind of
> combat or action adventure, real or simulated, the most popular forms being bas-
> ketball and videogames. They resonate for the same reasons mythic figures have
> always resonated. Only now, the audience numbers in the millions, and the object
> is not to celebrate ancestors or teach lessons or curry favor with the spirits. It's
> commerce. And the people transmitting their stories to the next generation aren't
> priests or poets or medicine women. They're multinational corporations. And they
> are not trying to appease the gods. They are trying to appease the shareholders.
> (p. 170)

It is not just video games, it is everything in our mass culture. We can just see it more clearly in video games. And we are just a little edgy about the attraction of this series of *Harry Potter* books. Violent entertainment is the most blatant form of popular culture, but it is all about taming mythic monsters. The difference with the video games is that the monsters are inside the games, and we can try them on ourselves. Such gods and monsters used to scare people. Now people manipulate the gods and monsters (see especially *Black and White*). So we see once again why Harry Potter is the character of the moment; he, too, trains and controls monsters and goblins just like a player of *Magic*, a player of the *Pokemon* card game, or a video game master.

In her writing, Herz seems to be claiming an evolution, a new breed of freaks that adults need to study and live with. Perhaps she agrees with Bruce Mazlish (1993) that, "In making machines, humans have become themselves Creators who endow their creations with movement."

Automata . . . express this form of creation dramatically. An automobile, a locomotor, an airplane, these also move under human inspiration. Until the Renaissance, it appears . . . that Western Man [sic] built automata and other machines not so much to dominate nature, but to copy it; not to rival God, but to imitate him [sic]. Increasingly, however, in the West, humans came to smudge the image of God as the Creator and to substitute their own, first turning God into a Newtonian machine, and then merging him with nature as an evolutionary process. In doing so, humans united within themselves extraordinary powers of destruction . . . and of creation. Whether in taking on creative powers, humans are also able, in the form of their machines, to bring into being a new evolutionary step remains our next question. If Man [sic] succeeds in taking this step, he would certainly be doing something admittedly unique. (pp. 213–14)

Curriculum and the Technologies of Morality

Throughout, my main curriculum argument is that educators need to learn from children what it is they are experiencing—that ol' Margaret Mead adage that our contemporary situation is one of migration into a new culture; children are the translators while adults are the keepers of tradition. Adults need to learn from children in order to survive, yet children gain valuable narratives through which to interpret action by listening to stories of the old country from the elders. The "answer" for curriculum is not to try to compete with technoculture because we will always fail at the imitation; instead, we need to develop organized experiences that respond to life in and with technoculture. More proactive would be for educators to work toward a biculturalism, and finally for a diversity that embraces both traditions and the multiplicities of what Herz calls "superhero sushi." This includes adult cultures and technocultures, mass and consumer cultures, and youth subcultures, and cross-over memberships and participations in multiple cultures at once. At the same time, we must be wary of constructing teachers themselves as the *anime* heroines, themselves progenitors of technohyperbolic change. If teachers read the *Harry Potter* books and then fashion themselves as the wizards with the children as the magical beasts to be tamed, then teachers become the technochildren themselves. Indeed, teachers are often urged to try on new prototypes of technology in order to experience a new sense of their powers of perception, production, and destruction (e.g., new technologies of assessment, instruction, surveillance). At other times, they experience the melancholia of the gundam; they conceive themselves as capable of harnessing the sometimes terrifying applications of scientistic pedagogical techniques in order to lead the student-monsters in an effort to save society from invasion or technological disasters (Appelbaum, 1999).

As the narratives reproduce themselves and their hegemonic themes, there is the parallel story in which we enter a new phase of cyborg technoculture. Even in this context, magic and technology are not distinct categories for children. They are attracted to technology for its ability to perform magic, and they are attracted to magic for its potential to be used as a tool.[7] In working with children, I find that magic is not special despite its amazing surprise or apparent impossibility; for a child, anything is possible. The intriguing thing is the secret of how it is done. It is no wonder to me that the *Harry Potter* books coincide with the unprecedented popularity of television specials in which magicians reveal their secrets, despite being exiled forever from the community of magicians. It is no longer the "magic" of magic, but the cleverness of the technique that matters. Whereas the technical ingenuity of a particular tool is no longer of interest, the technological possibility is replaced by the cleverness of the magic it can perform. Regardless of how incredible the actual task is, it is ordinary unless it is relatively unique, arcane, or unexpected.

O'Har (2000) turned to Jacques Ellul (1967) in working through the popularity of *Harry Potter*. If we imagine that magic and science were once "one," then we can create a narrative of their split; one path went the way of technique, into technology; material technique leads to a multiplication of discoveries, each based on the other and, thus, writes in itself a myth of progress. Magic, the other path, promotes only endless beginnings; it also answers all questions by preserving spirituality. The part of magic that was lost to our world in the dominance of science and technology was that aspect of magic that functioned in this spiritual realm. The fundamental message of *Harry Potter*, according to O'Har, is that magic saves Harry from turning into a Dursely; instead, it provides a whole new set of endless beginnings.

Oddly, though, these beginnings carry the trappings of everything we already know about how people live and work together. Here is the "literary beauty" of the school in the *Harry Potter* books; it is no better than any other school we know of simply by virtue of being school. Once magic is the subject matter it is nothing special. In its commodification, it has become another technology, another collection of technical skills to be mastered. Everything exciting, all of the real magic the children acquire, comes from the technological tricks they need to perform outside of school. Outside the books, however, the magic (when read about) serves a different function. For us, reading along, it is the magic that captivates us because of its presentation as technology. This new technology, the magic, is ironically a technique for solving all of the problems that technology and science have always failed to solve. For us, too, the magic provides a set of beginnings. The difference between school for Harry and his friends and the schools that readers experience outside the books, however, is that everyone at Hogwarts School of Witchcraft and Wizardry is learning stuff that they know they will use (Block, 2001). Students at Hogwarts are training to be wizards, and they know that what they are learning will be useful to them in their lives.[8] Outside the books, the uses of school learning are remote at best, good for a promised future; inside the books, kids use what they have learned immediately to solve life-threatening puzzles and to save the fate of the world as we know it.

Technologies of the Self: Morality and Magic

A particularly powerful element of the *Harry Potter* books is the unification of Harry's self-knowledge with his self-care. Who is this Harry, where does he come from, why is he so important, and why is he at the center of so much good-evil carnage so many times in his life? Only by strapping on the technoculture of magic can he seek the self-knowledge that he, we, and everybody else crave. For example, Harry looks into the magic mirror and sees his family; indeed, he initially learns that he is a wizard through a message sent to him from Hogwarts. In this process of strapping on the magic, a process of externalizing and realizing his self-potential, he wields the tools that lead to self-understanding. Harry is a personified conflation of self-knowledge and self-care. His self-knowledge leads to care of the self, indeed saves his life; and, in taking care of himself and his potential, he is able to achieve self-knowledge. The books thus present what Michel Foucault (Martin et al., 1988) named a "technology of morality": the transformation of self by one's own means or with the help of others—that is, in the operations upon one's body, soul, thoughts, conduct, and way of being. Foucault postulated that this technology of morality enunciates a hierarchy between knowing oneself and taking care of oneself. Harry doesn't yet enunciate a hierarchy, and he therefore lives the more nuanced notion of morality that Foucault initially suggested. Harry's life project does not place knowing oneself above caring for oneself, nor does it value care of the self over knowing who he is. Either he has not been transformed yet (J. K. Rowling plans to write several more books for each of Harry's years at Hogwarts, so as this chapter is composed, there is no clear conclusion), or he is a symbol of a shift away from Foucault's binary toward an independent coexistence with the technology of morality. This is parallel to videogamers channel-surfing through the strategies of what, in adult terms, are violent images but in young people's terms are mere strategy games devoid of the realistic violence these young people say they would condemn. For *Harry Potter* fans, the convention of good-evil contestation is a context for the real cleverness and intrigue of the story, the details about how Harry and his friends collect more trinkets of magic in their quest to be "cool." Similarly, a fifth grader can buy status at recess by recounting details of last night's *WWF* show and claim he is not in the least interested in the "fake" violence, but instead in the intricacies of the particular combinations of moves that the fighters made. In any of these examples, the cultural shift has moved the focus away from the binary and the potential hierarchy to the placement of the binary in an independent context.

When magic is treated as technologies and technology is treated as magic, what can we say about the morality of magic and about the magic of morality? Self-development is an enlightenment project, and self-development leading to self-knowledge is, again, an enlightenment project. We can see this clearly in *Pokemon*. The main characters, Ash and his friends, and the other Pokemon trainers are traveling around looking to understand themselves, using different Pokemon to understand and strengthen themselves. The Pokemon that children train and fight with are externalizations of their inner drives and desires. Only in striving to become a true Pokemon trainer does an aspirant achieve, eventually, self-knowledge and the ability to care for oneself. So we are again up against this idea that postmodern technoculture is spawning a fulfillment of Enlightenment fantasy. If we think about the degree of bourgeois optimism that was so prevalent in the nineteenth century—that by knowing things you could enrich yourself, make yourself happier, and be a better person, and in the process implicitly help society and if we think about the role of this technology of morality in supporting the accomplishment of cultural forms of optimism like capitalism and industrialization, it is possible to understand why and how this new scientific optimism and notions of new possibilities through technologies can blind us to terrible things that are going on in the world, such as genocides, slave labor in factories, or environmental racism. People are smugly not thinking about horrible famines in Ethiopia and instead are celebrating their technological power, a wealth-plus-knowledge equation that enables them to do what they want when they want in the world through technology—which is magic! In the end, the morality of magic is an Enlightenment ideology of post-modern technoculture. And this is Harry Potter's world. In the books, there are really serious concerns about the impending triumph of the dark arts to contend with; outside the books, we can turn our local concerns into major focal points for self-development and ignore the major ethical concerns that plague our postmodern world.

Children growing up in a state of enlightenment technoculture may indeed experience the technologies of morality as both a blinding scientific optimism and a more immediate celebration of individual prosthetic enhancement. As consumers of books, children are represented in our culture as a "hostile audience" since they are depicted as choosing other forms of entertainment over reading a new book. As science fiction and fantasy increasingly permeate the entertainment of children, adolescents, and young adults, members of contemporary society are effectively growing up in a fantasyland. It becomes imperative to analyze examples of these popular forms of entertainment (no matter how inconsequential or artless they may at first appear); we should understand what we are learning from these stories, and what sorts of adults we are becoming as a result (Westfahl, 2000). Yet I believe that the most important use of the popular is an interrogation of the culture through the popular. One significant feature of the *Harry Potter* phenomenon is the presence of continued items in a series and the need to continually market to an audience of consumers who will "need" to buy the next product, whether this product is a new book in the series, a home design product, a video game, a film based on the books, or fanware. Advertising and promotion of products have become the dominant element of the *Harry Potter* culture since the first book. One might posit children as social change agents in turning the books into major marketing products through word-of-mouth advertising. Yet the overriding nature of consumer culture is that one is trying to sell something to a cynical audience. As adults purchase a *Harry Potter* T-shirt because of its connection to reading a book, children want the T-shirt for its value as a commodity. However, for both, the T-shirt serves as a symbol of membership in a cultural subgroup.

Reading *Harry Potter* with children requires more than reading the books. Reading includes participation in and reflexive analysis of all forms of cultural text. Indeed, reading especially means interpreting the uses of fanware. This chapter has focused mainly on the introduction of the *Harry Potter* phenomenon through the books themselves because the fanware hype occurred mostly after the success of the books. Nevertheless, as we look forward to understanding what the *Harry Potter* books can teach us about ourselves, we will need to address more carefully these multiple sites of meaning beyond the books. The multiple "texts" of *Harry Potter* can be popular only if they are open enough to admit a range of negotiated readings through which various social groups can find meaningful articulations of their own relationship to the dominant ideology (Fiske, 1987). The "dominant reader" identifies with Harry, the hero, and can believe that everyone might just have magic in them. If we play down the fact that many muggles do not get an invitation to Hogwarts, while some wizard folk, squibs, are unfortunately lacking, we might just hope that hard work and careful practice can help us get ahead. The dominant reading maintains a commonsense belief in meritocracy. Negotiated readings emerge when people make use of the images presented to interpret their own lives, as when readers think of the ways they are like and unlike Hermione, or why they would never be able to become a teacher like Snape. Issues of class and race, underplayed by the dominant reader, may be foregrounded in negotiated readings. If the negotiation is more "against" than "with" the text, then a reader might use the texts as blatantly sexist or racist, or perhaps antireligious.

In any reading of the texts of *Harry Potter*, however, we will find magic and technology confused, or thrown into disarray, to be unraveled and comprehended in ways that are consistent with the reading that emerges. Arthur Weasley, who works for the Ministry of Magic, eccentrically collects electric plugs and batteries, and he secretly keeps a flying car until it ends up in a magic forest in a later book. The Dursleys want nothing to do with magic and fill their home with all of the latest technological gadgets and toys one could ever want.[9] It is Vernon Dursely who points out the peculiar place of technology in the arts of magic; in the end, it is technology that is the symbol of one's path to wizardry, as everyone takes the Hogwarts Express train to get to this school of witchcraft and wizardry. He asks why wizards need to take a train. He never gets his answer. Harry's story provides the larger context; in the end, technology/magic has to do with who one is and what one does. And because who one is and what one does is so intertwined with the technologies of magic and the magic of technology in the service of self-knowledge and self-care, who one is and what one does is a technology of morality and an essential node of the construction of ethics.

Hogwarts confronts the ethics of magic and science directly. Its purpose is to help its students harness and focus their powers. These powers might be called magic or they might be called technology; but in this case they are called magic. The problem for the educators in the books is that they cannot be certain that people (wizards) will use these powers for the common good. It boils down to a choice between the common good and the dark arts. And so we are confronted with the evil of Voldemort and the always-present danger of evil triumphing over good. Hogwarts was founded by four wizards, one of whom, Salazar Slytherin, at least dabbled and perhaps reveled in the dark arts. He used his powers for questionable, if not specifically evil, purposes. (For centuries many of the young wizards who reside in Slytherin House have exhibited the same tendency.) Albus Dumbledore, who heads the school, needs to figure out how to train students not just in the "technology" of magic but also in the moral discernment necessary to avoid the continual reproduction of the few great Dark Lords like Voldemort and their multitudinous followers. The problem is exacerbated by the presence of faculty members who are not wholly unsympathetic with Voldemort's aims.

Good and evil are not just cartoonized in the books. As Alan Jacobs writes, Harry Potter is unquestionably good; yet a key component of his virtue arises from his recognition that he is not inevitably good. When first-year students arrive at Hogwarts, they come to an assembly of the entire school, students and faculty. Each of them sits on a stool in the midst of the assembly and puts on a large, battered old hat—the Sorting Hat—which decides which of the four houses the student will enter. After unusually long reflection, the Sorting Hat, to Harry's great relief, puts him in Gryffindor, but not before telling him that he could achieve real greatness in Slytherin. This comment haunts Harry; he often wonders if Slytherin is where he truly belongs, among the pragmatists, the careerists, the manipulators and deceivers, the power–hungry, and the just plain nasty. Near the end of the second book, after his third terrifying encounter with Voldemort, he confesses his doubts to Dumbledore.

"So I *should* be in Slytherin," Harry said, looking desperately into Dumbledore's face. "The Sorting Hat could see Slytherin's power in me, and it—"

"Put you in Gryffindor," said Dumbledore calmly. "Listen to me, Harry. You happen to have many qualities Salazar Slytherin prized in his hand–picked students. Resourcefulness . . . determination . . . a certain disregard for rules," he added, his moustache quivering again. "Yet the Sorting Hat placed you in Gryffindor. You know why that was. Think."

"It only put me in Gryffindor," said Harry in a defeated voice, "because I asked not to go in Slytherin. . . ."

"Exactly," said Dumbledore, beaming once more, " . . . which makes you very different from [Voldemort]. It is our choices, Harry, that show what we truly are, far more than our abilities." Harry sat motionless in his chair, stunned.

Harry is stunned because he realizes for the first time that his confusion has been wrongheaded from the start; he has been asking the question, "Who am I at heart?" when he needed to be asking the question, "What must I do in order to become what I should be?" His character is not a fixed, preexistent thing, but something that he has the responsibility for making. "In this sense," writes Jacobs, "the strong, [Enlightenment] tendency of magic to become a dream of power makes it a wonderful means by which to focus the choices that gradually but inexorably shape us into certain distinct kinds of persons."

In the *Harry Potter* books, magic is often fun, often surprising and exciting, but also always potentially dangerous—much like the technology outside the books that has resulted from the "victory" of experimental science. The technocrats of this world hold in their hands powers almost infinitely greater than those of Albus Dumbledore and Voldemort; how worried are we about them and their influence over our children? If we could only measure technique by other criteria than those of technique itself. *Harry Potter* is more helpful than most children's literature in prompting such ethical and cultural reflection.

Notes

1. After weeks on the *New York Times* bestseller list, *Harry Potter* books found themselves on the newly created list of "Children's Best Sellers." Thus *Harry* ushered in a new awareness of the field of children's literature and the need to pay attention to the field as a major market niche. But more important, *Harry* books found themselves as markers of a new boundary, effectively denying it "real" status even as it was celebrated as a cultural phenomenon. No longer a book for adults, it continued to be read by many "older" readers. See Kathy Malu's chapter elsewhere in this volume.

2. Filk are new words to well-known songs, sung together by fans at gatherings.

3. *Gundam* is a term from Japanese animation for the hero who dons technology in order to fight the unleashed threats resulting from previous human efforts with technology and science.

4. See Charles Esler's chapter in this volume.

5. See Heather Sevarty and Deborah Taub's chapter, this volume.

6. How do you cope with the aggravation from strongly religious people against witchcraft? J. K. Rowling: "Well, mostly I laugh about it I ignore it . . . and very occasionally I get annoyed, because they have missed the point so spectacularly. I think the Harry books are very moral but some people just object to witchcraft being mentioned in a children's book unfortunately, that means we'll have to lose a lot of classic children's fiction." (Comic Relief 2001)

> Q: What are your feelings towards the people who say your books are to do with cults and telling people to become witches? (reader's question, didn't give name)
>
> A: Alfie. Over to you. Do you feel a burning desire to become a witch?
>
> Alfie: No.
>
> A: I thought not. I think this is a case of people grossly underestimating children. Again. (Southwest News 2000)

7. "Any smoothly functioning technology gives the appearance of magic." Quote attributed to Arthur C. Clarke (Jacobs, 2000).

8. *Hogwarts School Song*: *Hogwarts, Hogwarts, Hoggy Warty Hogwarts/Teach us something, please/Whether we be old and bald/Or young with scabby knees/Our heads could do with filling/With some interesting stuff/For now they're bare and full of air/Dead flies and bits of fluff/So teach us things worth knowing/Bring back what we've forgot/Just do your best, we'll do the rest/And learn until our brains all rot.* ("And now, before we go to bed, let us sing the school song! Everyone pick their favorite tune and off we go!")

9. Toys in Dudley Dursley's spare bedroom: computer, PlayStation, two televisions, racing bike, video camera, remote control airplane, large numbers of computer games (including MegaMutilation Three), VCR, gold wristwatch, working model tank, bird in a cage, air rifle, tortoise, sports bag, books (unused), computerized robot.

References

Appelbaum, Peter. *Popular Culture, Educational Discourse, and Mathematics.* Albany: State U of New York P, 1995.

———. *Cyborg Selves: Saturday Morning Magic and Magical Morality.* Ed. Toby Daspit and John A. Weaver. New York: Garland, 1999.

Appelbaum, Peter, and Stella Clark. (2001). Science! Fun? A Critical Analysis of Design./Content/Evaluation. *Journal of Curriculum Studies* 33 (5): 583–600.

Babbitt, Natalie. *Tuck Everlasting.* New York: Dell, 1987.

Block, Alan. Personal communication. Department of Education, School Counseling, and School Psychology, University of Wisconsin–Stout, Menominee, WI, 5475, USA.

Comic Relief. Live Webchat March 21, 2001. http://www.comicrelief.com/harrysbooks/pages/transcript.shtml.

Daspit, Toby, and John Weaver. *Popular Culture and Critical Pedagogy: Reading, Constructing, Connecting.* New York: Garland, 1998.

De Certeau, Michel. *The Practice of Everyday Life.* Berkeley, CA: U of California P.

Eco, Umberto. *The Role of the Reader: Explorations in the Semiotics of Texts.* Bloomington: IN: U of Indiana P, 1979.

Electronic Arts. *The Sims.* Computer game. Electronic Arts, 2000.

Ellul, Jacques. *The Technological Society*. New York: Random House, 1967.

Fiske, John. "British Cultural Studies and Television." In *Channels of Discourse*. Ed. Robert Allen. Chapel Hill: U of North Carolina P, 1987. 254–89.

———. *Reading the Popular*. New York: Routledge, 1990.

Giroux, Henry A. *Stealing Innocence: Corporate Culture's War on Children*. New York: Palgrave, 2000.

Gough, Noel. *Laboratories in Fiction: Science Education and Popular Media*. Geelong, Australia: Deakin UP, 1993.

Hendrix, Air. "Off to Be a Wizard." *GamePro*. June 2001. 36–41.

Herz, J. C. *Joystick Nation: How Videogames Ate Our Quarter, Won Our Hearts, and Rewired Our Minds*. New York: Little, Brown, 1997.

Jacobs, Alan. "Harry Potter's Magic." *First Things: The Journal of Religion and Public Life* 99 (2000): 35–38.

KISS Institute for Practical Robotics. Botball Technology Education website. 2001. http://www.kipr.org/botball/index.html.

Levi, Antonia. *Samurai from Outer Space: Understanding Japanese Animation*. New York: Open Court, 99.

Lowry, Lois. *The Giver*. New York: Houghton Mifflin, 1993.

MacDonald, James. "A Transcendental Ideology of Education." In *Theory as a Prayerful Act: The Collected Writings of James MacDonald*. Ed. B. J. MacDonald. New York: Peter Lang, 1995. 69–98.

Martin, Luther H., Huck Gutman, and Patrick Hutton, eds. *Technologies of the Self: A Seminar with Michel Foucault*. Amherst: U of Massachussetts P, 1988.

Mazlish, Bruce. *The Fourth Discontinuity: The Co-evolution of Humans and Machines*. New Haven: Yale UP, 1993.

Napier, Susan. *Anime: From Akira to Princess Mononoke*. New York: Palgraye, 2001.

O'Har, George. "Magic in the Machine Age." *Technology and Culture* 41:4 (2000): 862–64.

Plant, Sadie. *Zeros and Ones: Digital Women and the New Technoculture*. New York: Doubleday, 1997.

Poitras, Gilles. *Anime Essentials: Every Thing a Fan Needs to Know*. New York: Stone Bridge, 2000.

Provenzo, Eugene. *Video Kids: Making Sense of Nintendo*. Cambridge: Harvard UP, 1995.

Pullman, Phillip. *The Golden Compass*. New York: Knopf, 1996.

Rowling, J. K. *Harry Potter and the Chamber of Secrets*. New York: Scholastic P, 1999a.

———. *Harry Potter and the Prisoner of Azkaban*. New York: Scholastic P, 1999b.

Rushkoff, Douglas. *Playing the Future: How Kids' Culture Can Teach Us to Thrive in an Age of Chaos*. New York: HarperCollins, 1996.

Southwest News. Webchat July 8, 2000. http://www.southwestnews.com/rowling.htm.

Tierney, John. "Here Come the Alpha Pups." *New York Times Magazine*, 5, 2001, 38–43.

Waught, Coulton. *The Comics*. Jackson: UP of Mississippi, 1947.

Westfahl, Gary. *Science Fiction, Children's Literature and Popular Culture: Coming of Age in Fantasyland*. Westport: Greenwood P, 2000.

Wright, Bradford. *Comic Book Nation: The Transformation of Youth Culture in America*. Johns Hopkins UP, 2001.

Yolen, Jane. *Wizard's Hall*. New York: Harcourt, 1991.

Chapter Three

Controversial Content in Children's Literature: Is *Harry Potter* Harmful to Children?

Deborah J. Taub and Heather L. Servaty

Even as the *Harry Potter* books have been heralded as a publishing phenomenon the likes of which has "not been seen since the days of Charles Dickens" (Masson, 2000, p. 68), which have made "boys who hate to read drop their Nintendo and open a book" (Wilgoren, 1999, p. A21), they also have been the subject of challenge and controversy. The American Library Association reported that the *Harry Potter* books were the most challenged books of 1999 and 2000 (472 reported challenges in 1999 and 646 in 2000) and forty-eighth on their list of the 100 most challenged books of the decade (www.ala.org/alaorg/oif/top100bannedbooks.html). In all likelihood this is just a small portion of the actual challenges to the books; the ALA estimates that only 20 to 25 percent of the challenges to a book are reported (www.ala.org/alaorg/oif/top100.pdf). Objections to the books stem from their controversial content—from the centrality of magic to the topic of death to scenes that some believe are too violent, intense, or scary for children.

Controversy over children's books is not new. According to Shannon (1989), "The history of the struggle over the content of children's and adolescents' reading material is nearly as long as the history of schooling in America" (p. 97). Historically, many groups have been seen as weak, including women and those from the lower class, and as needing to be "protected from certain kinds of literature" (Stevenson, 1996, p. 305); "the one group that remains in this category is children" (p. 305). At the heart of challenges to such books is the objectors' idea of "what knowledge they think is valid, valuable, and virtuous for school curricula and library shelves" (Shannon, 1989, p. 97); those who challenge books "may believe that the materials will corrupt children and adolescents, offend the sensitive or unwary reader, or undermine basic values and beliefs" (www.ala.org/alaorg/oif/censormotives.html).

This chapter explores the controversial content of the *Harry Potter* books and whether the books might be harmful to children. The chapter focuses particularly on the issues of violence, scariness, magic, and death. The chapter concludes with guidelines for teachers and parents.

Challenges to Harry Potter
The Religious Argument

In his book about censorship of books in schools and public libraries, Foerstel (1995) states "there is no hotter topic among today's bookbanners than the devil and witchcraft . . . materials about witchcraft and the occult account for the largest number of challenges to resources in libraries today" (p. 109). This can be seen in many of the challenges to Harry Potter. Many of the objections to the *Harry Potter* books have been based on religious objections (www.elycia-webdesign.com/harrypotter/debate/antiharry.html; www.crossroad.to/text/articles/Harry9–99.html; www.mugglesforharrypotter.org/index.htm). *Education World*, reporting on the banning of *Harry Potter*, quoted Mark West, professor of children's literature at UNC–Charlotte: "During the 1980s, most of the censorship cases were anything that pertained to the body, sex, and swear words. [Now], although books like those written by Judy Blume are still under attack, what has taken over is fantasy stories" (www.education-world.com/a_admin/admin157.shtml).

Most religious objections to the magic in the *Harry Potter* books are based on various passages of scripture, most commonly Deuteronomy 18:9–12:

> When you come into the land which the Lord your God gives you, you shall not learn to follow the abominable practices of those nations. There shall not be found among you any one who burns his son or his daughter as an offering, any one who practices divination, a soothsayer, or an augur, or a sorcerer, or a charmer, or a medium, or a wizard, or a necromancer. For whoever does these things is an abomination to the Lord; and because of these abominable practices the Lord your God is driving them out before you. (Revised Standard Version)

Most of the information about the dangers of *Harry Potter* from a Christian perspective can be found on the Internet under such titles as "Harry Potter and the AntiChrist" (www.pawcreek.org.Harry%Potter.

htm); "Bewitched by Harry Potter" (www.crossroad.to/text/articles/Harry 9–99.html); "Harry Potter Lures Kids to Witchcraft—with Praise from Christian Leaders" (www.crossroad.to/text/articles/Harry&Witchcraft. htm); and "Harry Potter and D&D—Like Two Peas in a Pod?" (www.crossroad.to/text/articles/D&D&Harry.htm). The religious concerns include assertions that the books portray magic as harmless, fun, or good and that they may encourage children to dabble in the occult. (Similar arguments are made about the role-playing game *Dungeons & Dragons* ["D&D"] and certain rock music [Blimling, 1990; Hicks, 1990; Hunter, 1998; Kjos, 2000].)

The language of many of these websites is extreme, and both the reasoning and the interpretation of scripture frequently is convoluted. For instance, Joseph Chambers (www.pawcreek.org.Harry%Potter.htm) writes: "Without question I believe the *Harry Potter* series is a creation of hell helping prepare the younger generation to welcome the Biblical prophecies of demons and devils led by Lucifer himself." He continues by suggesting that the source of the inspiration for the *Harry Potter* books, which are widely reported to have just popped into author J. K. Rowling's head fully formed, is Satan. Many may find it difficult to take such extreme ideas seriously or to believe that others might. To many it will appear ridiculous that so many are taking a fantasy seriously.

In their discussion of how religious beliefs influence parental attitudes about children's fantasy behavior, Taylor and Carlson (2000) note that religion is a critical factor in that there are stark differences between what is considered real and what is considered fantasy from one religion to the next. They continue by describing how specific religious orientations (e.g., Hinduism, fundamentalist Christianity, and Mennonite) impact parent's views of childhood fantasy-related behavior. Taylor and Carlson address two primary objections to fantasy offered by parents with fundamentalist Christian beliefs. First, those with fundamentalist beliefs appear to equate fantasy with deceit and express concerns that fantastical activity and storytelling will lead to lying and other deceitful behavior. In addition, members of fundamentalist groups who are focused on issues of "spiritual warfare" believe that it is necessary to protect their children from evil forces in the spiritual world. Some in this latter group have even expressed concern about public elementary schools, stating that they expose children to dangerous ideas about witchcraft, occult practices, and Halloween.

Taylor and Carlson (2000) also discussed their research on the imaginary companions of children. They found a qualitative difference between the responses of parents with fundamentalist Christian beliefs and the other parent participants. In general, parents who expressed concern regarding the behavior usually did so in relation to the inconvenience of including the imaginary companion in family activities and worries that the behavior was developmentally inappropriate and/or that it might indicate that the child was struggling with distinguishing fantasy from reality. In contrast, parents with fundamentalist Christian beliefs associated imaginary companions with the devil. Taylor and Carlson argue that these disparate views of the same behavior "reflect a divergent perception on the part of the adults of what is real and what is fantasy" (p. 248).

This divergence of viewpoint can be seen in the reactions to *Harry Potter* by members of various Christian groups and denominations. Olsen, in *Christianity Today* (Olsen, 1999), cites several Christian leaders who support and admire the books. These leaders find the books promoting values such as courage and loyalty, with a moral approach of good versus evil. The magic, more than one points out, is not occult but mechanical.

In contrast, Gish (2000) presents a clear explanation of the fundamentalist religious concerns about the *Harry Potter* books. She points out that for fundamentalist Christians "witchcraft is as real to us as any other religion" (p. 263). This belief—that witchcraft is real and is necessarily evil—lies at the heart of the religious objections. To those who believe this, the threat of the *Harry Potter* books is that they might desensitize children to the sinfulness of magic and that "children may learn to see them [occult or Satanic practices] as acceptable" (p. 264). "Once again: when you believe that witches and occult practices are real, and contrary to God's laws, those books are quite different from what the authors probably intended" (Gish, 2000, p. 264). Gish provides a useful gloss of Deuteronomy 18:9–12 as those verses are applied to *Harry Potter*. (Those interested in a detailed and excellent description of the religious objections to the Harry Potter books and other popular children's fantasy books are directed to Gish's 2000 article.) She points, for example, to the Divination course offered by Hogwarts (Book Three) and, obviously, the fact that Harry and his friends are learning to be wizards.

Occult

What of the concerns and assertions that exposure to magical ideas, such as spells, wizards, and potions, puts young people in danger of becoming dabblers in the occult or members of a cult? On her website in her discussion of the dangers of *Harry Potter*, Kjos (2000) asserts:

> For most children tutored in paganism by popular authors and computer programmers, there will be no turning back. . . . A little dabbling in the occult usually fuels urges to explore other practices. . . . Packaged for our youth as D&D [Dungeons & Dragons] or as Hogwart's School of Witchcraft and wizardry, they desensitize their captive fans to the dangers of occult forces. They can become irresistible. (www.crossroad.to/text/articles/D&D&Harry.htm)

Hunter (1998) also cites the progression from fantasy role-playing games to dabbling in satanic rituals to cult membership. Some people even assert that satanists use *Dungeons & Dragons* to recruit members (Foerstel, 1994).

Hicks (1990), a law enforcement expert whose book, *In Search of Satan*, addresses alleged satanic crime, debunks the notion of a causal link between fantasy games such as Dungeons & Dragons and occult dabbling. Leeds (1995) studied a stratified random matched sample of fantasy role-playing gamers, satanic "dabblers," and students who were neither game-players nor dabblers. He found the gamers and the uninvolved comparison group to be similar to one another in terms of their beliefs in the paranormal and personal stability and the satanic dabblers to be different from the other two groups in both of those areas. Based on his study, Leeds concluded: "the occult and satanism are two distinctly different realms, and . . . one does not necessarily lead to the next" (p. 158). He continued:

> These results do not support popular media suggestions that involvement in fantasy role-playing games are the direct antecedents to satanic practices, beliefs in magical spells, and demon-summoning in impressionable youth. (Leeds, 1995, p. 158)

Hicks (1990) deplores the notion, suggested by the popular media, "that teens have so little judgment where fantasy is concerned that parents must absolutely control all that they read and hear" (p. 271). Can children and adolescents exercise judgment about fantasy?

Fantasy and Reality

Beyond the religiously based concerns expressed well by Gish (2000) are those of parents who do not believe that magic, of the type presented in the *Harry Potter* series, is real. These parents may express concerns that their children, however, could begin to view such practices as real. In addition, if a child is developmentally unable to distinguish fantasy from reality, the frightening fantastical content of the books (e.g., Lord Voldemort, the dementors) might provoke significant fear responses.

In her thorough review of the fantasy/reality literature, Woolley (1997) begins by highlighting a distinction made by Chandler and Lalonde (1994) between fantastical/magical thinking and thinking about fantasy/magic. She notes that the first of these terms describes a *process* of thought, while the later addresses the *content* of thought. One can think fantastically about realistic content such as when one thinks about an apple flying across the room when requested to do so. One can also think realistically about fantastical/magical content such as when one thinks about the tooth fairy having difficulty entering a house because all the doors and windows are closed and locked. Woolley discusses various definitions of magical/fantastical thinking and she concludes that "magical thinking involves reasoning without knowledge of, or on the basis of some sort of misconception about, causality, or about the natural laws more generally" (p. 993).

Prior to addressing the developmental issues associated with these two concepts as they relate to the magical/fantastical content in the *Harry Potter* series, it seems important to note the place that magical/fantastical thinking holds in current understandings of human development. Piaget (1929) began discussing magical thinking as one of the primitive forms of causality found in the child. He contended that such thinking emerged as a result of the child's "confusion between reality and thought" (p. 132). More specifically, children experience a time in development when they believe that they can modify reality through their thoughts, actions, or desires. Piaget noted that children struggle with this confusion up until the age of eleven or twelve, through his concrete operations period of cognitive development.

Rosengren and Hickling (2000) note that, in contrast to previous researchers and theorists (e.g., Piaget), they believe that magical reasoning emerges during the preschool years rather than existing as a cognitive operation present from birth. They found that children under the age of four years were not aware of and did not use the term "magic." Rosengren and Hickling cite a longitudinal investigation by Hickling (1996) in which she found that "children's first use of magical explanation in everyday conversation occurred on average at forty-two months, six to twelve months later than initial uses of physical, biological, psychological, or social explanations" (p. 84). They contend that "magical beliefs emerge as young children come to recognize shortcomings in the more conventional belief systems" (p. 80). This is in sharp contrast to Piaget's (1929) belief that magical thinking is a primitive thought process that children work to outgrow. Rosengren and Hickling, in fact, refer to magical thinking as a concept that "reflects a degree of cognitive sophistication" not previously present in the child's thought processes (p. 78).

Although the area of "fantasy" has been a neglected subject, particularly in the field of developmental psychology (C. N. Johnson, personal communication, 26 April, 2001), there is valuable information to be gleaned from the research that has been done. Woolley (1997) states clearly that the ability to distinguish fantasy from reality, at a very basic level, is in place by three years of age. She and her colleagues have found that around the age of three years children express differences between reality and pictures, reality and pretense, and reality and toys in their everyday conversations (Woolley & Wellman, 1990). In addition, Estes, Wellman, and Woolley (1989) found that similarly aged children can articulate that a difference exists between a mental representation and the real physical object it represents. In contrast to these achievements, Woolley and Wellman (1993) found that many three year olds believe that imagining something can make that something come into being. An additional interesting developmental note is the fact that children's concept of what magic is appears to change over time. For example, Rosengren and Hickling (1994) exposed children to impossible events and found that many four year olds described these events as "magic," whereas five year olds described them as "tricks."

Woolley (1997) argues that the research she reviewed suggests that children tend to use magical thinking in a rather selective way. She contends that the focus of the question shifts from the age at which children can distinguish fantasy from reality to what situations foster what modes of thought and what types of entities appear to confuse children. The following is a discussion of select factors, primarily noted by Woolley (1997), that seem to affect children's ability to distinguish fantasy from reality.

To begin, there appears to be no evidence that the reading of the *Harry Potter* series, or any other books, disrupts children's basic ability to distinguish fantasy from reality (C. N. Johnson, personal communication, April 26, 2001; J. D. Woolley, personal communication, April 5, 2001). Johnson goes on to note that "on the contrary, the attraction of the books involves playing with the boundary" between fantasy and reality. Another factor that seems to affect whether or not children will make accurate judgments regarding fantasy versus reality has to do with the emotional tenor of the object/entity being imagined (Woolley, 1997). In general, children tend to erroneously believe, regardless of the actual status of the entity, that positively charged entities are real and negatively charged entities are unreal (Samuels & Taylor, 1994). Woolley (1997) states the possibility "that children's judgments about imagined entities may reflect whether or not they *want* the entity to appear" (p. 995). In relation to the *Harry Potter* series, children may be more likely to believe in the existence of the Marauder's Map or the Patronus than they are to believe in Lord Voldemort or the dementors.

Subbotsky (1993, cited by Woolley, 1997) found that the presence of an adult can often inhibit children's use of magical thinking and subsequent behavior. This finding suggests that concerned adults might want to read the *Harry Potter* books to their children or at least be present during the child's reading of the books to be available for any questions that the child may wish to ask. Several researchers have similarly emphasized the importance of context and conditions for the understanding of fantasy versus reality. Bateson (1972) describes fantasy as a "communicational mode" and contends that it is actually the metacommunication (verbal and nonverbal) that accompanies an event that affects how that event will be interpreted. Vanderberg (1998) states that "it is crucial that children know what is serious and what is not, and that they understand and trust the regularities and particularities of communication that are essential for appropriate participation in intersubjective mutuality" (p. 298). Golomb and Galasso (1995) found that when children were clearly informed at the end of the pretense conditions that "they had to end the game," few made errors with regard to believing that fantasy could create reality.

In a similar vein, Subbotsky's (1993/1994, as cited in Woolley, 1997) research suggests that children are more likely to espouse magical beliefs when they have first been exposed to another individual who has endorsed such beliefs. This finding may suggest that children reading the *Harry Potter* books could begin to believe in magic because Harry believes in magic. However, there is also a strong role to be played by parents and other adults in the lives of these children. Rosengren, Hickling, Jurist, and Burger (in preparation, as cited in Rosengren and Hickling, 2000) asked parents to keep a record of their child's questions and parental responses to these questions during the week following attendance at a magic show. They found that parents of preschoolers generally provided magical explanations and affirmed the existence of magic, whereas parents of older children tended to respond to children's questions by describing the events as tricks or by providing physical/natural explanations. Parents and other concerned adults need to become more aware of the informal messages they send to children regarding the actual existence of magical phenomena (Rosengren & Hickling, 2000).

Phelps and Woolley (1994, as cited in Woolley, 1997) found that children's knowledge of the physical world greatly influenced their tendency to use magical explanations of events. The less information children had about certain phenomena, the more likely they were to incorporate magical concepts. Children with an understanding of principles and scientific facts such as gravity are, therefore, likely to recognize that the flying broomsticks and game of Quidditch in *Harry Potter* are imaginary.

The focus of this chapter thus far has been on the distinction between fantasy and reality. Concerns parents may have about fantastical thinking and variables that may be considered if one wished to minimize the level of fantastical thinking in which children engage have been addressed. The flip side of this issue is presented by Johnson (1997) and Vanderberg (1998) who speak about the *benefits* of fantastical thinking and play, respectively. They both address how these processes allow humans to think beyond the constraints of their culture in order to think more abstractly and theoretically. Johnson (1997) argues the need to acknowledge the positive and productive nature of fantastical thinking and the fact that it is not just mistaken thought processes gone awry, but is actually something that we as humans have the capacity to engage in and utilize intentionally as a tool. He offers Einstein as an example of his understanding of a person who used fantastical thinking in its most productive sense.

In addition, Vanderberg (1998) notes that in play "real experiences are rendered 'not real,' the serious made playful, thus allowing for it to be seriously reconsidered" (p. 300). Speaking in a similar tone about fantastical literature, Johnson (personal communication, April 26, 2001) offers that "it is a mistake to think that this genre is an escape from reality. Fiction/fantasy can vividly portray very real issues. In fact, it may amplify these issues, making them more vividly real." Perhaps the realistic issues faced by Harry (e.g., isolation, conflicts with friends, difficulty with authority, etc.) could provide catalysts for discussion about issues that would be too difficult for children to discuss in a direct manner, as pertaining to their own lives. It may be that the fantastical presentation of these topics actually makes such discussions safe and possible for children.

Scary

It is common to refer to certain movies, television programs, and books as "too scary for children" or too scary for children *of a certain age*. However, adult perceptions of what is "too scary" for children may be inaccurate and may be based on flawed reasoning (Stevenson, 1996). Adults label books as too scary based on an adult understanding of what is frightening to children; they also make the assumption that children need special protection from the content of such books. Often, adults make the argument that a given book or scene would have frightened them as children but, as Stevenson (1996) argues, "we can never really re-experience the children we were without bringing along the adults we've become; our adult-imagined children often do not judge or respond to books as would real contemporary children or even as our younger selves would have" (p. 310).

As noted earlier, there is, in fact, no research on the effects of given books on children. The focus in research has been placed on movies and television (Cantor, 1998). This research suggests that *visual images* have a much greater capacity to frighten children than do the word portrayals in books.

According to Cantor (1998), books are different from TV and movies because, for young children, an adult is present as the reader and provides a reassuring presence. (This is similar to the findings reported earlier about the effects of the presence of an adult on magical thinking.) When reading aloud, the adult can edit and interpret as s/he reads. The child who is reading independently has the ability to control the pace of the story rather than being at the mercy of the pacing of the movie or TV show—pacing that often is designed to heighten the tension and suspense of scenes and is accompanied by a soundtrack designed to further intensify the experience. The reading child has a number of options including putting the book down, skipping over the scary paragraphs or pictures, reading more quickly or more slowly, peeking ahead at the ending to reassure him/herself that everything comes out OK, and so on. (Stevenson [1996] gives the example of Ramona in *Ramona the Brave* opening and closing her book in which there is a frightening picture.) Furthermore, as Cantor

(1998) points out, the images in movies and TV are larger than book illustrations and they have the added power of movement and sound.

What is specifically frightening to children appears to depend on their developmental level. According to Cantor (1998), young children (2–7) are frightened of both realistic and fantastic visual images of frightening things, of physical transformations of characters, of the depiction of a parent's death, and of vividly presented natural disasters. Children ages 7–12 (more the age range of *Harry Potter* readers) find realistic threats and dangers, violence, and child victims frightening. Children ages thirteen and older are frightened by realistic physical harm, sexual assault, and threats from aliens and occult forces.

It has been suggested that "scary" books intended for children can help them learn mastery and control of fear (Stevenson, 1996). (Similar results have been found with some movies and TV programs [Cantor, 1998].) These books typically portray protagonists who learn or demonstrate mastery over the threat present in the book. These protagonists can serve as models for children about controlling fear. As Johnson (personal communication, April 26, 2001) observed about the utility of fantasy literature, the ability to deal with issues of fear through books is an example of an opportunity for children to confront real issues in the safe venue of a book.

Death

A particularly powerful example of the portrayal of very real issues in fantasy literature is the topic of death in the *Harry Potter* books. In an interview with *Newsweek* (Jones et al., 2000), Rowling clearly posited that "death and bereavement and what death means . . . is one of the central themes in all seven books" (p. 56). This has raised concerns for both parents and teachers. Is death—particularly the vivid portrayal of death—too sad, too frightening, or even appropriate for children's books?

Gray, Gleick, and Sachs (1999) note that Rowling has indicated that the books will become "darker" as the series progresses in that "there will be deaths" (p. 72). A critical issue that must be addressed here is the necessity to separate the topic of death from issues of violence and evil. It is problematic that all of the deaths in the *Harry Potter* series do occur as the result of violence/evil, in that death cannot and should not be equated with these concepts. Death is not "dark" in and of itself. The inappropriate representation of these ideas as consistently merged has engendered, and is likely to continue to perpetuate the mistaken notion that death is some kind of abnormality of our existence: an evil force. In reality, death is the inevitable end for all living beings. It is a natural stage in development. Society's continuing tendency to link the experience of death with evil fosters difficulties such as death denial (Becker, 1973), the avoidance of dying individuals (Kalish, 1966; Sweeting & Gilhooly, 1991–1992), and the isolation of grieving persons (Corr, Nabe, & Corr, 2000; Kastenbaum, 1998).

With this criticism of Rowling's representation of death duly noted, the fact that she does address issues of death, dying, and bereavement is actually to be commended. The growing body of literature focused on the childhood experience of death is virtually unanimous in its recommendation for straightforward discussions about death at an early age, prior to the occurrence of a death-loss crisis (DeSpelder & Strickland, 1995; Fitzgerald, 1992; Silverman, 2000). In fact, Grollman (1990) contends that "death education begins when life begins" (p. 3).

Despite this call for openness and candor, adults continue to struggle with addressing the topic of death with children. This hesitancy is likely due to a number of factors, including a desire to protect children from the pain of grief, an underlying philosophy of "let kids be kids," and the fear associated with the direct death-related questions children are likely to ask (Schaefer & Lyons, 1993; Silverman, 2000), as well as a basic feeling of inadequacy regarding how to broach the subject. The paradox that arises when death-focused conversations do not occur is that children are left to make sense of death from the wide array of examples they are exposed to on a daily basis through media, such as cartoons, video games, and TV news programs. Grollman (1990) aptly summarizes that "the question is not whether children should receive education about death, but whether the education they are receiving is helpful and reliable" (p. 1). When children are isolated from the truth of death, they are likely to create "a wild fantasy, much worse than the facts" (Schaefer & Lyons, 1993, p. 5) and are also left alone in their grief (Grollman, 1995; Silverman, 2000).

It is highly unlikely that the *Harry Potter* books will be children's first exposure to the idea of death. Children are quite aware of and frequently experience death and dying within their own lives (Corr, 1996; Schaefer & Lyons, 1993). In their overview of the major research findings on children's understanding of death, Speece and Brent (1996) concluded that despite considerable variability among studies, most children have a mature understanding of death by the age of seven years. The notion of a mature understanding of death hinges upon the idea that the concept of death is most accurately represented as incorporating the distinct subcomponents of universality, irreversibility, nonfunctionality, and causality.

Death due to magical causes could be confusing for some children. They are in the midst of learning about the abstract and realistic internal (e.g., loss of blood) and external (e.g., visible cut) causes of death (Corr, 1995). Children often struggle with "magical thinking" when faced with death experiences believing that their thoughts or actions actually produced the death (Grollman, 1990; Schaefer & Lyons, 1993; Webb, 1993). Although there are no clear cases of reversible death in the *Harry Potter* series thus far, it may be confusing for children to read about Harry's parents emerging from his wand in the fourth book. Rowling attempts to make it clear that Harry's parents do not come back to life, as when Dumbledore states, "No spell can reawaken the dead . . . all that would have happened is a kind of reverse echo. A shadow of the living . . . " (pp. 697–98). However, children could easily struggle with the idea of a life "echo" or "shadow" that gradually fades away. Children may also grapple with understanding the level of existence experienced by the vast number of ghosts who roam the halls of Hogwarts.

Looking beyond these unrealistic representations of death, Rowling addresses many accurate and insightful aspects of grief and bereavement in a realistic manner. The first death losses the reader is confronted with are those of Harry's parents. Lily and James Potter are murdered by the evil Lord Voldemort. These deaths occur when Harry is just an infant and he has little if any actual memories of his parents. A realistic aspect of Harry's grief experience as described by Rowling is that he grieves the deaths of his parents even though they died before he knew them. Although not directly addressed within the parental death literature, Davies (2001) found that siblings who experienced the death of a sibling prior to their own birth grieved in similar ways to those experiencing the death of a sibling subsequent to their own birth. Although Harry cannot grieve actual, physical relationships with his parents, he can and does grieve the relationships he was never able to establish with them.

Related to this idea is the continuing relationship Harry *is* able to maintain with his deceased parents. Harry makes frequent references to his parents and actually interacts with them in the first book through the use of the Mirror of Erised (p. 207), in book three during Harry's production of the Patronus, and in book four when his and Lord Voldemort's spells become connected (p. 667). Although these are instances when magical forces allowed Harry to have contact with his parents, his relationships with his deceased parents are examples of "continuing bonds," an emerging and strengthening concept within the grief and bereavement literature (Klass, Silverman, & Nickman, 1996). In contrast to the traditional Freudian (1919) notion that ties to the deceased must be severed for healthy adjustment to take place, the continuing bonds movement within the field acknowledges the human need to maintain, albeit in an altered state, a connection with deceased loved ones who are no longer physically present. More specifically, Silverman, Nickman, and Worden (1992) found that children with a continuing, though altered, relationship with their deceased parent appeared better able to cope with the death loss as well as other accompanying life changes. Silverman (2001) directly connected Harry's experience with her understanding of continuing bonds as she referenced the following statement made to Harry by Dumbledore at the end of book three: "You think the dead we loved ever truly leave us? You think that we don't recall them more clearly than ever in times of great trouble? Your father is alive in you, Harry, and shows himself most plainly when you need him" (pp. 427–28).

Another realistic, though unfortunate, aspect of childhood grief addressed by Rowling is the fact that Harry was shielded from the truth regarding his parents' deaths. He was not informed of the true cause until the latter part of his childhood, an experience that not only was confusing and difficult for him but that also put him at risk. There are many children who are misled about the causes of death, particularly those experiencing death as the result of homicide or suicide. Despite the anxiety and difficulty adults experience while engaging in or even contemplating discussions of such topics with children, experts in the field of children and death invariably call for truthfulness and honesty (Fitzgerald, 1992; O'Toole & Cory, 1998; Schaefer & Lyons, 1993). Although it is clearly not necessary to reveal all the explicit details of such death losses, truthful and developmentally sensitive reporting is of utmost importance. The manner in which Rowling (book four) has Dumbledore honestly state in a direct manner to his students that "Cedric Diggory was murdered by Lord Voldemort" (p. 722) is an example of respecting adolescents with regard to a death loss by providing them with an honest explanation of the death.

The most controversial death in the *Harry Potter* series, thus far, may be that of Cedric Diggory. Cedric was a seventeen-year-old student at Hogwarts, Harry's acquaintance, and fellow Triwizard Tournament competitor. As with Harry's parents, Cedric's death is sudden and caused by evil magical forces. Although deaths resulting from magic are obviously unrealistic, Rowling's portrayal of an adolescent male dying a sudden and violent death is alarmingly true to life. In fact, 1998 U.S. statistics indicate that the top three leading causes of death for males aged 15–24 years are accidents and adverse effects, homicide and legal intervention, and suicide, respectively (Stillion, 2001). Another unsettling, but accurate aspect of this death loss experience is that research indicates that up to 87 percent of all adolescents may experience the death of a peer (Schachter, 1991). In addition, Dise-Lewis (1988) surveyed 681 11–14 year olds (Harry was fourteen at the time of Cedric's death) and found that 12 percent had experienced the death of a peer within the previous twelve-month period. Although Cedric's death may be shocking and disturbing, the sudden death of a peer is far from an uncommon occurrence for children and adolescents. Other aspects of Cedric's death that are quite realistic and actually provide positive models include the appreciation expressed by Cedric's parents to Harry for bringing back the body of their son (p. 716) and the acknowledgment of Cedric's death and call for remembrance of his life led by Dumbledore during the Leaving Festival in the fourth book (pp. 721–24).

Also realistic is Harry's primary initial response to Cedric's death, which is shock and numbness (Corr, Nabe, & Corr, 2000; Kastenbaum, 1998). His subsequent emotion is one of intense guilt (p. 714). Grollman (1990) contends that children are more likely to feel guilt than grieving adults, particularly due to their ongoing struggle with magical thinking and their belief that their thoughts/actions somehow caused the death. Harry is appropriately cared for and comforted by Mrs. Weasley who whispers "It wasn't your fault, Harry" (p. 714).

Guidelines

Given the convergence of the popularity of the *Harry Potter* books and the concerns that they raise for many, how can parents and teachers best approach these books? Because the books have become part of American popular culture, children will be exposed to them. The publicity that will attend the publication of future books in the series and the release of the films and inevitable related merchandising (action figures and so on) will make Harry Potter even more ubiquitous.

1. *Forbidding the books is not the answer.* Gish (2000) cautions even religiously concerned parents against forbidding children to read the *Harry Potter* books, recognizing the temptation of the forbidden fruit.

2. *Know your child.* Although some age-related developmental generalizations can be made, most research suggests that age is not the primary determining factor in what content children find frightening, in children's ability to make sense of fantasy, or in children's understandings of death. A specific child may be "old enough" to read Harry Potter and possess the reading skills to tackle such a long chapter book but may be particularly sensitive or easily frightened. The recommendations of experts should not substitute for parents' judgment.

3. *Discuss the topics raised in the books.* Gish (2000) suggests that parents with religious concerns about the content of the *Harry Potter* books take this as an opportunity to discuss their beliefs and concerns with their children. Likewise, the theme of death in the books presents ready "teachable moments" (Ryan, 1988) for discussions of death (DeSpelder & Strickland, 1995; Fitzgerald, 1992; Wass, 1991). Discussing death with children prior to an immediate and personal loss experience allows adults, unencumbered by their own grief, the ability to provide reasonable and deliberate responses to questions and concerns. In addition, children are likely to gain knowledge and a sense of control/mastery, empowering them for when the inevitable does occur. The *Harry Potter* books also present opportunities for parents and teachers to discuss topics such as isolation and loneliness, conflicts with friends, and difficulty with authority—problems that many children experience in their own lives—in the safer context of the books.

4. *Help children distinguish fantasy from reality.* Adults should discuss with children their understanding of what is real and what is imaginary in the books. Further, adults should overtly and covertly reinforce with children an awareness that the content of the books is fantasy and not real. Because an understanding of the laws of science and the natural world contribute to a child's ability to distinguish fantasy from reality, concerned parents and adults should expose children to information about the physical world such as would be present at science museums, but also information that can be understood through home experiments and through watching educational television programs.

5. *Provide an adult presence.* The presence of an adult, whether as reader at home or in a classroom read-aloud or merely as a companion in the room with an independently reading child, can reduce the likelihood that fantasy and reality will be confused and the likelihood that the scariness of the books will be overwhelming.

6. *Distinguish between the books and the movie.* The fact that a child was "old enough" to read the *Harry Potter* books and found them fun and entertaining does not necessarily mean that he or she will not be overwhelmed or frightened by the movie. The power of movies to frighten is much greater than that of books (Cantor, 1998). Hollywood's depiction of Lord Voldemort, the dementors, the basilisk, and Aragog, the enormous spider, all may be much more frightening than the depictions in the child's imagination—and they have the added power of size, movement, and sound. Furthermore, the child will be unable to control exposure and pacing.

7. *Respect others' beliefs and viewpoints.* Some families may wish for their children to "opt out" of *Harry Potter* read-alouds. This is an opportunity to model understanding and respect.

References

Bateson, G. *Steps to an Eology of Mind: A Revolutionary Approach to Man's Understanding of Himself.* New York: Chandler Publishing, 1971.

Becker, E. *The Denial of Death.* New York: The Free P, 1973.

Blimling, G. S. (1990). "The Involvement of College Students in Totalist Groups: Causes, Concerns, Legal Issues, and Policy Considerations." *Cultic Studies Journal* 7 (1990): 41–68.

Cantor, J. *"Mommy, I'm Scared": How TV and Movies Frighten Children and What We Can Do to Protect Them.* San Diego: Harcourt Brace, 1998.

Chandler, M. J., and C. E. Lalonde. "Surprising, Miraculous, and Magical Turns of Events." *British Journal of Developmental Psychology* 12 (1994): 83–95.

Corr, C. A. "Children, Development, and Encounters with Death and Bereavement. "In *Handbook of Childhood Death and Bereavement.* Ed. C. A. Corr and D. M. Corr. New York: Springer, 1996. 3–28.

Corr, C. A., C. M. Nabe, and D. M. Corr. *Death and Dying: Life and Living.* 3rd ed. Belmon: Wadsworth, 2000.

Davies B. "When a Child Is Dying: Fathers' Experiences." Paper presented at the King's College International Conference on Death and Bereavement. London, Canada. May 2001.

DeSpelder, L. A., and A. L. Strickland. "Using Life Experiences as a Way of Helping Children Understand Death." In *Beyond the Innocence of Childhood.* Ed. D. A. Adams and E. J. Deveau. 45–54. Vol. 1. of *Factors Influencing Children and Adolescents' Perceptions and Attitudes toward Death.* Amityville: Baywood, 1995.

Dise-Lewis, J. E. "The Life Events and Coping Inventory: An Assessment of Stress in Children." *Psychosomatic Medicine* 50 (1988): 484–99.

Estes, D., H. M. Wellman, and J. Woolley. "Children's Understanding of Mental Phenomena."

In *Advances in Child Development and Behavior.* Ed. H. Reese. New York: Academic P, 1989. 41–86.

Fitzgerald, H. *The Grieving Child: A Parents' Guide.* New York: Fireside, 1992.

Foerstel, H. N. *Banned in the U.S.A.: A Reference Guide to Book Censorship in Schools and Public Libraries.* Westport: Greenwood, 1994.

Freud, S. "Mourning and melancholia." *Collected papers.* Vol. 4. 1919. New York: Basic Books, 1957.

Gish, K. W. "Hunting Down Harry Potter: An Exploration of Religious Concerns about Children's Literature." *The Horn Book Magazine* 76 (2000): 262–71.

Goldman, L. *Breaking the Silence; A Guide to Help Children with Complicated Grief: Suicide, Homicide, AIDS, Violence, and Abuse.* Washington: Accelerated Development, 1996.

Goldman, L. E., and J. P. Goldman. *Bart Speaks Out: Breaking the Silence on Suicide.* Los Angeles: Western Psychological Services, 1998.

Golomb, C., and L. Galasso. "Make Believe and Reality: Explorations of the Imaginary Realm." *Developmental Psychology* 31 (1995): 800–10.

Gray, P., E. Gleick, and A. Sachs. "Wild about Harry." *Time,* 20 Sept. 1999: 66.

Grollman, E. A. *Talking about Death: A Dialogue between Parent and Child.* Boston: Beacon, 1990.

———. "Can You Answer Children's Questions?" In *Beyond the Innocence of Childhood.* Ed. D. A. Adams and E. J. Deveau. 9–13. Vol. 1 of *Factors Influencing Children and Adolescents' Perceptions and Attitudes Toward Death.* Amityville: Baywood, 1995.

Harris, P. L., E. Brown, C. Marriot, S. Whittall, and S. Harmer. "Monsters, Ghosts, and Witches: Testing the Limitations of the Fantasy-Reality Distinction in Young Children. *British Journal of Developmental Psychology* 9 (1991): 105–23.

Hicks, R. D. *In Pursuit of Satan: The Police and the Occult.* Buffalo: Prometheus, 1990.

Hunter, E. "Adolescent Attraction to Cults." *Adolescence* 33 (1998): 709–14.

Johnson, C. N. "Crazy Children, Fantastical Theories, and the Many Uses of Metaphysics." *Child Development* 68 (1997): 1024–26.

Jones, M., R. Sawhill, C. Power, K. Springer, A. Cooper, and H. W. Scott. "Why Harry's Hot." *Newsweek,* 17 July 2000: 53–56

Kalish, R. A. "A Continuum of Subjectively Perceived Death." *Gerontologist* 6 (1996): 73–76.

Kastenbaum, R. J. *Death, Society, and Human Experience.* 6th ed. Needham Heights: Allyn and Bacon, 1998.

Kjos, B. (2000, June 28). *Harry Potter and D&D—Like Two Peas in a Pod?* <http://www. crossroad.to/text/articles/D&D&Harry.htm.

Klass, D., P. R. Silverman, and S. L. Nickman. *Continuing Bonds: New Understandings of Grief.* Philadelphia: Taylor & Francis, 1966.

Leeds, S. M. "Personality, Belief in the Paranormal, and Involvement with Satanic Practices among Young Adult Males: Dabblers versus Gamers." *Cultic Studies Journal* 12 (1995): 148–65.

Masson, S. "So What's All This about Harry Potter?" *Quadrant* Dec. 2000: 68–70.

Olsen, T. "Opinion Roundup: Positive about Potter." *Christianity Today* <http://www. christianitytoday.com/ct/1999/150/12.0.html.

O'Toole, D., and J. Cory. *Helping Children Grieve and Grow.* Burnsville: Compassion P, 1998.

Phelps, K. E., and J. D. Woolley. "The Form and Function of Young Children's Magical Beliefs." *Developmental Psychology* 30 (1994): 385–94.

Piaget, J. *The Child's Conception of the World.* New York: Harcourt and Brace, 1929.

Rosengren, K. S., and A. K. Hickling. "Seeing is Believing: Children's Explanations of

Commonplace, Magical, and Extraordinary Transformations." *Child Development* 65 (1994): 1605–26.

———. "Metamorphosis and Magic: The Development of Children's Thinking about Possible Events and Plausible Mechanisms." In *Imagining the Impossible: Magical, Scientific, and Religious Thinking in Children.* Ed K. S. Rosengren, C. N. Johnson, and P. L. Harris. New York: Cambridge UP, 2000. 75–98.

Rothbaum, F., and J. R. Weisz. *Child Psychopathology and the Quest for Control.* New York: Sage, 1988.

Ryan, M. "The Teachable Moment: The Washington Center Internship Program." *New Directions for Teaching and Learning* 35 (1988): 39–47.

Samuels, A., and M. Taylor. "Children's Ability to Distinguish Fantasy Events from Real-Life Events." *British Journal of Developmental Psychology* 12 (1994): 412–27.

Schachter, S. "Adolescent Experiences with the Death of a Peer." *Omega* 24 (1991): 1–11.

Schaefer, D., and C. Lyons. *How Do We Tell the Children?* New York: Newmarket P, 1993.

Shannon, P. "Overt and Covert Censorship of Children's Books." *The New Advocate* 2 (1989): 97–104.

Silverman, P. R. *Never Too Young to Know: Death in Children's Lives.* New York: Oxford, 2000.

———. "Bereaved Children and Adolescents: When Do Gender Differences Matter?" Paper presented at the King's College International Conference on Death and Bereavement. London, Canada. May 2001.

Silverman, P. R., S. Nickman, and J. W. Worden. "Detachment Revisited: The Child's Reconstruction of a Dead Parent." *American Journal of Orthopsychiatry* 62 (1992): 494–503.

Speece, M. W., and S. B. Brent. "The Development of Children's Understanding of Death." In *Handbook of Childhood Death and Bereavement.* Ed. C. A. Corr and D. M. Corr. New York: Springer, 1996. 29–50.

Stevenson, D. "Frightening the Children?: Kids, Grown-ups, and Scary Picture Books." *The Horn Book Magazine*, May/June 1996: 305–14.

Stillion, J. "Feminine Frailty and Masculine Might: Understanding Sex and Gender Differences in Dying and Death." Paper presented at the King's College International Conference on Death and Bereavement. London, Canada. May 2001.

Subbotsky, E. V. *Foundations of the Mind: Children's Understanding of Reality.* Cambridge: Harvard UP, 1993.

———. "Early Rationality and Magical Thinking in Preschoolers: Space and Time." *British Journal of Developmental Psychology* 12 (1994): 97–108.

Sweeting, H. N., and M. L. Gilhooly. "Doctor, Am I Dead? A Review of Social Death in Modern Societies." *Omega* 24 (1991–1992): 251–69.

Taylor, M., and S. M. Carlson. "The Influence of Religious Beliefs on Parental Attitudes about Children's Fantasy Behavior." In *Imagining the Impossible: Magical, Scientific, and Religious Thinking in Children.* Ed. K. S. Rosengren, C. N. Johnson, and P. L. Harris. New York: Cambridge UP, 2000. 247–68.

Vanderburg, B. "Real and Not Real: A Vital Developmental Dichotomy." In *Multiple Perspectives on Play in Early Childhood Education.* Ed. Olicia N. Saracho and Bernard Spodek. Albany: State U of New York P, 1998. 295–305.

Wass, H. "Helping Children Cope with Death." In *Children and Death.* Ed. D. Papadatou and C. Papadatos. New York: Hemisphere Publishing, 1991. 11–32.

Webb, N. B. *Helping Bereaved Children: A Handbook for Practitioners.* New York: Guilford, 1993.

Wilgoren, J. "Don't Give Us Little Wizards the Anti-Potter Parents' Cry." *New York Times*, 1 Nov. 1999.

Woolley, J. D. "Thinking About Fantasy: Are Children Fundamentally Different Thinkers and Believers from Adults?" *Child Development* 68 (1997): 991–1011.

———. "The Development of Beliefs about Direct Mental-Physical Causality in Imagination, Magic, and Religion." In *Imagining the Impossible: Magical, Scientific, and Religious Thinking in Children.* Ed. K. S. Rosenbren, C.N. Johnson, and P. L. Harris. New York: Cambridge UP, 2000.

Woolley, J. D., and H. M. Wellman. "Young Children's Understanding of Realities, Nonrealities, and Appearances." *Child Development* 61 (1990): 946–61.

———. "Origin and Truth: Young Children's Understanding of Imaginary Mental Representations." *Child Development* 64 (1993): 1–17.

Part II

Reader Response and Interpretive Perspectives

Chapter Four

Ways of Reading *Harry Potter*: Multiple Stories for Multiple Reader Identities

Kathleen F. Malu

Introduction

This chapter explores the tension between my personal interest in the *Harry Potter* series and my son's rejection of it as well as the reactions of other children and grown-ups to this literature. Questions I consider include: Why did this series appeal to me? Why did my son, Matthew[1], seem to reject this story? How have other children and grown-ups responded to this series? I begin by telling the story of how my son and I entered the world of Harry Potter. Next, I analyze this story using reader-response theory and the framework of context, reader, and text. Then, I explore responses from Matthew's friends and classmates, my friends, and other individuals, analyzing these as well. I conclude with suggestions to parents and teachers.

Memories of a Family Bedtime Read Aloud: Getting "Hooked" on *Harry Potter*

It all began innocently enough. A few summers ago, I found myself browsing through the books at my favorite children's bookstore when I noticed a few signs promoting a new book about someone named Harry Potter. I filed the information away, as I usually do, into some deep mental file-folder and promptly forgot about it!

A few weeks later, my sister asked Matthew if he had read *Harry Potter and the Sorcerer's Stone*. "No," Matt replied. So, my sister purchased it as a gift for Matthew's eleventh birthday, informing me that it was a "very popular" book. At that point I resurrected my bookstore observation and became conscious of other *Harry Potter* sightings: various newspaper and magazine articles and other bookstore promotional posters.

Matthew, meanwhile, forgot about *Sorcerer's Stone*. So, it gathered dust on his desk until I reminded him about it and proposed that we read it aloud as our next bedtime book. We began our reading at the end of September, a few weeks into the new school year.

As I read aloud during the first few nights I found myself stumbling over names that held little meaning for me (and currently for spellcheck as I stare at the red underlines that follow!): Dursley, Dedalus Diggle, Muggle, and, of course, Albus Dumbledore and McGonagall. Matthew would promptly fall asleep after three or four pages each evening. Since we didn't get very far very fast, I was perpetually struggling to hold Matt's interest in the text. Yet, I was sympathetic to his disinterest since I didn't find the story particularly appealing either. But I reminded Matthew of my "50" page rule, read fifty pages before rejecting a book, and insisted that we get to at least page fifty.

It took us about seven days of reading to reach the "boa constrictor" episode (*Sorcerer's Stone*, p. 28). Even with all of my prompting, cajoling, and encouraging, I just couldn't help Matthew stay awake each night, much less enter the story. Meanwhile, I was slowly becoming enraptured with this book, reading late into the night after Matthew's eyes shut. By the time Matthew and I reached page 50, I was finished with the book myself and felt compelled to begin the second book immediately! The very next day, as I found myself modifying my route to work so that I could stop at the local bookstore to purchase *Harry Potter and the Chamber of Secrets*, I knew that I was "hooked." Matthew, meanwhile, informed me that his teacher had begun to read *Sorcerer's Stone* aloud to his class and he preferred to follow along with them. So, we abandoned our read aloud of *Sorcerer's Stone*.

As soon as I finished *Chamber of Secrets*, I again found myself, the very next day, modifying my travel plans to include a brief stop at the bookstore, where I purchased *Harry Potter and the Prisoner of Azkaban*. Once I had devoured that book, I waited, like the rest of the Harry Potter fan club in the summer of 2000, for *Harry Potter and the Goblet of Fire*.

As for Matthew's school experience, he did not seem to enjoy the class read aloud experience, writing in his journal, "I don't like this book. I like action stories." He told me that he spent many days listening to the book without interest. At his November family conference, his teacher, Angela, noted that Matt seemed "disinterested" during the read aloud time, sitting quietly, but inattentive to the story. Only occasionally did he engage in any of the class discussion. When we asked about this he said, "It's boring. I don't like the book." From that point forward, Matthew did not talk further about his school activities with *Harry Potter*.

So, I was quite surprised at the end of the school year to discover that his class had written and performed a shadow puppet show. I learned of this when I went to Matt's classroom to collect his portfolio and noticed a handpainted poster, "Harry Potter and the Golden Snitch." It was quite serendipitous that I had a camera with me and was able to take a photo of it. Later that day, when I asked Matthew about the poster, he told me that the class had written and performed a shadow puppet show about the Quidditch match from *Chamber of Secrets*. Then, he added:

> It was kind of fun. I didn't really understand the game but I was one of the quid-ditch match announcers and sometimes I [had to move] the snitch [shadow puppet] and that was fun.

So, I thought, he didn't remain completely distant and "turned off" as I had originally imagined. What did this all mean, I wondered?

As I step back to analyze these experiences with the *Harry Potter* texts, I am most struck by the conflict between my enchantment with this story and Matthew's apparent dislike of it. What did I find so appealing about this series and why? What did Matt dislike about *Harry Potter* and why? What tensions did this create for us?

The Tools of Analysis

To conduct this analysis, I draw upon current reader response theory and research. According to Rosenblatt (1978), there is no one right way to read a text. Rather, readers make connections to their past experiences and create their own meaning from the written word, the "poem." Thus, reading is a transactional process between readers and text in which meaning is constructed each time readers read. Reader-response theory highlights the importance of individual responses to what readers feel is the author's message.

This theory of reading indicates that there are several perspectives to consider when analyzing and interpreting reading. Broadly viewed these perspectives include a focus on the context of the literacy event, the reader, and the text and author (Moje, Dillion, & O'Brien, 2000; Rogers, 1999). Rogers (1999) urges that these perspectives be situated within and beyond the classroom. An examination of reading that incorporates these perspectives is not distinct, fixed, and stagnant. Such an examination reveals that these perspectives are dynamic, fluid, and interdependent.

The nature of this dynamic movement becomes clearer when a

sociocultural lens is used to examine literacy and learning. The perspectives of context, reader, and text become blended and blurred (Galda & Beach, 2001). As the broader contexts of learning and readers "constructing texts as cultural worlds" are studied, further insights and understandings about how readers transact with texts are gained (Coles, 1998; Galda & Beach, 2001; Gee, 2000).

Our current understanding of the role that context plays in reading calls for us to move beyond the immediate to consider influences from family, friends, and peer groups even when these influences may not be readily apparent to the reader. Context also includes environments that the reader may not be aware of or immediately involved in, or such as an after-school play group or family holiday gathering. Children's experiences and cultural and academic backgrounds contribute to their way of responding to text. Sipe (1999) urges a focus on ever-expanding context circles that move from the individual reader to the classroom and from the classroom community. Moje, Dillon, and O'Brien (2000) note that contexts, dynamic and always changing, are constructed by learners. Understanding context offers significant insights into readers' literacy experiences.

Readers bring multiple identities to their reading experiences and these identities are in a constant state of flux, shifting as readers engage with text. Such identities are shaped by a reader's gender, age, ethnicity, social class, sexual orientation, language use, and religious (Moje, Dillon, & O'Brien, 2000), personal, and academic experiences (Alvermann, 2001), as well as family stories (Chandler, 1999). For example, Alvermann (2001) wonders whether the identification of some readers as *struggling* may shape the ways in which they read texts. Chandler (1999) suggests that parents have the potential to provide valuable information regarding their teenager's literacy identities within the context of home reading and family book talks. Understanding these identities and the roles they may play for readers as they read provides valuable information and insight into a reader's interpretation of text.

Rosenblatt (1978) defines text as the "poem" created by the active participation or "transaction" of a reader with text. This definition holds true today, even though "text" is no longer defined as simply the printed word. In today's technoculture, researchers (Leu & Kinzer, 2000; New London Group, 1996) have broadened the definition of text to include multimedia text with graphics, design, color, layout, and audio. Talk is text (Heath, 1994). Responses to literature that take the form of dramatic performance

(Wolf, Edmiston, & Enciso, 1997) create new "texts" to be read. Gee (2000) identifies talk as a tool that can carry culture and establish identity. Carico (2001) notes the complexities inherent in classroom small group talk, specifically for middle-school girls, and calls for a literacy of talk, urging teachers to value the process of talk in similar ways as the writing process is valued today. Lehr and Thompson (2000) studied the oral responses of children to multicultural texts and found that they made connections that were personal, that were scaffolded to other children's comments, and that revealed background knowledge. Text and the meanings it carries link readers to others and others to readers.

Studies that explore resistance to text focus on authors' (Sutherland, 1985) and readers' (Enciso, 1994) resistance to issues or experiences within society. Just as authors may accept or reject, destroy or promote a variety of stances toward social issues and experiences, might not readers do the same as they transact with text? Enciso (1994) suggests that this may be the case.

While we all know the pleasure of reading a "good" book (Trelease, 1995), there is little exploration of pleasure within reader-response theory (Sipe, 1999; Touponce, 1996). Yet, studies of intertextual connections clearly reveal children's pleasure with personalizing stories (Sipe, 1999) and questioning the story line or revealing textual gaps (Sipe, 1998).

Let me preface this analysis by explaining how I created it. In preparing this chapter, I drew upon my memory to revisit and reflect upon the family story and our experiences with reading *Sorcerer's Stone*. I reviewed my personal and professional calendars; conversed with Matthew to explore his memory of events; examined my notes from his family conferences and his school artifacts such as his report card, writing journal, shadow puppet show script, and classroom photos; reread *Sorcerer's Stone*; and shared and discussed various drafts of this manuscript with Matthew, asking for and integrating his input and feedback.

Who is Matthew? From my perspective, Matthew is an energetic, athletic, independent-minded pre-adolescent, who, at the time of our reading of *Sorcerer's Stone*, spent more time playing baseball, soccer, basketball, and video games and talking on the phone than he did reading. Matthew agreed with this description and added, "I like to read magazines a lot." Beginning when he was three years old, Matthew attended progressive public schools in New York City: Marble Hill Nursery School and Central Park East I Elementary School. At the time of our reading of

Sorcerer's Stone, he was eleven years old and in sixth grade. Currently he is an eighth grader.

Who am I? I have been an educator for many years and have taught in a wide variety of settings (see elsewhere in this volume), working for twenty years predominately with individuals for whom English is not their first, home, and/or primary language. For the past ten years I have been involved with teacher preparation at the undergraduate and graduate levels. Currently, one of my most exciting professional challenges is teaching a graduate reading course in cyberspace. I enjoy reading, discussing, thinking about, and conducting educational research that focuses on theory and practice issues, diversity, and social justice. Whenever I can, I spend my free time with my two sons, Joe (who began his second year of college at the time we began reading *Sorcerer's Stone)* and Matthew, and I particularly enjoy watching them play on their various sports teams. I began reading *Sorcerer's Stone* just as I was trying to learn how to roof garden without killing plants!

Exploring Contexts

Matthew and I chose to read *Sorcerer's Stone* because this gift book was waiting to be read and I hadn't read aloud to Matthew at bedtime for much of August. At the beginning of the school year, I proposed that we take up this ritual again because it gave us some quiet time together before Matthew fell asleep. However, there was a natural paradox inherent with reading at bedtime: Reading gave us some time together to share a story and also helped put Matt to sleep. Matt reported, "I like when you read out loud before I go to bed," and added, "Whenever you read, I fall asleep."

Today, I wonder why I was so passionate about continuing this nightly ritual. As a professional and a mother, I value reading aloud to children. Was it also significant that Joe had returned to college the first week in September? I missed Joe and reading with Matthew seemed to allow me to recall Joe's presence and my memories of reading with him. Losing Joe to college made me aware of time's speed! This nightly reading ritual with Matthew would not last forever, I knew. Within a few years, Matthew would be gone, too. Did I think I might be able to try and stop time by continuing to read to Matthew?

In the context of "Joe" memories, Matthew recalls roughhousing with Joe in their shared bedroom, "When I'm in a head lock with Joe, I feel like Harry Potter," living in the small cupboard room under the stairs. Harry's plight provoked a poignant memory for Matthew, framed within Matt and Joe's shared bedroom.

Another context for our read aloud undoubtedly came out of my fear of Matthew's disinterest in reading *Harry Potter*. Matthew and I recalled comments I made to him that seemed to transform the bedroom read aloud experience into a teacher-centered classroom. Matthew, in total agreement with this bedroom-as-classroom image, recalled my asking him, "Can you figure out what *Muggle* means? Listen again to this sentence."

A close rereading of the first few pages of *Sorcerer's Stone* supports this complex context shift for us. We didn't just read in Matt's bedroom-as-classroom. My recall of my struggles with the unusual, strange names supports my image of this transformation of Matt's bedroom-as-classroom to Matt's bedroom-as-*my*-classroom—with me as the student, reading a difficult passage aloud.

The importance of my passion for reading with my children is well supported by national calls for parents to "get involved" with their children's reading (Anderson, Richard, Hiebert, Elfrieda, Scott, Judith, & Wilkinson, 1985; Scholastic, Chrysler Learning Connection, American Federation of Teachers, Association for Supervision and Curriculum Development, 1995) and research on family literacy and parent involvement in reading. Bissex's (1980) seminal work documents her son's literacy growth and development and encourages parents to take an active role in their children's literacy learning. Trelease (1995), drawing upon a variety of research studies, urges parents to read aloud to their children each night, and Taylor (1997) notes that, while there are many different family literacy styles, they all have value and should be supported. Chandler (1999) notes that reading relationships between parents and their teenagers might be used to inform and improve the teaching of literacy at the secondary level. Research on parental involvement in schools suggests that children whose parents are involved with their children's teachers, schools, and school work are more successful in school than children whose parents do not become involved (Epstein, 1990; Hoover-Dempsey & Sandler, 1997).

Matthew's reluctance to read *Sorcerer's Stone* contradicts both my expectations about what I thought would happen and my experiences with Joe. Because Joe enjoyed our nightly read aloud before he went to sleep, I assumed that Matthew found this pleasurable as well. In fact, from infancy, Matthew joined us each night, nestled in my arms, listening quietly to this nighttime ritual. From these positive family experiences, I saw no reason why Matthew and I should not continue reading together, finding pleasure in each other's company and a shared text.

Research findings about the literacy habits of boys tend to set off alarm bells in my head as I struggle to make sense of Matthew's reluctance to read *Harry Potter*. Boys, regardless of their age, fail more often than girls in the area of reading (Flynn & Rahbar, 1993; Riordan, 1999). There is also a much higher percentage of boys in remedial reading classes (Vogel, 1990; Riordan, 1999). I wonder about the influence of female teachers on Matthew and his work in school. Out of seven teachers, Matthew had only one male teacher, who was quite rigid in his expectations of children and their learning. I am sympathetic to Brozo and Schmelzer's (1997) suggestion that gendered social practices of literacy teaching and learning may have an "insidious" effect on boys' perceptions of and attitudes toward reading.

Creating Texts

There are occasional accounts in the literature regarding parents-who-are-teachers/researchers and the literacy struggles their children encounter (e.g., Nierstheimer, 2000). Yet, the great volume of literature reports on the merits of family involvement in literacy and reading, failing to adequately address what can happen when parents begin to seem like teachers and a "fun" text begins to feel like a school text to a child. In reexamining *Sorcerer's Stone* today and recalling my struggle and Matthew's struggle to make sense of the story, I am struck by how much of a "school text" I created as we read this magical story. School-type text memories are so much a part of my memory of our *Sorcerer's Stone* read aloud, I wonder whether Matthew abandoned our nightly reading for his class read aloud in part to avoid the tension inherent in the teacher-mother text I read to him at bedtime ("school" time from Matthew's perspective, perhaps).

What was this teacher-mother text that we read? The words on the pages of *Sorcerer's Stone* created one text. I suspect that the tone of my reading and the talk Matthew and I shared created a second text. It is this second text, long swept into the memories of our minds, that troubles me, as a teacher, mother, and researcher. What is it, I wonder, about this profession of teaching that compels me to use text in ways that transform a familial bedroom into a classroom and a bed into a school desk? In what ways did I contribute to the creation of this familial school text for Matthew? I don't have answers, only memories.

Yet, this reading was not for my child alone. There were numerous other ways in which I read once Matthew was asleep. Reading late into the nights with Harry Potter, I was transported back to my childhood home, recalling a powerful reading memory I hold vividly today. I recall as a child in seventh grade reading *Jane Eyre* late into the night, aware that I was the only one awake in our dark, creaky house. I was scared of the night but desperate to follow Jane's story. It was a kind of becoming-of-age experience in which I deliberately stayed awake to read long after my parents were asleep, willfully disobeying their sleepy calls to "turn out the lights and go to sleep because you won't be able to get up for school." With *Harry Potter*, it was my professional voice urging me to return to correcting student papers or writing another draft of a manuscript I needed to produce.

As I reflect further, my mind moves fluidly with the smallest text images. An early scene of the cat, McGonagall, sitting on a wall transports me to the Congo and the houses there that are enclosed within walls. The adventures at Hogwarts recalls a few of my boarding school activities, including a few nighttime escapades to the kitchen for a few cookies when most of the boarders were asleep! Thus, the text for me was multilayered and complex, provoked by powerful personal connections within and outside of the text and linked to many varied settings, including adult and childhood locations. Besides the garden wall image, I didn't find anything appealing in the early pages. In fact, when I discovered "Muggle" I found myself drawing upon my "school" reading strategies as I tried to find a definition for this word. I remember feeling annoyed and distracted. I tried to attract Matthew's interest but I think that this only served to remind him that I teach. I remember saying:

> Well Matt, what do you think this word *muggle* could mean? . . . Can you figure it out? . . . What other word could we put in its place? You have to listen carefully to figure out what a muggle is. It looks like we're going to have to learn some new vocabulary if we want to read this book.

In revisiting my memories of these new words, I remember thinking that Matthew and I would need to learn them quickly. I questioned: Is this book really going to be worth the struggle? Will we ever need to use these words? Couldn't we read something a bit more exciting and less complicated, with fewer unusual words? It wasn't just the words. It was also their pronunciation (particularly the names, as I indicated earlier).

This text provoked shifts in contexts that propelled and provoked shifts in my identities. I moved frequently between mother, child, and teacher. Initially, I read ahead so that I could better "teach-read" with my son to help him enter the text. As the weeks passed and I became more aware of the popularity of the *Harry Potter* series, I puzzled over the disconnect with Matt. I was enthralled with the story, attending to Harry's plight as an unwanted, orphaned relative, the mystery of the wizard world, and eventually the Hogwarts classroom stories and thrilling adventures (see Alton, chapter 8, for her references to the bildungsroman, school stories, and adventure genres fused into the series).

As I progressed through the *Sorcerer's Stone*, I occasionally chatted with a colleague about Harry and, through our conversations, I became aware of just how much I was compelled to read because I wanted to "see" how Rowling depicted schools, schooling, students, and teachers. I mentally challenged and protested her rigid stereotyping of girls (good students) and boys (troublemakers). I recalled my days at boarding school, easily relating to the camaraderie. I challenged the image of "good food" (at any institution!), recalling my fair share of "mystery meat" days with mousy brown pudding for dessert. The text became, for me, a living memory, transporting me, after Matthew's eyes closed, into my childhood world that I linked into Harry's world.[2]

For Matthew, just the opposite seemed true. In revisiting his experiences he told me:

> The book was boring and I'm not patient. I didn't like listening to it because Angela [his teacher] reads it late, after recess and I'm exhausted. I just want to lay down. . . . It's like a cartoon and I don't like that kind of cartoon . . . the names were so weird.

In trying to probe for further information, I was struck by how little I understood about his disinterest and how difficult it was to help him reveal anything further. He had written only a few journal entries at school that gave me further clues. My family conference notes supported only what Matthew continued to say, "I didn't like the book." In reviewing some of his school artifacts including the photos I took of the shadow puppet theater and a copy of the "Harry Potter and the Golden Snitch" shadow puppet show script, featuring the Quidditch match, Matthew responded:

Oh, you found that! That's what I was looking for! See, I was a game announcer and sometimes moved the ball and the other ball with wings, like this. [Matt shows me with his arms how he had to move the two balls, substituting one for the other.]

This sports story (see Alton, chapter 8) appealed to Matthew, within the context of the puppet show. This spark of interest appears to lend support to reader-response theory and text as performance. The call for more drama and performed texts in schools (Moffet & Wagner, 1992) should not be ignored, particularly for boys.

Revealing Readers' Multiple Identities

It was impossible to find the identities that Matthew used when hearing the *Sorcerer's Stone* or *Chamber of Secrets* at school. It is difficult to capture the multiple identities I recalled throughout my reading of the *Harry Potter* series. Sometimes, I was the diffident little girl who read independently into the night; I was the shy school girl constantly stumbling when asked to read aloud in school; the growing-in-confidence boarding school student who enjoyed living with friends and playing the occasional trick or two; the grief-filled teen whose beloved father died much too soon; the progressive educator who grew up during the 1960s protests for civil rights and peace; the educator who worked and traveled in Africa; and a proud wife and the mother of two thoughtful, independent sons.

Across the global community of Harry Potter readers, some of my identities may be a bit unusual. I wonder how many young teens have experienced the sudden death of a parent, even though Alton (chapter 8) notes the broad appeal of this theme. If I use my own childhood experience as a guide, out of a class of fifty students, I and one other classmate experienced the death of a parent during four years in high school. My father died suddenly when I was fifteen; hers, when she was ten. This loss resonates today each time I read Dumbledore's words:

> You think the dead we loved ever truly leave us? You think that we don't recall them more clearly than ever in times of great trouble? Your father is alive in you, Harry and shows himself most plainly when you have need of him. (*Prisoner of Azkaban*, pp. 427–28)

While my school experiences were quite normal and undoubtedly universal, I think I was a bit unusual in that I attended a boarding school, unusual for children in the United States, as well as for children in many other countries. My experiences in boarding school helped me connect immediately to the Hogwarts community. My life in Africa came immediately to mind as I read the first pages of *Sorcerer's Stone* when the cat McGonagall negotiated the Dursley's garden wall. I so easily recall gated and walled compounds where I visited and lived in the Congo.

My identity as a progressive educator may also not be the norm for *Harry* readers. Nevertheless, other identities I held as a reader are quite common, including the identities of mother and diffident little girl. In fact, reading is dependent upon an individual's experiences, and several of my experiences have been no different from those of most individuals. Consider, for example, reading *Harry Potter* as a parent. There are any number of intriguing themes to follow. The opening pages begin as bildungsroman (see Alton, chapter 8) when we learn of the Dursleys' deep fear and hatred of the Potters, labeling them "unDursleyish." They just couldn't fit in with the Dursleys' lifestyle. What parents cannot relate to the fear-filled nightmare of a sudden, horrific death that leaves their beloved child orphaned and forced to be unwelcomely admitted into an unfamiliar extended family. Parents can easily imagine the animosity and hatred Harry suffers at the Dursleys'! The fear that such a fate may befall any child can easily leave parents, including parents in blended families, and guardians, with many, many sleepless nights!

Then there is the incessant teasing and antagonism between Dudley and Harry that parents may also find tragic, frustrating, and totally believable, perhaps because they are living it in their own families! There are so many plausible experiences, namely, fights between Harry and Dudley, that this theme may not require much imagining on the part of parent readers. The episode at the zoo when Harry's anger gives the boa constrictor magical powers that this reptile uses to belittle and embarrass Dudley might also touch a parent's fancy but probably will be more appealing to sibling readers. This theme of sibling rivalry may be a lived experience for readers who wear parent hats! As this rivalry continues throughout the series and becomes more sophisticated and convoluted as Harry and Dudley reach adolescence, it continues to pit the slim, athletic, thoughtful leader, Harry, against the overweight, dim-witted Dudley. Fortunately for parents, this story-theme appears to vanish as these two characters grow older and Harry spends less and less time at the Dursley's. Yet, sibling rivalry may be one of the most universal themes that parent readers can identify.

In reading the *Harry Potter* series with a parent identity, readers may find this story further and further troubling, uplifting, and perhaps melodramatic. Lily and James Potter, sacrificing their lives for Harry, to protect him from Voldemort with their unconditional parental love, represent the most noble and loving of parents. As the characters of Lily and James gradually "appear" and develop through the series, parent readers' interest with this story-theme may become more and more intense as the characters of these two loving parents become further revealed.

Considering Others' Responses to *Harry Potter*

As I became more and more intrigued with the tensions and conflicts between my pleasure with this series and Matthew's disregard of it, I became curious about the responses of Matthew's classmates. Did they enjoy this series as much as I did or were they as disinterested as Matthew? One afternoon I met with thirteen children from his class of twenty-six, fifth and sixth graders who represented a cross-section of the rich mosaic of New York City children, coming from a variety of socioeconomic, cultural, and ethnic backgrounds with a wide variety of experiences outside of the classroom. I tape-recorded our conversations and transcribed them later for analysis. The children volunteered to participate.

At the time we spoke, their teacher, Angela, had read *Sorcerer's Stone* and was on chapter 9 of *Chamber of Secrets*. In analyzing these conversations using the framework of context, text, and reader, there appear to be five themes in our conversations. The children used metaphors linked to personal experiences to explain their experiences with reading the books. They discussed their feelings about reading the books, particularly at the beginning. Other themes that were prevalent throughout these conversations include memory, imagination, and knowing and understanding the character of Harry Potter.

The metaphor Matthew used to describe the book was a "cartoon," the kind he didn't like. His classmates compared their reading experiences to watching a movie, a book/story, a former teacher, and a different world/culture:

Iris: It's like watching a "G" rated movie . . . for general audiences.

Luigi: Yeah! . . . Ron, Hermione, and Harry Potter. They're like The Three Musketeers.

Tia: When I was reading I was thinking about school and which teacher was like my teacher in the story. I had a teacher like Professor Snape in my old school.

Nicole: It's also like explaining a different world that we've never been to. Different vocabulary words. In this book of *Harry Potter* we would be muggles. I feel weird. I want to be a wizard too!

A second theme that the children focused on was their feelings, their emotional responses to the book, particularly at the beginning of the story. When they shared these feelings of boredom with Angela, her response played an important role in helping them to enter the story:

Austin: We all voted that we didn't want to read [*Sorcerer's Stone]* anymore until Angela just said, "This part is good" and we just kept on going . . . sometimes it gets boring but like you have to really stay with it. It's a good book. Like in the beginning I thought it was boring but then like when I started really listening, it was really good . . .

Adriana: Yeah, a lot of us were complaining . . .

Luigi: I think the book is good but like in the beginning it was real boring. I didn't get it. I was wondering what I was going to write because Angela said to write about what happened. . . . Then in the middle and after Harry went to school I started liking it. But first, I said, "Angela, no it's boring. No, another book." Then she said, "No, no, this book's good because they said it in the *Nickelodeon* magazine." I said like *wooow!*

The children's entrance into the story and Harry's world was not easy; however, with Angela's support and help, some of the children eventually entered the story. Others, like Kenny, Natasha, and Matthew, had difficulty entering the story:

Natasha: I couldn't remember who all the teachers were. I loose [sic] the memory of the story and I can't keep it in my head.

Kenny: The story was complicated . . . hard to remember like, where Harry Potter was, who the people were. The people were just showing up.

These children's difficulty with enjoying the story focused on their memory and the complicated text. There appeared to be very little information that they could make personal connections to and this made their reading experience difficult.

On the other hand, Michael reported the same feeling of "addiction" that I had, "getting hooked."

Michael: I used to spend mainly all my time going down[stairs] to my friend's [apartment] playing computer games all day long. When Angela began reading it, the first couple of pages were boring but then when we got deeper into the book, I was hooked.

The fourth theme that the children discussed was the role of the imagination. Here, there were conflicting views about how much or how little imagination children needed to have when reading. All the children agreed, however, that J. K. Rowling had lots of it!

Tia: It's making kids imagine.

Michael: It's very imaginative and children like me use our imagination. It's more of a way of expanding your imagination.

Krystalyn: *Harry Potter* uses a lot of imagination.

Nicole: Anyone can read it. People have to have an imagination.

Krystalyn: Yeah! It's very fun to read this book! You don't need imagination. After you're finished reading you have all the imagination in the world.

Luigi: I give lots of credit to K. J. [sic] Rowling. I think she has lots of imagination.

Children: Yeah!

A fifth theme that was revealed throughout the conversations was the children's connection to Harry as a character/child. Several children noted the appeal Harry had for them:

Danielle: Harry is like me because he is always looking for trouble.

Michael: He is like me because he's always finding out small secrets. I like looking for stuff. I am always finding out small secrets or something hidden in my house.

Krystalyn: He's living at the same time we are. I was like Harry, always getting into trouble and everybody knows that my teacher was trying to help me out.

Nicole: He's a brave person and I find some pieces of me in him.

In general, for those children who liked the book, they highlighted themes that have been discussed by Appelbaum (technoculture) and Alton (a variety of genres):

Luigi: The sports, the quidditch match.

Austin: The wizardry, the imagination. It attracts the kids. The magic parts. I liked it all.

Betty: It has adventure, imagination, so scary . . . and magic.

Iris: The best part that is good to me is that they get to use magic. I wish I could go turn a rat yellow or something like that.

Danielle: This author is so detailed. It has so much detail. It goes right down to the details . . . in this book you don't need pictures. You will understand without pictures.

Adult responses to this series mirrored the children's responses. The adults with whom I spoke and whose published comments I read reveal parallel themes of metaphors, feelings, memory, and imagination. The metaphor of addiction was repeated by adults. This addiction begins with the magical, quick entrance into Harry's world and the sense that time stands still while reading. I remember one day in my office when I just couldn't find a paper I knew I'd had in my hand a minute earlier . . . for a flash of a moment I thought, "a magical disappearance?" Or in the context of a conversation about a group of people, I found myself calling them "Muggles." Did I enter Harry's world or did he enter mine? Johnson notes similar themes:

> After reading J. K. Rowling's first installment, I knew I was addicted. I could not for the life of me put it down . . . I began to use my imagination and the barrier between fantasy and reality blurred. When reading in a public place, I felt as if I were the only person left in the world and I wished I could borrow Harry's invisibility cloak to disappear for awhile. (Johnson, 2001)

For an adult who did not enjoy *Sorcerer's Stone,* Cawkwell (2001) notes similar experiences of struggle with the text that mirror Natasha and Kenny's comments above and highlight the role that memory and imagination play in reading:

> I kept forgetting what had happened before . . . I suspect that the problem I have with reading this book is mine. The events seemed "out there," detached from me . . . I could not enter Harry's world. . . . If imagination is what is needed then I don't seem to have the right kind. I am left wondering if the plot and character development are what readers of the intertextual world of multimedia computer game narratives like to read today . . . Harry Potter exists in the space of the reader's imagination. (Cawkwell, 2001)

If "the *Harry Potter* series is written for people who love reading" (Zuleika in Nicola, p. 748), then what about Natasha who ended her conversation with me by saying, "I don't like reading?" What obligations do we have to help readers like Natasha enter the world of literacy? How can we help them enter?

Where Do We Go from Here?

Rogers (1999) has articulated a question I hold dear to my heart as Matthew's mother, a researcher, and a teacher of teachers: How do we interpret reading, identity, and resistance in classroom spaces and communities? And, I would add . . . in families? How do we do this honestly and respectfully, while maintaining the spontaneity and joy of learning? Rogers (1999) likens literacy learning to a complicated dance in which we engage as we travel through the journey of life. This journey takes us through various communities and institutions and bestows upon us multiple identities that make us unique. Our individuality should not be lost but there is a danger in losing it when we try to institutionalize our reading experiences. Rogers (1999) also asks how we might choreograph this dance. I wonder if we can do this, and, if we can, then do we have the right to do so? What should be our guidelines for shaping this dance called literacy learning?

On a personal level, I have much to ponder about Matthew's experiences with *Harry Potter*. What else can I do to help Matthew enjoy a wider variety of genres? Need I be so concerned that he doesn't love a book that I do and that he doesn't seem to read by making personal connections as I do? There's that mother's guilt that we all feel at one time or another! Then, part of me whispers, "I must remember to keep my *teacher voice* quiet and out of this house!"

As a professional, I wonder about this teacher's voice. Is it really the voice of the progressive educator I pride myself in being? If I think I'm not the "sage-on-the-stage" but I suspect I still have *that* voice, then maybe I need to do some deeper reflecting and, perhaps, tape myself as I teach so that I can monitor myself a bit more closely.

What about Angela's strategy of encouraging the children to stay with the story? The children reported that they were allowed to vote—but it seems that their decision was overruled. What did that mean for the children? Did Angela talk to the children about it? She worked to convince them to stay with her reading for a bit longer, even invoking the *Nickelodeon* magazine for support.

What did Angela do to help Natasha and Kenny feel more welcomed and knowledgeable about Harry's world? What might she have done differently and what might she have avoided? If I had spoken with them at the end of the year, might they have been more enthusiastic about the book?

We know that not everyone can or will like every text read, but what happens to individuals who do not like a text when the culture is so overwhelmingly enthusiastic about it? How might we work with children to help them not feel "left out" as I sensed that Natasha, Kenny, and Matthew were?

What are we doing to the "pleasure and fun" of reading when we impose school-type activities on reading the text? Luigi noted, "I was wondering what I was going to write because Angela said to write about what happened so I just copied off of Michael's paper," and Daniel wrote:

> School comprehension tests on this would be OK but just plain reading is much better. If anyone extracted pieces from this book, even if it were a few sentences for school use, it would be torture to the readers. . . . (in Nicola, 2001, p. 750)

On the other hand, the school activity of creating, producing, and performing the shadow puppet show helped Matthew enter Harry's world in a way that he didn't with the more traditional school activities. I wonder if this activity also helped Kenny and Natasha. Did this activity offer these children an opportunity to construct individual responses to this text as the play was written and performed? Wagner and Moffet (1992) would suggest that this is the case.

When individuals read texts, they search for different narrative themes. Inevitably readers are drawn to texts because these themes resonate with them or captivate them. One of the many remarkable events that the *Harry Potter* series helped to promote was the creation of the *New York Times* bestseller's list of children's literature (Thompson, 2001). The creation of this new category of text acknowledges and legitimizes what children's librarians and many readers have known for years: Texts, including children's literature, that become "classics" stand the test of time, in part, because they can appeal to a wide variety of readers. The *Harry Potter* series may become just such a classic!

Epilogue

The activity of writing this chapter prompted me to interview a wide variety of individuals, including my sister, who had initially given Matthew

Sorcerer's Stone for his birthday. You can imagine my surprise, and Matt's, when my sister said:

> I never finished *Sorcerer's Stone*! I just didn't like it. . . . It didn't resonate with me. I wasn't captivated by the story. I usually give every book a try and read to about page fifty but I can't even remember now what I read.

When I asked her to reread the first few chapters, she did and added:

> After rereading, I still didn't enjoy it and found that I didn't remember too much. The character sketches were stereotyped to me and so the plot just seemed to be something like, "in the end Harry would enjoy freedom and not be tormented anymore."

Matthew's turn: A week before my final draft of this chapter was due, Matthew and I were driving on a city highway when he noticed a billboard promoting the *Harry Potter* movie debut on November 16, 2001. Matthew told me:

> I didn't know they are going to make a movie. I'll tell you what, Mom . . . I'll go see the movie and then I'll read *Chamber of Secrets*. I think *then* I'll like to read that book!

So, this *Harry Potter* family story continues.

Acknowledgments

I wish to thank several individuals for their help, support, and feedback on various drafts of this chapter. First and most important, to Matthew for patiently answering all my questions and reading this chapter many times over. Thanks to friends Kevin Hayward and David Alvarado, who spoke with Matthew and me during a few sleepover breakfasts. Also, Marie Grace Mutino, Peter Appelbaum, Elizabeth Heilman, and Betsy and Mary Figlear gave me valuable insights and suggestions. I am very grateful to each of you.

Notes

1. All names are real, including Matthew's (nicknamed Matt).
2. Please see Peter Appelbaum's definition of Harry's world elsewhere in this volume.

References

Alton, Hiebert Anne. "Generic Fusion and the Mosaic of Harry Potter." In *Harry Potter's World: Multidisciplinary Critical Perspectives*. Ed. Elizabeth Heilman. Forthcoming.

Alvermann, Donna E. "Reading Adolescents' Reading Identities: Looking Back to See Ahead." *Journal of Adolescent & Adult Literacy* 44.8 (2001): 676–690.

Anderson, Richard C., Elfrieda H. Hiebert, Judith A. Scott, and Ian Wilkinson. *Becoming a Nation of Readers: The Report of the Commission on Reading*. Champaign-Urbana: Center for the Study of Reading, 1985.

Appelbaum, Peter. "Harry Potter's World: Magic, Technoculture, and Becoming Human." In *Harry Potter's World: Multidisciplinary Critical Perspectives*. Ed. Elizabeth Heilman. Forthcoming.

Bissex, Glenda. L. *Gyns at Wrk: A Child Learns to Write and Read*. Cambridge: Harvard UP, 1980.

Brozo, William, and Ronald Schmelzer. "Wildmen, Warriors, and Lovers: Reaching Boys through Archetypal Literature." *Journal of Adolescent and Adult Literacy* 41.1 (September 1997): 4–11.

Carico, Kathleen M. "Negotiating Meaning in Classroom Literature Discussions." *Journal of Adolescent and Adult Literacy* 44.6 (2001): 510–18.

Cawkwell, Gail. "Not Spellbound by *Harry*." *Journal of Adolescent and Adult Literacy* 44.7 (2001): 669.

Chandler, Kelly. "Reading Relationships: Parents, Adolescents, and Popular Fiction by Stephen King." *Journal of Adolescent and Adult Literacy* 43.3 (1999): 228–39.

Coles, Gerald. *Reading Lessons: The Debate over Literacy*. New York: Hill & Wang, 1998.

Enciso, P. "Cultural Identity and Response to Literature: Running Lessons from *Maniac Magee*." *Language Arts* 71 (1994): 524–33.

Epstein, Joyce. (1990). "School and Family Connections. Theory, Research and Implications for Integrating Sociologies of Education and Family." In *Families in Community Settings: Interdisciplinary Perspectives*. Ed. D. G. Unger and M. B. Sussman. New York: Hawthorn P, 1990. 99–226.

Flynn, I., and M. Rahbar. "The Effects of Age and Gender on Reading Achievement: Implications for Pediatric Counseling." *Developmental and Behavioral Pediatrics* 14 (1993): 304–7.

Galda, Lee, and Richard Beach. "Response to Literature as a Cultural Activity." *Reading Research Quarterly* 36.1 (2001): 64–73.

Gee, James Paul. "Teenagers in New Times: A New Literacy Studies Perspective." *Journal of Adolescent and Adult Literacy* 43.5 (2001): 412–20.

Heath, Shirley Brice. "The Children of Trackton's Children: Spoken and Written Language in Social Change." In *Theoretical Models and Processes of Reading*. 4th ed. Ed. R. B. Ruddell, M. R. Ruddell, and H. Singer. Newark: International Reading Association, 1994. 208–30.

Hoover-Dempsey, Kathleen, and Howard Sandler. "Why Do Parents Become Involved in Their Children's Education?" *Review of Educational Research* 67.1 (1997): 3–42.

Johnson, Shaun. "The *Harry Potter* Craze: From Skeptic to Addict." *Journal of Adolescent and Adult Literacy* 44.7 (2001): 666–67.

Lehr, Susan, and Deborah L. Thompson. "The Dynamic Nature of Response: Children Reading and Responding to *Maniac Magee* and *The Friendship*." *The Reading Teacher* 53.6 (2000): 480–93.

Leu, Donald, and Charles K. Kinzer. "The Convergence of Literacy Instruction with Networked Technologies for Information and Communication." *Reading Research Quarterly* 35.1 (2000): 108–27.

Moffet, James, and Betty Jane Wagner. *Student-Centered Language Arts, K-12*. 4th ed. Portsmouth: Boynton/Cook, 1992.

Moje, Elizabeth B., Deborah R. Dillon, and David O'Brien. "Reexamining Roles of Learner, Text and Context in Secondary Literacy." *Journal of Educational Research* 93.3 (January–February 2000): 165–81.

New London Group. "A Pedagogy of Multiliteracies: Designing Social Futures." *Harvard Education Review* 66.1 (1996): 60–89.

Nicola, Ruth. "Returning to Reading with *Harry Potter*." *Journal of Adolescent and Adult Literacy* 48.8 (2001): 748.

Nierstheimer, Susan. "'To the parents of . . .' A Parent's Perspective on the Schooling of a Struggling Learner." *Journal of Adolescent and Adult Literacy* 44.1 (September 2000): 34–36.

Riordan, Cornelius. "The Silent Gender Gap: Reading, Writing and other Problems for Boys." *Education Week*, 17 November 1999, 46, 49.

Rogers, Theresa. "Literary Theory and Children's Literature: Interpreting Ourselves and Our Worlds." *Theory into Practice* 38.1 (1999): 138–46.

Rosenblatt, Louise, M. *The Reader, the Text, the Poem: The Transactional Theory of the Literary Work*. Carbondale: Southern Illinois UP, 1978.

Rowling, J. K. (1997). *Harry Potter and the Sorcerer's Stone*. New York: Scholastic P, 1997.

———. *Harry Potter and the Chamber of Secrets*. New York: Scholastic P, 1998.

———. *Harry Potter and the Prisoner of Azkaban*. New York: Scholastic P, 1999.

———. *Harry Potter and the Goblet of Fire*. New York: Scholastic P, 2000.

Scholastic, Chrysler Learning Connection, American Federation of Teachers and Association for Supervision and Curriculum Development. *Reading Together: Celebrate National Family Reading Week*, 1.2 New York: American Federation of Teachers and Association for Supervision and Curriculum Development, 1995.

Sipe, Lawrence R. "First and Second Grade Literary Critics: Understanding Children's Rich Responses to Literature." *Literature-based Instruction: Reshaping the Curriculum*. In Taffy Raphael and Kathryn Au. Norwood: Christopher-Gordon, 1998. 38–70.

———. "Children's Response to Literature: Author, Text, Reader, Context." *Theory into Practice* 38.3 (1999): 120–29.

Sutherland, R. "Hidden Persuaders: Political Ideologies in Literature for Children." *Children's Literature in Education* 16 (1985): 143–57.

Taylor, Denny. *Many Families, Many Literacies: An International Declaration of Principles*. Portsmouth: Heinemann, 1997.

Thompson, Clifford. *2000 Current Biography Yearbook*. New York: H. W. Wilson, 2001.

Touponce, W. F. "Children's Literature and the Pleasures of the Text." *Children's Literature Association Quarterly* 20 (1996): 175–82.

Trelease, Jim. *The Read-Aloud Handbook*. 3rd rev. ed. New York: Penguin Books, 1995.

Vogel, S. "Gender Differences in Intelligence, Language, Visual-Motor Abilities and Academic Achievement in Students with Learning Disabilities: A Review of the Literature." *Journal of Leaning Disabilities* 23 (1990): 44–52.

Wolf, S., B. Edmiston, and P. Enciso. "Drama Worlds: Places of the Heart, Head, Voice, and Hand in Dramatic Interpretation." In *A Handbook for Literacy Educators: Research in the Communicative and Visual Arts*. Ed. J. Flood, S. B. Heath, and D. Lapp. New York: Macmillan, 1997. 492–505.

Zuleika. "Upper Primary Students Respond to *Harry Potter*." In Ruth Nicola, "Returning to Reading with *Harry Potter*." *Journal of Adolescent and Adult Literacy* 48.8 (2001): 748.

Chapter Five

Reading *Harry Potter* with Navajo Eyes

Hollie Anderson

As I read the *Harry Potter* books as a Navajo graduate student at Purdue University in Indiana, 1,400 miles from my home, I felt that many of the themes were pertinent to me personally as an alien student disconnected from the familiar and also to the experiences of my parents, both of whom attended boarding schools. As the daughter of Navajos who had experienced enculturation through assimilationist boarding schools, it was impossible for me to read the books without the stories of my parents echoing in the shadows of the text. I experienced themes of alienation and disconnection strongly as I read. And yet, I found familiar and comforting themes as well. In this chapter I will share my observations about the ways that the *Harry Potter* books connect to my story, my family, and my culture.

I was raised on the Navajo Reservation in the Four Corners area of the United States covering parts of Arizona, New Mexico, and Utah. This area is traditional land for the Navajo. Stories are many landforms encircled by four sacred mountains the Navajo believe are their protectors. Within these mountains you can find a rich culture that was almost lost due to the U.S. government plan to assimilate all cultures to the European American culture. The culture of the Navajo people has lived on despite all the energy put into removing it. One of the instruments the United States employed in doing this was schooling. In the beginning, from the late 1800s to the early 1900s, Native American education centered on civilizing. Before the Meriam Report, the United States viewed the native ways as wrong, and school was to save them from themselves. As historian Joel Spring (1998) reflects, "one might consider this plan of Indian education as one of the great endeavors to destroy cultures and languages and replace them with another culture and language" (p. 33). After the Meriam Report clearly stated that the problem with Native education was the government's attitude, there was a change made in approaches to Native schooling. It was declared that the students should interact more with their families instead of being isolated, and it was a policy goal that their culture and language would not be discouraged. Although the original plan to rid Native people of their culture and language through education was formed in the late 1800s and changed after the Meriam Report, the effects of the assimilation reappeared in the 1950s and 1960s when my parents were in school, due to the reaction to the civil rights movement (Spring, 1997).

The Boarding School

Both my parents attended Bureau of Indian Affairs' boarding schools in the 1960s. My mother attended an off-reservation boarding school at Fort Wingate in New Mexico. Here she was unable to speak her native language. The students there would be punished anytime they would speak Navajo. Punishments, such as washing their mouths out with soap, getting slapped on the hands with rulers, doing extra chores, or even getting paddled, were common. One thing that my mom always remembered was that the teachers would assign different students to monitor the language they spoke. The monitor would write down the names of all the students who spoke Navajo and report it to the teachers. The students who had their names reported got punished. This was hard on students because they had to tell on each other and that made barriers to having really good friends. There were similarities in the *Harry Potter* series with Harry being denied the culture he belonged to, although at first he was not even aware of it. He could not even mention anything about the "M" word, magic, in the Dursley home, but he did not know why. There are not many barriers at Hogwarts. Students are encouraged to help each other, although there are times when other students try to "monitor" one another, but usually end up getting into the same trouble. Draco tries a few times to get Harry in trouble, for example, when he finds out that Harry, Ron, and Hermione are out after hours, trying to get Norbert on his way, or when he thinks Harry is getting in trouble for flying his broom when he was told not to. Draco usually ends up unhappy with the results.

Most of the Navajo kids stayed at the dorms all the time. My mom hardly ever went home. The faculty and staff were mostly made up of older white people who expected the students to believe the religion they believed and speak the language they spoke. There was no sign of encouraging the Navajo culture there. My mom did not understand this. She just knew she was not at home and missed her family. In the *Harry Potter* books the children often stay at boarding school through holidays. Yet, this is portrayed as a positive experience, which is the children's preference. By contrast, many Navajo children longed for home. Also, the muggle children show no signs of concern that their muggle values, language, dress, and other habits are being lost.

Home to my mother was where she could freely express herself and practice the culture she had grown up in. Strong ties to the Navajo way of life ensured that my mother stayed connected to her culture and the language she spoke. My grandmother never discouraged speaking Navajo and often took my mother and her siblings to ceremonies other members of the family participated in. Never did my grandmother tell my mother to stop being Navajo. Although my grandmother was married to a non-Navajo Danish man, my grandfather, she did not assimilate to his way of life. They were able to live in two worlds and make it one for their family. In contrast, Hogwarts, the school, was the safety zone for Harry to be who he wanted to be, and "home" with the Dursleys was where he felt unknown.

This world that my mother grew up in was very different from what most Navajo kids grew up in. First of all, my mother was racially one-half Navajo and one-half Danish. The fact that she looks more Danish than Navajo contributed to the bad experience she had growing up in a boarding school. Everyone who grew up with her and knew her did not see the difference that was so apparent to everyone else. She knew she was Navajo, but when she got to the boarding school, the other students saw her as a little white girl and she experienced discrimination from people she thought were the same as her. With the students discriminating against her and the teachers not wanting her to speak her language, life was tough. Being among her family made her appreciate who people are and not what they look like. My mother speaks very fluent Navajo and English with no hint of the other's accent.

Cross-Cultural Experiences

In the *Harry Potter* books, students who are bicultural, who belong to both the muggle and magical worlds, are also targets for derision and attack. Just because they are of muggle families, they are discriminated against although they are quite capable of succeeding in performing magic like any full-blooded wizard. Hermione and Neville are examples of people coming from two different cultures, each with the same expectation, namely, to be a good wizard. Hermione, on one hand, is a full-blooded muggle who proves her wizarding talents in her magic classes at Hogwarts and usually does better than most classmates. Neville, on the other hand, is a full-blooded wizard who has difficulty using his common wizard sense to get through everyday tasks. This is a case that shows that just because you are born into a culture, it does not mean you are automatically better than someone who is taught the culture. This part of the text also sends readers the positive message that where you come from should not matter.

In many ways my experience going to Purdue University from the Navajo Nation is similar to how Harry felt going to Hogwarts. As a graduate student in education, I often felt isolated, but still excited and glad to be somewhere new, in a different culture. I felt isolated because I was so far away from home. My culture was far away. Everything was different. I had to watch everything from the things I laughed at, and the way I pronounced words. At times I just wanted to get in my truck and drive home, and at times when I was home, I could not wait to get back to Indiana. My experience is similar to what other Navajo students experience. As Wilder, Jackson, and Smith (2001) describe Navajo students' transitions to postsecondary education:

> Participants reported feeling uneasy and somewhat "disconnected" when they left
> their homeland to pursue work or educational opportunities. They also reported feel-
> ing confused about mixed messages to (a) leave their reservation to be successful, and
> (b) maintain their traditional connection to their tribe, land, and culture. (p. 123)

Harry was put into a culture that was nothing like the one he had been growing up in. He had to learn on his own what things are and what they mean to the people who are of the culture in which he was placed. Although Harry was glad to have left the Dursleys, he was still uncertain of the new environment. The smallest things confused Harry because he did not know what every wizard grew up knowing. The whole idea of being a wizard and practicing magic seemed very uncommon to Harry, who had grown up as a muggle. When he first met Hagrid, who was sent to pick up Harry from the Dursleys, he found out more about himself than the Dursleys had ever let him know and he could hardly believe any of it. It all was very shocking for Harry to find out he came from a wizard family with very famous parents and that he, too, was very famous. Once

Harry stepped into the Leaky Cauldron and attention came to him, he knew that everyone knew something that he did not. When Hagrid led Harry into Diagon Alley, the physical setting was something that Harry had never seen before, although any wizard kid his age would not have been so excited because it was a normal thing to see cauldrons of all shapes and makes or shops that sold magic wands. The encounter that made Harry feel very unsure and stupid was when he went into Madam Malkin's Robes For All Occasions and had his first experience with another first-year Hogwarts student. This encounter brought out the given knowledge that every wizard should know. The boy Harry came in contact with, which we later find out is Draco Malfoy, expects that just because Harry is of a wizarding family and he is going to Hogwarts, he should know the simple things. Although Harry did feel stupid for not understanding why a first-year was trying to smuggle a broomstick into school, or what on earth Quidditch was or why it was a bad thing to be in the Hufflepuff house, he did not let the other boy know this. Harry probably did not want to embarrass himself or just the fact that he already disliked the boy's attitude made him not ask questions.

As a graduate student at a Midwestern university I found that I, like Harry, often questioned what people were talking about because I did not know some things that were everyday knowledge for someone from the local culture. One day, in one of the classes I taught called "Multiculturalism and Education," one of my undergraduate students was telling us that his grandfather did the eulogy for Norman Dale. Apparently, everyone knew who Norman Dale was, whereas I was wondering what was so special about him. The students had to explain to me that Norman Dale was the coach that Gene Hackman portrayed in the 1986 movie *Hoosiers*. I do not know if it was Indiana culture, or just college basketball culture that I lacked knowledge about, when, on another occasion the students were talking about the situation that was happening with Bobby Knight. They were all talking about it and after listening awhile, I asked, "Who is Bobby Knight?" They looked at me as if I came from another planet. I was a living example of cross-cultural experience for my students. Aside from what other people were talking about that I was unfamiliar with, small things like the commercials on the local television stations did not make too much sense. There was a commercial for Pizza King pizza and their line was something about how Pizza King was as traditional to Indiana as cow tipping. Is cow tipping really a tradition? Not only were some of the things in the new culture not making sense, but there were times when what I said did not make sense to people I was talking to. It did make sense, but not in the way I wanted it to. The full context was missing. I had to watch how I said things, such as when I talked about the reservation I often said, "the rez." I would realize that people did not know what "the rez" was until I explained it, starting back to when the U.S. government came up with the idea of reserving land for different tribes. The word rez, so simple in my culture, is an entire history lesson in another culture, the same as Norman Dale was simple enough in one culture and a history lesson to me.

The culture shock that Harry was experiencing is also similar to what happens in the Navajo culture when a child grows up off the reservation and then returns back to the reservation. The Navajo who grows up without the Navajo culture can find himself feeling embarrassed or lost because things that are learned growing up Navajo are things that are a part of everyday life. There is not a class to take to learn how to be Navajo. The norms that Navajo children come to know are things they pick up from their environment. When children who might have been adopted return to the Navajo reservation, there is no way they could know culturally specific details and norms because not even the Navajo kids who do know these realize that these things, such as how to be funny or polite, are different. If you asked Navajo kids why they do things the way they do they probably couldn't explain it. So, when Navajo kids come into contact with other kids who are not Navajo they do not realize that there is a difference. The children are not the ones to blame for discriminating in such circumstances, but it is important to have these children aware of what can be harmful or hurtful. In the *Harry Potter* books, Draco Malfoy might have known he was discriminating. He did not realize he was talking to someone who, he would later find out, was Harry Potter the famous wizard.

A contemporary example of children growing up off the reservation and returning with no clue as to what being Navajo means are the children of the L. D. S. Mormon Church placement program. Navajo Mormon families sometimes send their children off to school and to live with someone else to learn more about the Mormon Church, which is always off the reservation. These children typically grow up in a white household with little connection to their Navajo roots. After the children complete their schooling in the placement program, which they might have been in for several years, they return to their families on the reservation and are expected to live within a culture they have not experienced in the past few years. This causes profound culture shock and feelings of being lost. It is very difficult for such young people to adapt to the way of life of the Navajo because there are so many differences between these cultures. Parents who send their children on these placement programs believe it is for the good of the children, but what most of them do not understand is that this program uses this tactic to assimilate Native American children into the American culture. The sad thing is that it works.

Feelings of embarrassment and stupidity based on cross cultural misunderstanding are sensed as Harry Potter listens to Draco talk. The good thing is that Harry comes across some nice people to help him understand this new culture in which he was placed. Harry's friend plays a vital role in his understanding of this new culture. Like Harry, I found nice people to help me understand the new culture in which I was placed. A friend of mine was at Purdue a year before I went there. She was originally from Staten Island in New York City but she helped me understand some of the "normal" things done in West Lafayette, Indiana. She did not understand some things out there either, but she knew they were done. I guess you could say she taught me how to go through the motions, but not the reasons why, just because she merely shared what she was told. Another friend of mine who was also Native American, helped me understand the Indiana culture from what she had experienced in the four years she lived there. I think just talking with her about the differences we had both noticed was what helped me get along more easily. My professors also had a lot of input in helping me understand my position and exactly what I was doing in Indiana by asking me questions that made me think critically about what my true thoughts were about where I was. They also helped me put words to my feelings. One incident occurred when I was talking with a professor who was also not from Indiana but had been there several years. She said, "It's like someone cut your image out of a picture and placed it in another picture with a different scene and it just doesn't look right." It made sense because I did feel like I was somewhere that was just two-dimensional to me, everything was just backdrop. I did not really get into any of the third dimension of West Lafayette, which I would consider to be the culture. The only place that was real to me and made sense was the classroom. Many aspects of classroom culture are shared across regions. I think also that in the back of my head I kept thinking I was out there only for school and, thus, I did not think I had to get rooted into the culture.

Types of Families

The biggest change in being in Indiana was being without my family, with whom I had lived closely for twenty-three years. Family is very important to most people and it is a significant theme in the *Harry Potter* series. As I read, I noticed that there were also many similarities between the idea of family in the *Harry Potter* series and the idea of family in Navajo culture. There are also differences. Navajo families can be related to on either side of what we consider good or bad families. The first family that we come across in the *Harry Potter* stories is the Dursley family. The Dursley-like family occurs in every culture. This family was ashamed of being related to a wizarding family. Navajo people that know they are related to people who use witchcraft with negative motivations usually react the same way. They want nothing to do with them. They will not relate to these people unless they have to because they are still family and sometimes involvement in negatively motivated witchcraft is not even their fault.

Although the Dursleys did not want anything to do with Harry, just because he was of a wizarding family, they still took him in. Kinship made the Dursleys keep and raise Harry. The fact that Aunt Petunia was Harry's maternal aunt seems like the most logical explanation. This explanation might be logical to me because, in Navajo culture, maternal aunts are considered mothers to the babies of their sisters. Because clans and identity are passed through the mother's bloodline, which makes the Navajo people a matriarchal one, it is a simple explanation as to why the Dursleys did not give up Harry Potter. They might not have done the same things for him as they did for Dudley, or even consider him one of their own, but they still gave him what he needed.

Another family that the readers are introduced to is the Weasley family. Although the Weasley family was totally different from the Dursleys, they, too, show Navajo characteristics. The generosity that the Weasleys demonstrated even though they were not blood relatives of Harry's, showed their concern for his well-being in giving him what he needs emotionally. The Weasleys are a family who many Navajo can relate to because, although, they might not be as well off financially as the dominant culture might suggest is adequate, they emit the feeling that they are happy and thankful that they have their family. Of course, there are always going to be people in the family who show their gratitude differently. Mr. and Mrs. Weasley were proud of their family and made sure that they all had what they needed even though it might mean that Ron got the hand-me-downs. Although some of the children might have had to put up making do with secondhand things, they all had plenty of respect for their parents for they knew that their father loved his job and that he did the best he could for them and that their mother was always there to give them what they needed emotionally and, if necessary, materially. We do see Mr. Weasley trying to do a little more for them when he took the boys to the Quidditch World Cup. Charlie, Bill, and Percy seemed to be happy with what they had, and although they were determined to live on their own, in their own jobs, they still show their respect to their mother and father. These family dynamics will be familiar to the Navajo reader.

Magic and Nature and Culture

In addition to the broad themes of schooling and family, there are also many details about culture, magic, and nature that a Navajo could relate to in the *Harry Potter* series. The parts that might seem fiction to a mainstream American reader such as the cloak of invisibility or animagi would be something that is possible to understand and believe to a traditional Navajo reader. Traditional Navajos, like myself, can understand that there is witchcraft out there and all people have their own magic. Whether they choose to make it good or evil is what will shine through. There are always good and evil in every culture. Along with the good and evil in every culture, all cultures have a way to protect themselves from what opposes them. In the case of Harry Potter, his lightening-bolt shaped scar was a mark of the protection that came from his mother. Lightening is also a symbol of protection to the Navajo people because lightening was used by twin heroes as swords to defeat "monsters."

What people consider frightening varies across cultures. Some things in Harry Potter made me feel uncomfortable. Little things like the death day party disturbed me. Talking about death is taboo, so it is usually not mentioned or discussed. What made me uncomfortable reading this was that it was a party and there were these kids attending this party with the ghosts and rotten food. Another thing that is taboo in Navajo culture is the owl. The owl is usually a bad omen or a messenger of bad news. For Harry, having an owl was a good thing. In both Harry Potter and Navajo culture, animagi are real. Sirius Black, Professor Lupin, and Wormtail were able to transform from a human figure to an animal. It is said that certain people in the Navajo culture are able to transform themselves into animal figures. The people who can do this are considered witches and it is done by magic. The ability to transform into an animal was developed for the purpose of necessity and travel for the Navajo centuries before modern transportation was available. It goes all the way back to the beginning of man. Like the wizards in the book, the Navajo culture has both good and bad practitioners of magic. These days, it is oftentimes used for personal gain in a negative way. Although it was never meant to be a bad thing, the idea of animagi has become a negative one.

Teaching *Harry Potter* to Navajo Children

I am currently a fifth grade teacher in a school on the Navajo Reservation. As I read these books, I have reflected on how I would use the *Harry Potter* series in my classroom. It has many multicultural issues that need to be addressed in a fifth grade classroom. Being a fifth grade teacher has made me aware of the many issues that our students face every day. These texts can be a valuable resource in discussions about cross-cultural experiences. Themes can be taught from both a broadly historical and a personal and immediate point of view. I would be concerned that Navajo children not bring exclusively positive connotations to the idea of boarding school based on their readings of the *Harry Potter* books. As I grew up, the term "boarding school" was painfully evocative of my parents' experiences. By contrast, my fifteen-year-old brother reading these books may have both more positive and more contradictory associations with this term. This issue can stimulate an important discussion among fifth graders. Ideas of magic and evil can also be discussed. There are many books that students need to have written permission to read, which I understand, but the *Harry Potter* series is something that students should be reading. As a Navajo teaching Navajo students, I would not perceive the *Harry Potter* books to be an evil thing or even a bad thing to read. The creativity in itself is a factor that students at about the fifth-grade level need to explore. For many students, this series involves the most "real" characters that have been written in a long time.

Core issues of multiculturalism are very apparent throughout the series. The ways that different races are portrayed can be profitably discussed with students. Socioeconomic status is the most dominant difference among groups at Hogwarts and should also be examined. The socioeconomic difference is something that I related to most. There are many times that dominant cultures try to use their power to oppress another culture. Using the series to help kids understand that there are biases in the world might encourage them to reflect upon themselves and about what kind of people they will be in our society. Do they want to be like Draco and his family? Or do they want to be like Harry and the Weasley's? All students who read these books, with whom I am acquainted, are able to relate to them somehow—from ten year olds at my school to my fifteen-year-old brother in high school, to people who study behind the scenes of *Harry Potter*. Navajo students and teachers and the traditional Navajo family who believe in balance and harmony can enjoy these books for their entertainment value and for the "realness" of these characters and events, but they will inevitably be read with Navajo eyes.

References

Hoosiers. Dir. D. Anspaugh. Prod. C. DeHaven and P. Angelo. Hemdale Films, 1986.

Meriam, L., *The Problem of Indian Administration*. Baltimore: Johns Hopkins UP, 1928.

Spring, J. *Deculturalization and the Struggle for Equality: A Brief History of Dominated Cultures in the United States*. New York: McGraw-Hill, 1997.

Wilder, L.K., A. P. Jackson, and T. B. Smith. "Secondary Transitions of Multicultural Learners: Lessons from the Navajo Native American Experience." *Preventing School Failure* 45.3 (2001): 119–25.

Chapter Six

Writing Harry's World: Children Coauthoring Hogwarts

Ernie Bond and Nancy Michelson

The *Harry Potter* books have inspired numerous young people to write. In school and in their free time, students are actively creating and extending histories, characters, and storylines, which arise out of the world of Hogwarts but which then take on lives of their own. In this chapter, we explore the theoretical underpinnings for the participatory authoring of literary worlds and then examine some examples of student writing in response to the *Harry Potter* series. The lens through which we view student coauthoring of *Harry Potter* narratives includes these foundational points:

- Reading is a constructivist process of meaning-making.

- Reading and writing are intricately connected processes.

- New technologies mandate an expansion of the constructs of text, reading, and even literacy.

For the majority of practitioners in the educational community, reading has come to be viewed as constructivist: Meaning unfolds as a reader draws upon personal knowledge and experience to guide developing understanding of the text being read. Langer (1991) describes four stances a reader may assume as s/he develops an envisionment of a text. An envisionment, as opposed to understanding, is described as "an act of becoming" (Langer, 1991, p. 5). While understanding implies a single, static response to text, envisionment is a dynamic process, in which meaning and reaction change as the reader progresses through a text. Thus, according to Langer, readers may be "out and stepping into an envisionment" (p. 6), as they use their own existing knowledge and the surface features of the text to enter the narrative world. A reader is "in and moving through an envisionment" (p. 6) when prior knowledge and the emerging envisionment involves greater immersion in the deep structures of the text. "Stepping back and rethinking what one knows" (p. 6) occurs when the reader reflects on what has been read in order to consider how prior understandings might have changed as a result of the reading experience. Finally, when a reader is "stepping out and objectifying the experience" (p. 7) s/he is reacting to what has been read, or even the experience of reading itself. Langer notes that these four stances do not necessarily occur in linear fashion; however, readers who utilize all four of these stances will consciously bring personal experience to a text to shape understandings of the text itself, as well as using their envisionments of the text to reshape their prior experience and knowledge.

When the literature a person has previously read is consciously used as a model, it provides the reader with a sense of narrative and allows her to internalize story structures and conventions; these then provide schema for readings of new texts. The reader in effect apprentices the craft of each writer encountered. Narratives familiarize the reader with writing craft, allow her to gain familiarity with character possibilities, and provide schemata for story creation.

Thus, reading allows children to develop their sense of genre and its conventions, becoming the source of knowledge on writing and all its subtle variations. Literature provides models of narrative structure with which children can then experiment. Students can learn to write with a particular audience in mind without publishing, but as Atwell (1998) has suggested, audience is an important element of a student's writing development, and instruction in writing should include such factors as determining appropriate audiences. Teachers of writing should create opportunities for students' writing to be read and heard, according to Atwell. A complex transactional process occurs in which each borrowing is echoed within a cumulative response to a variety of previous readings and experiences. Online fiction has the added potential of allowing students to dialogue with peers about the writing—creating a virtual writing workshop atmosphere.

Terry Rogers (1991), for example, found that students who had learned to approach texts in this sort of intertextual way were more interpretive in their reasoning. Being familiar with and having in their repertoire different types of textual responses enables learners to apply their knowledge flexibly in novel situations (Greene & Ackerman, 1995). The range of possibilities open to authors and protagonists alike expands or contracts within the intertwining narratives they encounter. So, the story-lines created by the author and the storylines interpreted by the reader will, in both instances, be conditioned by previous literary encounters and lived experiences. Likewise, a reader with varied experiences might reject a storyline that does not necessarily fit within his or her range of possible understandings of the world.

Terry Rogers builds on Iser's (1978) conception of the indeterminate nature of literary works, asserting that interpretation is not a static activity; rather, it involves ongoing dialogue and constantly evolving interactions (Rogers, O'Neil, & Jasinski, 1995). Indeed, literature is never static and the interpretative process is always in flux due to any number of contextual factors. Unfortunately, studies of adolescent and pre-adolescent text constructions in school settings have revealed that the reading of text often occurs as a discrete act; indeed, Langer (1993) found that of her four stances, adolescent readers rarely took the third stance—applying their envisionment to experience outside the text under study. Rather than taking advantage of the potential for expanding meaning development, for young readers in school situations, textual study tends to establish an endgame: The purpose of envisioning the text often remains rooted in that text. Once the reading is complete, the envisionment ends abruptly. The reader's experience of the text often remains encapsulated, largely isolated from other meaning-making in the readers' lives.

However, the *Harry Potter* phenomenon has changed the experiences of many young readers. Because children and adolescents are reading these texts primarily outside of the classroom, they are establishing their own envisionments. Young readers of *Harry Potter* are entering a literary world and exerting upon it a creative force of their own. It is not a new phenomenon for young readers to occasionally extend a literary creation by becoming authors of new versions, sequels, or spin-offs of the story. However, the advent of *Harry Potter* has generated an unprecedented number of voluntary literary responses by adolescent readers. These young authors have been able to co-construct a web of meaning-making as they find a wide audience for their writings, facilitated by the increasing accessibility of the Internet.

The expanding influence of technology in modern society is not universally viewed as a positive influence on literacy. Carter (2000) expresses the fears felt by many book lovers that traditional print will eventually be displaced, and indeed, disappear altogether, when she laments the disappearance—sometimes gradual, sometimes not so gradual—of books from school media centers. She finds it problematic that this shift signals a growing emphasis on children's reading of informational text at the expense of their reading of literature. Citing the empowerment that innumerable authors—Richard Wright and Annie Dillard, for example—found in their early reading of literature as they made connections between themselves and the characters and situations they encountered, Carter sees an increasing need for children to find such personal connections in an era of "virtual friends; e-commerce . . . and family dynamics . . . [that seem] more real on television talk shows than in their own kitchens" (p. 19). For Carter, an essential value of literature in a technological society is the opportunity that story provides for children to recognize the "connections between individuals and society" (p. 19).

Bishop (2000) expresses concerns about the effect of technology-based literacy, cautioning users of the Internet to question the "priorities and ethics" (p. 18) involved in this process. She, like Carter, champions literature as a significant foundation for the development of values since literature encodes a society's history and belief systems and provides a source of hope and comfort. Literary narrative is seen by Bishop, Carter, and many others as an important form of text for its role in the reader's constantly shifting understandings of self and the world (Bruner, 1986).

Indeed, Bronwyn Davies (1993) has suggested that we not only read and write storylines but also that we live them. Whether we are speaking of fictional texts or lived storylines, both allow us to envision possibilities for what we may become. Our storylines are socially constructed entities, which, in turn, inspire the types of fictions we create for and about ourselves. They suggest possibilities for what we may become, and they offer us cultural storylines that guide our presentation of self. Readers of literature vicariously experience dilemmas that allow them to make judgments, test the results of decisions, and imagine alternatives, and, in doing so, they prepare themselves to respond to moral issues.

Unfortunately, Internet technology tends to be used in schooling simply to gather and share information, rather than to foster aesthetic and ethical sensibility. However, there is no reason why this needs to be the case. Other scholars have a more optimistic vision of the power of technology to address existing societal problems. Rogers et al. (2000), for example, find technology to have a potentially transformative function that could level the playing field for children. Young people whose cultural histories are influenced by literacies, such as storytelling or the visual arts, may find that technology, with its emphasis on diverse modes of communication, can actually encompass and extend their language and story experiences.

Andrea Pinkney (2000) also believes in the power of the Internet to break down cultural barriers. Because of its ability to connect people of all walks of life throughout the world Pinkney believes that people will more easily come to understand those who are different from themselves. Furthermore, the faceless interactions that occur on the Internet remove many cultural markers that allow prejudices that otherwise may interfere with our ability to communicate. Pinkney observes, "When I go on-line . . . [n]o one makes assumptions based on my skin color, or the way I speak, or on my clothing" (p. 48). Rogers et al. (2000) and Pinkney (2000) then find that technology may have the potential to provide children with wider opportunities to make, and even extend, their personal connections. Rogers and her colleagues (2000) envision the Internet's role in providing the means to support "interactive, dialogic and collaborative models of learning" (p. 80).

It appears, then, that adult literacy experts are engaged in an active dialogue about the intersections between literature and the information superhighway. Meanwhile, young readers appear to have forged their own paths through the mire, finding ways to link their experiences with the characters and situations from the series in a format that allows them to also connect with other readers of *Harry Potter*. A number of wonderful sites exist on the World Wide Web (WWW), many of which are informational but some of which extend the fictional world through narrative, visual images and role-playing games.

The young authors whose work follows clearly have taken a constructivist approach to their reading. Their work signifies a breakdown of the borders that, as adults, many of us have accepted as natural. In fact, the abundance of child-authored literature on the World Wide Web takes the concept of expanded literacies a step further than the envisionments of most literary theorists. Until recent years it could be argued that there was no real "children's literature"—published narratives written by young people for young people. However, Internet browsing and publishing software have made this genre a reality. Some of these narratives are even edited and peer reviewed before they are published online. The sites are constantly being updated by their young webmasters, who show tremendous commitment to their work. As we have returned to these sites over the past few months, we have seen a variety of new work and an increasing number of site features. We are certain that when readers of this chapter visit the sites discussed below they will discover that they continue to grow and change.

One excellent project involving a number of young authors who are reading, writing, and extending the world of *Harry Potter* is the *Daily Prophet* with managing editors Liz "Malfoy" and Megora "McGonagall" (Malfoy & McGonagall, pseudonyms, retrieved 11/21/01). Based on Rowling's newspaper of the wizards and witches, these web writings dissolve the boundaries between informational and literary text in a display that should dispel the fears of book lovers such as Carter. The site takes the format of an online newspaper, but the articles display the imaginative realms of its authors: News items inspired by events in our Muggle world are combined with fan fiction columns on sports (Quidditch) (Malfoy & McGonagall, retrieved 11/21/01, p. 1), events, such as a robbery at Gringott's (Malfoy & McGonagall, retrieved 11/21/01, p. 1), and advice (Malfoy & McGonagall, retrieved 11/21/01, p. 1). An ongoing feature focuses on "magical creatures" (Malfoy & McGonagall, retrieved 11/21/01, p. 1) some of which are mentioned in the series, others of which are pulled from fantasy, folklore, or imagination.

Some of these articles take elements from Rowling's storylines and extend them in interesting directions. In a recent issue, an interview with Professor Snape appeared that was rather antagonistic (Malfoy & McGonagall, retrieved 11/21/01, "Classic Prophetonian: Interview with the Head of Slytherin House: Severus Snape Confirms Dumbledore's Prediction"). The same issue contained a letter to the editor from Professor Snape complaining about the way the reporter had harassed him (Malfoy & McGonagall, retrieved 11/21/01, "Classic Prophetonian: A Letter to the Editors"). In another article, "Muggle Magic," the story of Harry is extended in an interesting direction: A news article describes a possible attack by Voldemort on the Dursleys while Harry is away visiting the Weasleys:

> Mr. Dursley went down the stairs screaming for the man to go away. "We'll not have any of your kind here! I forbid you to come into this house!"
>
> Of course He-Who-Must-Not-Be-Named would not heed the words of a Muggle, especially one as Mugglish as was Mr. Dursley. You-Know-Who entered

the Dursley home demanding that they "hand over Harry Potter, or die a very painful death!"

"You would be a friend of his," muttered Mr. Dursley.

Meanwhile, Mrs. Dursley who was still wiping potatoes out of her hair sat cowering behind her great lump of a son on the stairs. She suddenly stood up, "Take him, we don't want him. We've never wanted him. If it weren't for my stupid sister Lily dying, I would have a normal life."

When the name Lily was mentioned, You-Know-Who turned his attention to her. "So, you are Lily Potter's sister, are you?"

As his mother stood frozen in fear, Dudley finally managed to heave himself up the rest of the stairs and squeeze through the door to his bedroom. He-Who-Must-Not-Be-Named slowly pointed his wand at Mrs. Dursley. Mr. Dursley knew that this wasn't going to be good, so he ran towards his wife. Unfortunately for Mr. Dursley, You-Know-Who was faster. He spun around and leveled his wand at Mr. Dursley, saying "Imperio," in a bored tone. Mr. Dursley fell to the floor in mid-stride and began counting his toes in a delighted manner.

In a moment of utter panic, Petunia Dursley began to glow a sickly shade of yellow. He-Who Must-Not-Be-Named turned back towards her, and his mouth dropped open in astonishment. The yellow light grew brighter at it slowly spread from her body to the stairs. You-Know-Who, the most evil wizard in the world, backed away from the light as he recognized one of the most ancient charms of protection in the wizarding world. (Malfoy & McGonagall, retrieved 11/21/01, "Classic Prophetonian: Muggle Magic," para. 2)

Under pressure, Harry's aunt (much to her dismay) displays some powerful magical ability. Knowing the Dursleys from Rowling's narratives, readers will recognize this as poetic justice of sorts and likely much more painful for the Dursleys than a simple death at the hands of He-Who-Must-Not-Be-Named. This turn of events also opens up a range of possible new storylines. Thus, the use of language in this writing illustrates intertextuality, as described by Barthes (1977):

The text is a tissue of quotations drawn from the innumerable centers of culture . . . the writer can only imitate a gesture that is always interior, never original. His only power is to mix writings, to counter the ones with the others, in such a way as never to rest on any one of them. (pp. 146–47)

In another recent article, an unnamed inhabitant of the Hogwarts world reports finding an abundance of cultural legends and myths throughout the world, which indicates that Muggles encounter far more magic than they realize (Malfoy & McGonagall, retrieved 11/21/01, "A Wizard's Travels through China"). This site is certainly evidence of young adults expanding their cultural awareness, as envisioned by Rogers et al. (2000) and Pinkney (2000). Another site, "Harry Potter Fan Fiction by Kim" (Anonymous, retrieved 11/21/01), also displays growing cultural awareness among young people. Kim, who is a recent college graduate, writes fan fiction based on Harry's universe, but sets it in other countries.

"Hagrid's Hut" is yet another site that exemplifies the power of technology to bring together young people from different cultural traditions (Hagrid, pseudonym, retrieved 11/21/01). The original site is now linked to "Hagrid's Hut" websites in South Korea, El Salvador, and Australia (retrieved 11/21/01). "Hagrid's Hut" provides information about the wizardly world, written in the voice of the caretaker character. One item was initially interactive: readers were encouraged to suggest new items with which Hagrid could fill his pockets. The webmaster, however, has discontinued further reader contributions to this feature, with his apologies for some inappropriate and "not mature" items that had appeared (Hagrid, retrieved 11/21/01, p. 1).

Other sites have had better success with eliciting reader contributions. "Harry Potter Fan Fiction" (retrieved 11/21/01) has more than 10,000 entries from Potter fans around the world. This site has inspired other Potter webmasters to include fan fiction links in their own websites. For example, at "Harry Potter Facts and Fun" (Alexandra, retrieved 11/21/01), the twelve-year-old webmaster allows site visitors to contribute to a "Rumors" section (retrieved, 11/21/01, p. 1) or to share favorite quotes and questions to ask J. K. Rowling (retrieved, 11/21/01, p. 1), in addition to accepting other readers' *Harry Potter* fiction (retrieved, 11/21/01, p. 1). In November, 2001, Elizabeth's story, "More than Friends: Harry and Hermione" (retrieved 11/21/01, "Written") appeared on the site, along with a note from the author critiquing her own story development of an imagined romance between the characters. Specifically, she criticized how she had portrayed the swift shift in Harry's devotions from Cho to Hermione; however, she explains that she had limited time to resolve the story's conflict and she was regretful that she had not created a more gradual change better suited to Harry's character ("Author's Note," para. 1). Elizabeth's interest in developing Harry's romantic relationships is echoed in fan fiction on many other sites. Clearly, young authors have found the value of literary reflections of self.

One possibility that the technology allows for is the seamless versioning of text. Not only is there no longer necessarily one fixed narrative but the reader can also, with a click, choose a different pathway or can even write her own ending. Although "choose-your-own-path" narratives have been around in print for years, the flow of hypertext is more suited to the format. Claire Field, age fifteen, has published "Til Death Do Us Part—The Wedding Day Blues" on her site (retrieved 11/21/01, "Fan Fiction"). This story, with two alternate endings, is set six years after graduation from Hogwarts. Harry has survived the disappearance of Cho on their wedding day several years earlier and is now set to marry Ginny, but with unexpected results (retrieved 11/21/01, "Transfiguration"). The author invites readers to comment on the two versions of this story and is especially interested in which version they prefer.

In "Til Death Do Us Part," Hermione has become the youngest Minister of Magic ever named. Strong female characters are another hallmark of much of the fan fiction created on the web by adolescent females. One teenage webmaster, Mena Baines, is particularly noted for her development of female characters (retrieved 11/21/01). Her website contains enough of her own fan fiction to fill several books. Her stories focus on the character of Hermione, although Harry still holds a major position in the storyline. And while there is considerable attention to romance in Baines's stories, Hermione is clearly cast in the role of hero, and her strength is a defining characteristic. For example, in "Hermione and the Muggles," she has to overcome Harry's bashful nature in order for them to kiss for the first time:

"You_" he began and then restarted with more composure. "You don't know how it feels . . . to . . . care about someone . . . and know that . . . that you're putting them in danger."

"That's a lot of rubbish." Hermione said. "A poor excuse for being too scared to take a chance, that's what I call it."

"I . . . take chances." Harry breathed, inching closer to her. Almost all of the other students were on the train now, save a few first years who were rushing to drag their bags into the luggage compartment.

"You never take chances with me." Hermione said boldly, taking a step closer to him. His hand brushed hers, and then held it. "You're more afraid of me than even Voldemort, that's what Ron thinks," she said, and Harry laughed. His breath smelled like candy canes and peppermint toads, from all the sweets they'd been eating.

"That's . . . not true." Harry said, his face leaning so close to hers that their noses touched. Hermione reached up and pulled off his glasses and they both giggled nervously. "What d'ya do that for?" he asked, whispering now because they were so close together.

"Why should we be afraid of anything, so long as we are together?" Hermione asked, her voice soft. She brought a trembling hand up to touch Harry's cheek, and he shut his eyes and put his other hand around her waist. "I think we could do anything." Hermione whispered, and she shut her eyes too, felt Harry's hand gently cup her cheek, and his lips softly touch hers—

"Hey Hermione, the train is leaving!" someone shouted loudly, and Harry looked up. Hermione turned to see Lavender Brown hanging out the window of the train, Pavarti and Cho Chang not far away, laughing. Lavender gave her a wicked smile as she stuck her head back inside, the train whistle sounded and it began to move out of the station. (Baines, retrieved 11/21/01, "Hermione and the Muggles," para. 53)

Despite the shift in emphasis, the events actually follow logically with what we already know about these characters. Throughout her fiction, Baines creates situations and events that foreground a reality appealing to numerous other young people. There is much discussion of relationships, mainly among female friends and boyfriend/girlfriend. It's likely that in Rowling's narrative, Hermione will get her first kiss from Harry before year seven, but Baines has concentrated on characters her own age, dealing with issues that likely appeal directly to her.

While the above are examples of adolescent-authored third-person narratives, in which the authors are the storytellers, some young web authors, inspired by the *Harry Potter* series, have found ways to actually invite their readers and coauthors more intimately into the world of Hogwarts. "The Hogwarts School" site (Newton, retrieved 11/21/01), "Hogwarts School of Witchcraft and Wizardry" (Anonymous, Black, Moon, Drowelf & Spinnet, retrieved 11/21/01), and "Calypso and Artemis' Hogwarts Page" (Wolfe & Parkinson, retrieved 11/21/01) are interactive sites in which players must create Potter-style characters, sign up for classes, and complete homework assignments to earn house points. Creative writing is the focus of most of the assignments, and the work of some of the players appears on the site.

In addition to their prolific storytelling, young webmasters have utilized the capabilities of computer technology to expand literacy beyond print. Many have created fan art, in addition to their fan fiction. In one such site, Tealin Raintree (retrieved 11/21/01) features multiple examples of her own creations. This young author is particularly interested in readers' dreams about Harry Potter, and when her visitors submit descriptions of their dreams, she will draw the described scenes for them (p. 1). Tealin does not limit herself to one format; she also writes fan fiction. She is especially interested in imagined wizard and witch characters who represent earlier and later generations of the families of Harry and friends.

These young authors have certainly explored the diverse modes of communication envisioned by Rogers et al. (2000). In addition to fan fiction and art, Alexandra has numerous games, puzzles, and role-playing opportunities that are not based on enrolling in Hogwarts. Mena Baines has created an interesting yearbook on her site ("Hogwarts," retrieved 11/21/01), and many of these fan sites include their own wizardly newspapers. While the majority of the features on the sites discussed are text-based, there are certainly a range of writing forms and purposes represented in the work of the young webmasters.

It is important to note that their efforts to create, re-create, and co-create storylines have met with some unexpected obstacles. One young webmaster, Claire Field (site password protected, 12/3/01), has been at the center of a demand by Warner Brothers that owners of these fan sites give up their *Harry Potter* domain names. Claire has refused to do so, and she has received strong support from Alistair Alexander, creator of "Potter War," a site that provides information about the legal issues faced by Claire and other young webmasters (retrieved 11/21/01). Many young site creators have responded to the threatened legal actions by including disclaimer statements on their sites, acknowledging that they have not created trademark Harry Potter characters.

It is widely believed that people learn effectively by becoming agents in their own learning. *Participatory literacy*, in its broadest sense, describes the multiple ways readers take ownership of reading and writing to construct meanings situated within their own sociocultural characteristics (Fingeret, 1989). We have argued in this chapter that reading, writing, and other responses to text are socioconstructivist processes in which learners interact to create worlds of meaning that incorporate a text, personal context, and prior knowledge (Kucer, 1985). Ways of seeing self and the world are co-constructed as people insert themselves and others into various storylines. Lived experience conditions and informs a person's inscription of self into the fictions s/he has encountered. These everyday discourses and practices are implicit and embedded in everyday social worlds, talk, and texts that children encounter. The possibilities children might adopt are defined by the available discourses through which their individual personalities and their social worlds are constituted. Where technology might best contribute to this constructive process is by providing an arena for publication of and communication about student narratives that take advantage of the potentials of hypertext.

Seymour Papert (1993) has posited that technology offers incentives to learning that are not present in schools. He contrasts the extraordinary cognitive growth of pre-schoolers, who learn through self-directed experiments with their environment, with the resistant behaviors of the same children when they enter a classroom and when encounters with real-world events are mediated by print. He questions the desirability of creating literate students when only "the literal sense of literacy" (p. 11) is what is meant. Papert, echoing Shirley Brice Heath, advocates that literacy be defined instead as "ways of knowing" (p. 10). Only when young people can use their knowledge of what Papert calls "letteracy" (p. 11) to transform themselves and their sense of the world around them do they become truly literate.

This is exactly what is happening among the growing number of young authors on the web. Their work displays control over a variety of textual forms: narrative and informational writing, as well as specialized formats, such as yearbooks, newspapers, and advertisements. They can use voice in an effective and flexible manner. They do not limit themselves to print as a means of expression, but they also use graphics and art as legitimate expressions of ideas. These young authors are engaging in activity that would be viewed by many educational practitioners as optimal for their growth as learners. Papert (1993) finds support in the influential educational theories of John Dewey, Paolo Freire, and Lev Vygotsky for the positive effects of the web-authoring of these young writers:

- children learn better if learning is part of lived experience;

- children learn better if they are truly in charge of their own learning processes;

- conversation plays a crucial role in learning.

While the websites discussed demonstrate all of these ideas in practice to a certain extent, the most crucial point is that the use of technology is not detracting from literature in these instances; in fact, these online interactions enhance reading and help young adults build envisionments of literature. In visiting these sites, young people continuously come into contact with intersecting storylines which will affect their understandings of the narratives and of self. The young Harry Potter fan fiction writers have clearly been able to "see the intersection between themselves as fictions (albeit intensely experienced fictions) and the fictions of their culture; which are constantly being (re)spoken, (re)written, and (re)lived" (Davies, 1993, p. 2). That these are by and large not related to school activities and tend to be child-initiated is a wonderful statement on the motivation *story* can provide for writing.

References

Alexander, A. *Potter War*. Retrieved 11/21/01 from http://www.potterwar.org.uk/home/index.html.

Alexandra. *Harry Potter Facts and Fun*. Retrieved 11/21/01 from http://www.hpfactsandfun.com.

(Anonymous), J., A. Black, S. Moon, K. Drowelf, and M. Spinnit. *Hogwarts School of Witchcraft and Wizardry*. Retrieved 11/21/01 from http://www.expage.com/harrypotteryhogwartstoo.

(Anonymous), K. *Harry Potter Fan Fiction*. Retrieved 11/21/01 from http://www.geocities.com/kim_2000rl/KimFanfic.html.

Atwell, N. *In the Middle*. 2nd ed. Portsmouth: Heinemann, 1998.

Baines, M. *Hermione's world*. Retrieved 11/21/01 from http://menarasin.tripod.com/hermioneworld.html.

Barthes, R. *Image, Music, Text*. New York: Hill and Wang, 1977.

Bishop, R. S. "Why Literature?" *The New Advocate* 13.1 (2000): 73–76.

Bruner, J. *Actual Minds, Possible Worlds*. Cambridge: Harvard UP, 1986.

Carter, B. "Literature in the Information Age." *The New Advocate* 13.1 (2000): 17–22.

Davies, B. *Shards of Glass: Children's Reading & Writing beyond Gendered Identities*. Cresskill: Hampton Press, 1993.

Field, C. *The Boy Who Lived*. Retrieved 11/21/01 from http://harrypotterguide.co.uk/.

Fingeret, H. A. "The Social and Historical Context of Participatory Literacy Education." *New Directions for Continuing Education* 42 (1989): 5–15.

Greene, S., and J. Ackerman. "Expanding the Constructivist Metaphor: A Rhetorical Perspective on Literacy Research and Practice." *Review of Educational Research* 65.4 (1995): 383–420.

Hagrid (pseud.). R. *Hagrid's Hut*. Retrieved 11/21/01 from http://www.hagridshut.com.

Hansen, J. *When Writers Read*. Portsmouth: Heinemann, 1987.

Harry Potter Fan Fiction. Retrieved 11/21/01 from http://www.fanfiction.net/master.cfm?action=story-listfiles&categoryID=224.

Iser, W. *The Act of Reading: A Theory of Aesthetic Response*. Baltimore: John's Hopkins University Press, 1978.

Kucer, S. L. "The Making of Meaning: Reading and Writing as Parallel Processes." *Written Communication* 2.3 (1985): 317–36.

Langer, J. A. *Literary Understanding and Literature Instruction*. Report Series 2.11. Albany: Center for the Learning and Teaching of Literature, 1993.

———. (1993). *Approaches toward Meaning in Low- and High-Rated Readers* (Report Series 2.20). Albany, NY: Center for the Learning and Teaching of Literature.

Malfoy, L. (pseud.) and M. McGonagall (pseud.). *The Daily Prophet*. Retrieved 11/21/01 from http://www.dprophet.com.

Newton, J. *Hogwarts School*. Retrieved 11/21/01 from http://www.harryPrpg2000.homestead. com/hogwarts.html.

Papert, S. *The Children's Machine: Rethinking School in the Age of the Computer*. New York: HarperCollins, 1993.

Pinkney, A. S. "Books and Megabytes: Good Friends in the Information Age." *The New Advocate* 13.1 (2000): 43–48.

Raintree, T. *Tealin's Harry Potter Page*. Retrieved 11/21/01 from http://www.geocities.com/ SoHo/Courtyard/8290/HarryPotter/index.html.

Rogers, T. "Students as Literary Critics: The Interpretive Experiences, Beliefs and Processes of Ninth-Grade Students." *Journal of Reading Behavior* 23.4 (1991): 391–423.

Rogers, T., O'Neil, and J. Jasinski. "Transforming Texts: Intelligences in Action." *English Journal* 84 (8), 41–46.

Rogers, T., C. Tyson, P. Enciso, E. Marshall, C. Jenkins, J. Brown, El Core, C. Cordova, D. Youngsteadt-Parish, and D. Robinson. "Technology, Media and the Book: Blurring Genres and Expanding the Reach of Children's Literature." *The New Advocate* 13.1 (2000): 79–83.

Wolfe, C., and A. Parkinson. *Calyso and Artemis' Hogwarts Page*. Retrieved 11/21/01 from http://www.gurlpages.com/other/calypso_artemis/index.html.

Part III

Literary Perspectives: The Hero, Myth, and Genre

Chapter Seven

Harry Potter—A Return to the Romantic Hero

Maria Nikolajeva

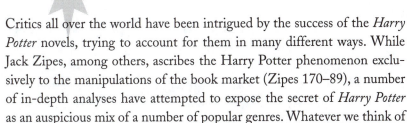

Critics all over the world have been intrigued by the success of the *Harry Potter* novels, trying to account for them in many different ways. While Jack Zipes, among others, ascribes the Harry Potter phenomenon exclusively to the manipulations of the book market (Zipes 170–89), a number of in-depth analyses have attempted to expose the secret of *Harry Potter* as an auspicious mix of a number of popular genres. Whatever we think of the novels in terms of their social or literary value, we can hardly dismiss them; instead, we should explore their allure in a critical way. It is my conviction, shared by a number of critics and scholars, that the attraction of the novels lies chiefly in the main character. But what exactly is it about Harry that appeals to readers, young and old, male and female, ardent and reluctant readers alike?

In his treatment of literature as the displacement of myth, Northrop Frye discerns five consecutive stages: myth, which presents characters as gods, superior to both humans and the laws of nature; romance, which presents characters as idealized humans who are superior to other humans, but inferior to gods; high-mimetic narrative, which presents humans who are superior to other humans, but not the laws of nature; low-mimetic narrative, which presents humans who are neither superior nor inferior to other humans; and finally ironic narrative, which presents characters who are inferior to other characters, such as children, the mentally handicapped, animals, and so on (Frye 33–34). By this definition, all child characters in children's fiction would appear at the ironic stage since they naturally lack experience and knowledge and are therefore inferior to adults. However, even a brief glance at a number of classical and contemporary children's novels demonstrates that this is not the case. Characters in children's novels are empowered in a variety of manners and operate on all the displacement levels. Harry Potter is in fact an excellent illustration of this. Being a wizard, he is omnipotent as compared to Muggles, not least his foster family. He is in many ways superior to his peers at Hogwarts: famous since birth, unbeatable in Quidditch, and indisputably more energetic and mischievous—virtuous in the eyes of his classmates, if not in those of his teachers. On the other hand, Harry and his fellow wizards are not free from the laws of nature: they can obviously get hurt, get sick, and even die. In some respects, Harry is inferior to his schoolmates; for instance, he is not particularly good in his academic achievements. Thus, Harry as a character is more complex than any of the archetypal figures in Frye's schema.

According to Frye, contemporary Western literature has reached the ironic stage, at which most of the characters we meet in novels are weak, disillusioned men and women. However, this is only true of quality literature since formulaic fiction operates within the romantic mode (romance, adventure, or fantasy). Children's literature is historically a recent form of fiction. Its emergence coincides with the establishment of realism (mimetic modes) in the mainstream; therefore, Frye's five stages seem to coexist more frequently in the children's literature than in the mainstream of any given period. In contemporary Western children's fiction, we meet characters from all of Frye's modes. Moreover, with Frye's model, we can also read one and the same text on different displacement levels, and again, the *Harry Potter* novels are a very good illustration of this. Indeed, they have already been interpreted by critics in a variety of ways (the present volume is no exception): as a heroic fantasy, a social satire, and so on.

Mythic hero is, however, not a common figure in children's fiction, for myth as such is absent in the history of Western children's literature. Since children's literature emerged long after Western civilization had lost its traditional mythical belief, this stage is not directly represented in children's fiction. The most important mythic figure is the cultural hero, who teaches his people to use fire, to hunt, and to cultivate land. Such stories were not relevant—as living narratives, essential for survival—for young readers at the time children's literature became a separate artistic form. It is, therefore, hardly possible to treat Harry Potter as a mythic hero in the conventional sense of the word since the stories are not based on belief (this, if anything, is a good argument against the adversaries who would like to ban the novels as propagating witchcraft). It is legitimate and fruitful to apply, for instance, Joseph Campbell's model for myth analysis toward the *Harry Potter* novels (see Deborah De Rosa's essay in this volume) since the movement of Campbellian monomyth, separation–initiation–return (Campbell 30), corresponds exactly to the master plot of children's fiction, home–away–homecoming, most tangible in all *Harry Potter* novels to date. Although myth as such is not a part of children's fiction, the mythic hero is a major source of inspiration for children's writers (see Stephens and McCallum). Yet, even though contemporary authors may lean heavily on myth, they will inevitably deconstruct it in some way (see Hourihan).

The romantic hero, on the other hand, superior to ordinary human beings, is one of the most common character types in children's fiction. We encounter it primarily in fairy tales and fantasy, where the child is empowered by being able to travel through space and time, by possessing magical objects, or by being assisted by magical helpers. In fairy tales retold for children, characters are usually empowered in a way that makes them superior to other human beings. They are endowed with magical agents enabling them to be transported in space, or to metamorphose into animals or other, presumably better, human beings (Cinderella's transformation from ashes to diamonds). However, fairy-tale heroes normally have helpers possessing stronger powers than they do, without whom they would not be able to achieve their goals. If fairy-tale protagonists are demi-gods, their helpers are gods. Ultimately, this reflects the power relationship between children and adults in society.

All these elements are well-matched in the person of Harry Potter and his environment. Harry is transported from the real world to the magical realm by means of the magical train, invisible to his Muggle family; he gets possession of a large variety of magical agents: his fantastic supermodern flying broom, his magic wand, an invisibility mantle, a magical interactive map, and so on. He also has a number of helpers who come to the rescue when his own magical powers prove insufficient; as in fairy tales, the adult wizards appear stronger than the hero himself. Thus, although empowered, the child is not given full control; and even though it is understood that Harry is the only one to match the evil force of Voldemort, until the ultimate battle Harry has to comply with the rules and laws imposed on him by adults. In the end, Dumbledore, the father substitute, has the final say.

With few exceptions, fairy tales have always been regarded as suitable for children, apparently because fairy-tale protagonists, like children, grow from being the underdog to being strong and independent. Indeed, Harry's triumphant ascent from his oppressed position in the Dursleys' home to fame, perpetual riches, and his privileged existence at Hogwarts is an easily recognizable fairy-tale pattern.

Another essential trait of fairy-tale heroes is their lack of complexity, considered appropriate for young readers from a didactic viewpoint. Fairy-tale heroes know no nuances; they are one hundred percent heroic, they never doubt, fear, or despair. In fact, they are seldom individualized. If described at all, they possess a standard set of traits: strong, brave, clever, kind, or beautiful. Their moral qualities are impeccable: they are just, loyal, and devoted to the cause they pursue. The premise for the romantic child hero is the idealization of childhood that developed during the Romantic era. It is based on the belief in the child as innocent and, therefore, capable of conquering evil. Although this ideal, fictional child is now being interrogated by some critics (see essays in McGavran), it affects the ways in which child heroes are still constructed in certain text types. Harry is no exception. His chief strength is the very fact that he is a child, and it is stressed that already, as an infant, he had the power to protect himself against Voldemort. His intrinsic goodness is his most momentous weapon.

The essential difference between mythic and romantic patterns in children's fiction is the return, in the latter, to the initial order, the disempowerment of the hero, and the reestablishment of adult authority. The classic mythic hero kills his father and usurps the father's place, which would be highly improper in a children's book (instead, Harry's father is, in accordance with children's literature tradition, conveniently killed off while Harry is still a baby). From magical journeys to alternative worlds or histories, the child hero is brought back to the ordinary, sometimes being explicitly stripped of the attributes of previous power, most tangibly seen in the transformation of the Kings and Queens of Narnia back to children at the end of C. S. Lewis's *The Lion, the Witch and the Wardrobe*. The magical object is irretrievably lost or loses its magical power (*The Story of the Amulet* by Edith Nesbit), the magical helper is removed (*Mary Poppins* by Pamela Travers), and the character once again stands alone without assistance, no longer a hero. Thus, in many children's fantasy novels, the characters become displaced yet further away from myth, onto low-mimetic and ironic levels. After each year at Hogwarts, Harry is returned to his inferior position with the Dursleys. Apart from being a suitable narrative element, providing a convenient and natural frame for each school year, the return serves as a reminder of Harry's temporary departure from the ordinary and his temporary empowerment through the magical setup. Rowling follows the tradition from the Grand Old Lady of contemporary fantasy, Edith Nesbit, who, according to interviews, was one of Rowling's childhood favorites. Magic, in Nesbit's novels, is never omnipotent and often tricky. It has its limits, and a return to the ordinary, magic-less world is inevitable. We do of course feel sorry for Harry, but for the sake of the plot his staying with the Dursley's is indispensable. The novels here adhere to the long tradition of children's literature based on the concept of carnival, as developed by Mikhail Bakhtin.

The essence of the medieval carnival, Bakhtin points out, was the temporary reversal of the established order when all societal power structures changed places. Fool was crowned king, while kings and bishops were dethroned and denigrated. The temporary nature of carnival presupposed the restoration of the initial order. Yet, as Bakhtin sees it, carnival had a subversive effect since it showed that social hierarchies were not unquestionable. Bakhtin applies the concept of carnival to literature, viewing it as a narrative device used to describe reality in a distorting mirror, in a state of temporary deviation from the existing order, as well as a total freedom from societal restrictions.

Carnival theory is highly relevant for children's literature. Children in our society are oppressed and powerless, having no economic resources of their own, no voice in political and social decisions, and subject to a large number of laws and rules that the adults expect them to obey without interrogation. Yet, paradoxically enough, children are allowed, in fiction written for their enlightenment and enjoyment *by adults*, to become strong, brave, rich, powerful, independent—on certain conditions and for a limited time. The most important condition is the physical dislocation and the removal, temporary or permanent, of parental protection, allowing the child protagonist to have the freedom to explore the world and test the boundaries of independence. The child may be placed in a number of extraordinary situations, such as war or revolution, exotic, far-away settings, temporary isolation on a desert island, extreme danger (common in mystery novels), and so on. All these conditions empower the fictional child, and even though the protagonist is most frequently brought back to the security of home and parental supervision, the narratives have subversive effect, showing that the rules imposed on the child by the adults are in fact arbitrary. Fantasy is another common carnivalesque device, as an ordinary child is empowered through transportation to a magical realm, through the possession of a magical agent (object or helper), and through acquisition of a set of heroic traits or magical force, impossible or at least improbable within the existing order of things—what we normally call "real world." Carnival, reversing the existing order, elevates the fictional child to the superior position of the romantic hero. Yet, the inevitable reestablishment of order in the end of a carnivalesque children's story brings the characters down to the high-mimetic, low-mimetic, or ironic levels, at which they are only slightly more powerful than their environment, equal to it or inferior to it.

High-mimetic characters, in Frye's model, are humans superior to other humans, for instance, in terms of bravery, wisdom, or patriotism. High-mimetic narratives for children emerged almost simultaneously with the early retold fairy tales. Two common types are hagiographies (lives of saints) and plutarches (lives of important historical and political figures). Being superior to other humans, including the reader, high-mimetic characters are supposed to serve as models not only for the other character in the story but for the readers as well. In children's fiction, such characters are used for educational and didactic purposes. In fact, adult co-readers may find Harry quite satisfactory as a model for children: he is humble, well-mannered, respectful toward his seniors, almost a perfect English gentleman. Young readers may appreciate other traits in Harry. As pointed out before, Harry is superior to his peers in terms of fame, bravery, and sports achievements. He is favored by his teachers, for instance, is chosen for the Quidditch team against the rules; in volume four, he is allowed to participate in the Triwizard Tournament, which is likewise against the rules (and as we learn later, the result of an evil conspiracy). There is still another element in the novels that allows Harry to be superior in a typically carnivalesque manner, and that is mystery. Mystery novels for children, such as *Nancy Drew* or the *Hardy Boys* series, empower the protagonists by letting them be smarter than the adults, to succeed where real detectives fail, and to happen to be at the right place at the right moment. Although devoid of supernatural features, mystery novels are no more "realistic" than the most incredible fairy tales, and the young heroes are far from ordinary. Indeed, they excel in everything: They can drive cars and fly airplanes, have quick brains, intuition and observation aptitude; they can perform chemical analyses, operate obscure machinery, and find their way around without maps or compass; and they certainly always come safely out of the most dangerous situations. Incidentally, Nancy Drew is also exceedingly good at sports and wins golf tournaments just in passing, while busy solving another mystery. Harry Potter is very much like these popular heroes. In each novel, he must solve a mystery, using his wits, courage, defiance, curiosity, deduction ability, and, not least, physical dexterity. His skills with his magic wand (a phallic symbol, as many critics have pointed out) are not to be neglected. I will in this context abstain from the statement, repeatedly made by critics, that it is invariably Hermione's wit that helps to solve the mystery. For my argument, Hermione is "merely" Harry's helper—in a Proppian or Campbellian sense—so that her special qualities are nothing but the extension of the hero. I see nothing sexist in this fact, at least no more than any male heroic tale is by definition sexist. Hermione and her intelligence are simply part of Harry's entourage, alongside magic wands and flying brooms.

Yet, the deconstruction of Harry does not stop at the high-mimetic level, but it goes further down to the low mimetic. Low-mimetic narratives present ordinary children in ordinary situations: domestic stories, school stories, and so on. As pointed out by many critics, boarding school story is a genre tangibly present in *Harry Potter*. In boarding school novels, with *Tom Brown's Schooldays* as an early model, the plot revolves around "ordinary" adventures: lessons, homework, sports, celebrations of the first and last day of school, competition among dormitories, mischief, nightly orgies, forbidden outings to off-bound places, spying for enemies, the arrival of new students and new teachers, bullying, revenge, and so on. Apart from the ongoing progressive plot featuring the struggle of good and evil, it is the never-ending chain of everyday episodes, albeit generously seasoned with magic, that the bulk of the *Harry Potter* volumes contain. For my taste, the dominance of these in volume four becomes tedious, edging on unbearable (but then I am not particularly fond of Tom Brown either). However, these everyday elements dilute the heroic nature of our hero, making him more like us, the readers.

The ordinariness of Harry is magnificently emphasized by his name, which clearly stands out as plain and unpretentious beside Dumbledore, McGonagall, or Draco Malfoy. While these associative names are used to contribute to their bearers' individuality, Harry's name underscores his "everyman" nature, signaling to the readers: "He is just like one of you."

Although "realistic" characters seemingly have existed in children's fiction from the beginning, I would argue that characters appearing on a low-mimetic level—neither superior nor inferior to other characters—are a relatively recent development. Considering the protagonists of some classic novels for children, we discover that they are portrayed as anything but ordinary. The four March sisters in *Little Women* are exceedingly virtuous and become still more so as they go through their self-imposed "pilgrimage." Tom Sawyer finds a treasure ensuring him of a pleasurable future in the adult world. Anne Shirley becomes a brilliant student and is eventually described as quite good-looking. Cedric Errol in Burnett's *Little Lord Fauntleroy* is nauseatingly blameless, in addition to inheriting great wealth.

Modern low-mimetic characters appear on a larger scale in Western children's literature after the Second World War as a result of major changes in society, rapid urbanization, changes in family structure, as well as the achievements of child psychology. Low-mimetic characters offer the most natural subject position for contemporary young readers: they are not freed from the obligation to attend school by eternal summer holidays; they are not extremely lucky to be in the right place at the right time to have exciting adventures; they are not exceedingly bright, nor brave, nor handsome; they do not marry princes or millionaires; and they do not find treasures that will allow them to live happily ever after. Contemporary characters are not meant as examples for young readers to admire, but as equal subjectivities. While Harry is undoubtedly more lucky than most of us, his exceptionality is balanced by his more down-to-earth qualities, including his poor sight. Yet, with his old-fashioned, broken glasses Harry sees better than any other Hogwarts student, a quality especially appreciated by the members of his Quidditch team.

It has taken children's fiction a long time to venture into the ironic mode and depict characters who are weaker, physically and spiritually, than their peers, in addition to being inferior to their parents and other adults. Unlike fairy-tale heroes, these characters are not empowered at the end of the story. At best, they remain the same, at worst they perish, incapable of coping with the surrounding reality. It can be questioned and has indeed been repeatedly questioned whether ironic characters are "suitable" in children's fiction. They do not provide models for young readers; they may even leave unsophisticated readers frustrated and confused. As adults, we supposedly have the ability to detach ourselves from failed, unhappy, disoriented protagonists and view their predicaments from a distance and with a condescending smile. Young readers, with their inherent strong sense of empathy, may have serious problems handling ironic characters.

It is not always possible and still less fruitful to draw a definite boundary between low-mimetic and ironic characters in children's fiction. As pointed out above, all child characters are by definition ironic, that is, inferior to their surroundings and, it would seem, to the readers. However, in children's fiction, the readers may be just as inexperienced and disempowered as the ironic character. In other words, young readers may find themselves at the same level as the character. Although adult readers may see the young protagonist's faults and mistakes, a young reader may fail to do so. Contemporary writers have developed means of drawing the readers' attention to the ironic status of their characters, for instance, through detachment and alienation.

In traditional fiction, children as well as adult readers are expected to identify and empathize with at least one character, to adopt a subject position coinciding with a character's. One of the main premises of postmodern aesthetics is subversion of subjectivity, often achieved by making the protagonist repulsive in some way: physically unattractive, obnoxious, morally depraved, a criminal, or even an inhuman monster. Some contemporary characters in children's fiction efficiently alienate the reader by being unpleasant and thus offering no clear-cut subject position. Whereas Mary Lennox in Burnett's *The Secret Garden*, repeatedly described as "disagreeable," quickly gains the reader's sympathy, being an orphan and exposed to the adults' indifference, a character staying unpleasant and destructive throughout the story may leave the reader concerned and even frustrated. In many contemporary psychological children's novels, notably by Katherine Paterson, the narrative device of filter—shifting the reader's point of view away from the character's—allows the reader to dissociate from the focalizing character (Nikolajeva, *Art*). This narrative strategy may seem more generous toward young readers since it enables them to feel superior to the protagonist. However, it presupposes a significantly higher degree of involvement on the readers' part; rather than passively flowing with the plot from the imposed subject position, the readers must resist this and detach themselves from the character's point of view. While as critics and scholars we may favor texts that put higher demands on young readers, the readers themselves certainly prefer texts with minimal resistance.

The eternal question in connection with the essence of children's fiction is the adult authors' capacity to adopt a child subject position. It is reasonable to assume that adult writers would feel most comfortable writing from their own superior position, presenting child characters as inferior physically, morally, spiritually, in terms of knowledge, experience, economy, and societal power. However, even a very brief glance at a number of children's novels reveals that the ironic mode is the most complex and demanding. On the other hand, the romantic mode allows adults to empower the child, thus creating an illusion for the character and the reader that such empowerment is indeed possible. On the high-mimetic level, adult writers can use characters to provide young readers with examples and ideals. Which endeavor is to be regarded the most successful depends exclusively on the purpose the authors have in writing for children. The development from hero to character in children's fiction is not a simple linear process. It reveals the attitude toward childhood and toward children's reading at any given moment in any given society. Writing for children at the turn of the third millennium, Rowling must necessarily take these factors into consideration.

Low-mimetic and ironic characters are the first ones historically and the only ones typologically who presuppose and allow a portrayal of internal life. Therefore, we are most likely to find such characters in contemporary psychological novels for children. If, according to Harold Bloom, a psychological human being was invented by Shakespeare (Bloom), in children's literature it was invented collaboratively by such authors as Katherine Paterson, Patricia MacLachlan, Beverly Cleary, Nina Bawden, Cynthia Voigt, and Michelle Magorian. Harry Potter is not a character encumbered by a complex inner life. Throughout the four volumes, we hardly ever know what Harry thinks or feels. True, we are told that he is scared or lonely, but these are narrator's statements, not representations of mental states, which some of the above-mentioned children's writers have elaborated with. Rowling does not use any of the more sophisticated narrative techniques for conveying psychological states: free indirect discourse, interior monologue, or psychonarration (see Cohn). The *Harry Potter* novels are clearly action-oriented rather than character-oriented, which, according to some critics, notably Perry Nodelman, is the intrinsic feature of children's fiction (Nodelman 192). If we see Harry reflect at all, he reflects upon what to do and how to do it best. Like fairy-tale heroes, he never has any ethical dilemmas or moral choices. He may misjudge some people or follow false clues, but this is indispensable in a mystery novel. Contemporary modes of conveying psychological states are demanding on the reader since they are ambivalent in allowing the reader to determine the source of utterance. The *Harry Potter* novels are unequivocal and straightforward.

What can be said in Harry's defense, if he needs defense, or rather in his creator's defense, is that, his machismo notwithstanding, Harry does not in fact present a gender stereotype. In fact, if we apply one of the many standard schemata for masculinity or femininity (see Stephens), we will discover that Harry displays quite a few traits we normally associate with feminine stereotypes. He is nonviolent, nonaggressive, emotional, caring, and vulnerable, which definitely makes him different from the conventional romantic heroes. Yet, he never comes any closer to the complexity of some contemporary fantasy protagonists.

To provide a better comparison of Harry Potter with an ironic character, we may turn to Diana Wynne Jones's novel *The Lives of Christopher Chant*, one of the many forerunners to Rowling featuring a school of wizards. The title character is similar to Harry Potter in that he, at a young age, discovers his magical powers. Yet, unlike Harry, Christopher's introduction into the world of wizardry is painful and reluctant. While most of Harry's adventures in Hogwarts are rather innocent pranks, Christopher repeatedly serves the abominable purposes of his greedy and evil uncle, bringing profitable loot from the many parallel worlds he visits, including mermaid flesh and dragon blood. As a true hero, Harry takes the right side in the struggle between good and evil, leaving no doubt to the readers as to where their sympathies should be. Even though some of the adults in Harry's immediate surroundings prove the opposite of what they initially seem to be, the basic distinction between right and wrong is still there, and Harry's choice does not present any serious moral dilemmas. In Christopher's world, nothing and nobody is ever what they seem to be; the adults are treacherous, and even the boy's parents are ambiguous in their ethical qualities. Since the novel consistently employs the young protagonist's naive point of view, the readers may feel superior to the character in their understanding of the actual events as well as the adults' motivations. The readers are enabled to see Christopher's horrible errors as well as his naive blindness and false loyalties. However, in order to do so, we have to free ourselves from the protagonist's subject position—a demand that is never placed on the recipient of a fairy tale or any other conventional romantic text. Certainly, we have no problems with subjectivity in the *Harry Potter* novels, sharing our literal and transferred point of view with

Harry irrespective of our age, gender, race, social group, or geographical anchoring. This is how romantic texts function: imposing the fixed and incontestable subject position on all readers indiscriminately.

Viewing the characters' ontological status from a historical perspective, we can clearly see that contemporary characters tend to become more like "real people," appearing on low-mimetic and ironic levels. Our shifting criteria for "plausible" characters depend on several factors, for instance, on our growing knowledge of human nature (which young children normally lack); on our changing values of human virtues and vices; and finally on the variety of human behavior. Examples of real heroes are found today only in formulaic fiction, including fantasy. As illustrated by *The Lives of Christopher Chant*, contemporary sophisticated fantasy contains a substantial amount of uncertainty and ambiguity, typical of postmodern thinking. Philip Pullman's *His Dark Materials*, which from the very start has been repeatedly compared to the *Harry Potter* novels, portrays characters with dubious moral qualities, including the young protagonists. Lyra, the heroine of Pullman's trilogy, has in fact caused the death of her best friend. Morally, she is not as pure and innocent as traditional fantasy prescribes. The ultimate battle between good and evil in *The Amber Spyglass* concerns Lyra, the chosen child who will decide the fates of all the parallel worlds. In this, she is not unlike Harry Potter. The problem is that in Pullman's novels, it is not self-evident which choice is the right one. As readers, we are given to understand that Lyra, like Eve in the Bible, will be subject to a temptation. It is, however, far from clear whether she is supposed to fall or withstand, and in the first place what consequences either of these actions will have. With Harry, on the other hand, we can be more or less sure that his task is to fight Voldemort, not to assist him.

The utter ambiguity of character in Pullman's trilogy is based on the postmodern concept of indeterminacy, of the relativity of good and evil. By intuition, we decide that the forces who wish to kill Lyra are evil, while those who seek to hide and protect her are good. However, the motivation of both sides is equally dubious. We also learn that the subtle knife, one of the major attributes of the trilogy, featured in the title of the second novel, is of a double nature. It is used to open passages between the different worlds, and as such seems to serve a good cause. What the characters only learn later is that the passages they create are the very source of the threat to the universe they are trying to save. The reader of Pullman's novels is not given any clues or guidance as to the true nature of good and evil.

Against this background, the tremendous success of the *Harry Potter* novels may be at least partially ascribed to the fortunate attempt to reintroduce the romantic character into children's fiction. Let us once again contemplate the character of Harry Potter and the necessary components of the romantic hero. First, there are mystical circumstances around his birth and infant years. He bears the mark of the chosen on his forehead, and he is—although unaware of this himself—worshipped in the wizard community as the future savior. The pattern is easily recognizable from a great variety of world mythologies, even though Harry is not claimed to be a god or a son of a god, which, as pointed out earlier, disqualifies him as a genuine mythic hero, instead displacing him to the level of romance.

Harry is born into the world of humans; he is dislocated from his rightful environment. A child deprived of his or her birthright is one of the most common mythical and folktale motifs, occurring in stories as diverse as Cinderella and the Bible. The romantic convention will, however, suggest to the reader that the weak and the oppressed will be empowered and returned to their proper position, their proper place in the social hierarchy. This happens, appropriately, on Harry's eleventh birthday, eleven being the common age of initiation in archaic societies. He is reintroduced to the community from which he has been temporarily expelled, and he is given seemingly unlimited power, even though, with a marvelous ironic twist, he is yet to learn how to make use of this power. Moreover, although restored in his rightful position, Harry is yet to prove himself worthy of it, and is therefore subjected to a number of trials. Each volume of the *Harry Potter* saga is a duplication of this trial pattern (I presume that the remaining three books will follow it as well), with a number of ingenious variations, yet basically identical (see also Zipes 176f). The conventions of the romantic mode dictate that the hero pass the trial and win the combat with the evil forces. In this, Harry is equipped with an army of gurus and supporters and an infinitely evil and powerful opponent. However, his innocence and his intrinsic benevolence make him superior to the evil—adult—powers.

It is of course not a coincidence that Rowling has chosen a male protagonist for her saga. The romantic narrative is by definition masculine, and any contemporary attempts to place a female character in a masculine plot merely results in a simple gender permutation, creating "a hero in drag" (see Paul; Nikolajeva, *From Mythic to Linear*, 147–49). More interesting is to contemplate the reason why the ultimate evil is represented by a male figure. However, even here Rowling faithfully follows conventions. As shown by critics, with few exceptions, fantasy authors present evil as figures of the opposite gender. The reason, psychoanalytically-oriented critics argue, is that we subconsciously see the opposite gender as abnormal and therefore evil (Veglahn). Whether or not we accept the explanation, the pattern is obvious. Frank Baum and C. S. Lewis have evil portrayed as females, while Astrid Lindgren has male villains in her two fantasy novels, *Mio My Son* and *The Brothers Lionheart*. Susan Cooper's *The Dark Is Rising* suite and Ursula Le Guin's Earthsea novels also have male evil figures. While more sophisticated contemporary fantasy novels show the ambiguity of good and evil, male and female (for instance, Lord Asriel and Mrs. Coulter in *His Dark Materials*, or Lugan and Lady Taranis in Susan Cooper's *Seaward*), Rowling certainly prefers traditional clearcut patterns, in which she also, most probably unconsciously, creates the utter evil as a figure of opposite gender.

Connecting the evil figure to the character, we could say that in meeting the opponent of the same gender, the protagonists face the dark side of the same-gender parent, which they must acknowledge and reconcile with (the Shadow in the Jungian model). Harry naturally idealizes his dead father; yet, he must learn to accept the uncomfortable truth that the father was perhaps not as perfect as the ideal Harry has developed. On the psychological level of the story, Voldemort is a reminder of this darker parental image. By the fourth volume, Harry has learned that one cannot flee from the Shadow, but must meet it face to face. This is the fate of romantic heroes.

Yet, Harry Potter is a child of his time, of the twenty-first century. He appears as a reaction to a long chain of ironic characters, showing ambiguity in their concepts of good and evil, gender transgression, and other tokens of the postmodern aesthetic. By contrast, Harry Potter is a very straightforward hero. We know what to expect from him. After decades of parody, metafiction, frame-breaking, and other postmodern games, it may feel liberating for the readers, young and old alike, to know where to place their sympathies and antipathies. Of course it is conceivable that Harry will eventually go over to the dark side. But such a development would almost feel trivial today, especially in the wake of *Star Wars—the First Episode*. After so many antiheroes in children's as well as adult literature, a hero is welcome. However, the appeal of Harry is exactly that he is not a hero of the Superman caliber, but an ordinary clumsy and bespectacled boy. A boy who turns out to have magical powers, yet a boy who receives most praise for his sporting achievements. A boy who is disobedient and curious, who is not at all brilliant in school, but quite average. A boy who has friends and enemies, who needs to eat and sleep, and who, in *Harry Potter and the Goblet of Fire*, is at long last awakening—very cautiously for his age—to the charms and mysteries of the opposite gender. Harry is of course brave, kind, and he has a strong sense of justice. Yet he is not above playing dirty tricks on his foster family by using magic, and he does not hesitate to wear the invisibility mantle to sneak around like a typical fairy-tale trickster. Harry Potter is at once human and nonhuman, with the same emotions we all know: longing for mom and dad, loneliness, insecurity, curiosity about his identity and origin. In this respect, he differs from the traditional romantic hero, devoid of any such sentiments. Thus Harry is repeatedly taken down to the mimetic and ironic levels, only to be elevated to hero status again at the moment of decisive struggle. The end of volume four is especially illuminating in this respect as Harry is finally put through a trial in which he can only count on himself. In a way, Harry is a hero of the same kind as Pippi Longstocking: the one we would like to be, but know we can never be—not because we are not born into a rich family or do not have Einstein's IQ or Cindy Crawford's looks but simply because we recognize the conventions of the genre. We are not envious of Harry's gift or his success, just as we are not envious of Pippi's strength. On the contrary, we feel an affirmative joy when following their adventures.

Harry Potter provides the sense of security for the reader that characters such as Lyra or Christopher Chant have subverted. In following Harry's adventures and misadventures, we are not interested in whether he will win or not, but in how he gets there. In volume four, Rowling has achieved a masterly balance of suspense and confidence in the final scenes. As in a James Bond movie, we know that the hero will be miraculously saved in the last moment, and we keep on reading to learn exactly how this happens. The extratextual knowledge of the three remaining volumes adds to our firm belief in the positive outcome. Rowling cannot possibly kill Harry and let the sequels go on without him. Neither can she kill him and resurrect him in the next volume since she has included the hero's mortality as a part of her universe. As stated earlier, Harry is not a mythic "returning god."

It seems that Harry Potter is a child of serendipity. He appeared at the time when the international children's book market was in acute need of a new type of character. The flat, one-dimensional, mind-numbing characters of formulaic fiction, though satisfying the basic desires of less sophisticated readers, had for decades vexed conscious critics, librarians, and teachers. The ambivalent, ironic, postmodern characters, praised by critics, have often been rejected by young readers as too complex and demanding. The fortunate blend of the romantic and the ironic, the straightforward and the reasonably intricate, the heroic and the everyday in Harry Potter appeared as a response to these contradictory needs, and, sarcastic voices notwithstanding, seems to have reconciled the incompatible desires.

References

Bakhtin, Mikhail. *Rabelais and His World*. Cambridge: MIT Press, 1968.

Bloom, Harold. *Shakespeare. The Invention of the Human*. New York: Riverhead Books, 1998.

Campbell, Joseph. *The Hero with a Thousand Faces*. 2nd ed. Princeton: Princeton UP, 1968.

Cohn, Dorrit. *Transparent Minds. Narrative Modes for Presenting Consciousness in Fiction*. Princeton: Princeton UP, 1978.

Frye, Northrop. *Anatomy of Criticism. Four Essays*. Princeton: Princeton UP, 1957.

Hourihan, Margery. *Deconstructing the Hero. Literary Theory and Children's Literature*. London: Routledge, 1997.

McGavran, James Holt, ed. *Literature and the Child. Romantic Continuations, Postmodern Contestations*. Iowa City: U of Iowa P, 1999.

Nikolajeva, Maria. *From Mythic to Linear. Time in Children's Literature*. Lanham: Scarecrow, 2000.

———. "The Art of Self-Deceit. Narrative Strategies in Katherine Paterson's Novels." In *Bridges for the Young*. Ed. Sarah Smedman and Joel Chaston. Lanham: Scarecrow (forthcoming).

Nodelman, Perry. *The Pleasures of Children's Literature*. New York: Longman, 1992.

Paul, Lissa. "Enigma Variations. What Feminist Criticism Knows about Children's Literature." In *Children's Literature. The Development of Criticism*. Ed. Peter Hunt. London: Rutledge and Kegan Paul, 1990. 148–66.

Stephens, John. "Gender, Genre and Children's Literature." *Signal* 79 (1996): 17–30.

Stephens, John, and Robyn McCallum. *Retelling Stories, Framing Culture. Traditional Story and Metanarratives in Children's Literature*. New York: Garland, 1998.

Veglahn, Nancy. "Images of Evil: Male and Female Monsters in Heroic Fantasy." *Children's Literature* 15 (1987): 106–19.

Zipes, Jack. *Sticks and Stones. The Troublesome Success of Children's Literature from Slovenly Peter to Harry Potter*. New York: Routledge, 2001.

Chapter Eight

Generic Fusion and the Mosaic of *Harry Potter*

Anne Hiebert Alton

We shall not cease from exploration
And the end of all our exploring
Will be to arrive where we started
And know the place for the first time.

—T.S. Eliot, *Four Quartets*

The *Harry Potter* phenomenon has taken the world by storm, and in many ways the series appears to be responsible for a renaissance in reading for children all over the world, despite its competition from the supposedly more accessible forms of entertainment available on videos, television, or the Internet.[1] While there are myriad reasons for its tremendous popularity, much of its appeal lies in J. K. Rowling's incorporation of a vast number of genres in the books.[2] Genres traditionally dismissed as "despised" genres—including pulp fiction, mystery, gothic and horror stories, detective fiction, the school story and the closely related sports story, and series books—appear throughout the *Harry Potter* books, along with more "mainsteam" genres (at least in children's literature) such as fantasy, adventure, quest romance, and myth. Rather than creating a hodgepodge with no recognizable or specific pattern, Rowling has fused these genres into a larger mosaic, which not only connects readers' generic expectations with the tremendous success and popularity of the *Harry Potter* series but also leads to the ways in which the series conveys literary meaning.

One of the primary functions of genre, at least in terms of readership, is as a marketing device: how books are generically categorized tends to influence how readers think about them even before picking them up. This tradition can be seen particularly clearly in works of pulp fiction and children's magazines in the late nineteenth and early twentieth centuries, and it is a tradition shared by the *Harry Potter* series. Though not pulp fiction in the strict sense since it lacks such defining features as sentimentality, eroticism, sensationalism, and (in a physical sense) the poor paper quality of tabloid fiction, the series does contain certain pulp elements, particularly in terms of titles and dust jackets. The titles—all beginning with the phrase "Harry Potter and"—suggest series books, while the rest of the phrase encourages readers to formulate more specific generic expectations. *Harry Potter and the Sorcerer's Stone*[3] suggests fantasy, magic, and myth, while elements of mystery, thriller fiction, or possibly even horror are evoked by *Harry Potter and the Chamber of Secrets. Harry Potter and the Prisoner of Azkaban* sounds like a racy crime thriller or perhaps a gothic tale, and *Harry Potter and the Goblet of Fire* invokes images of adventure, fantasy, and mysticism. The dust jackets demonstrate an even stronger link with pulp fiction. Like late-nineteenth-century pulp novels, whose visual appeal appeared in covers designed to capture purchasers' attention by representing, or claiming to represent, the "contents of the magazine in an appealing, vivid, alluring light" (Scott 42), the covers of the *Harry Potter* books tend to be connected to certain generic assumptions. For example, the American edition of *Sorcerer's Stone* shows Harry—a clumsy-looking, skinny boy with messy hair and glasses—flying on a broomstick and trying to catch the golden snitch, while the cover of the British edition portrays him as a skinny, puzzled schoolboy standing on Platform 9¾ before a red train engine labeled Hogwarts Express. While this cover appears to be somewhat less fantastic than its American counterpart, the colors—predominately pinks and purples, with orange and blue in the background—traditionally indicate fantasy. The rest of the covers have similarly powerful generic implications, though naturally these entail certain cultural differences.[4] These differences are perhaps best seen when contrasting the British and American covers for *Goblet of Fire*: the British cover—rendered in red, gold, and black—shows an intent Harry flying on his broomstick toward a golden egg and evading a realistic-looking dragon spewing fire, while the American cover—done in green, copper, and black—shows a beaming Harry holding a golden egg in one hand and a wand in the other, while three unknown teens stand behind him. The former hints at some of the book's serious content—the life-and-death struggle that appears in the three trials for the Triwizard Tournament, for example—and indicates to its reader that this will be a tale of fantasy, adventure, and conflict; in contrast, the latter seems far less threatening: the wand and the small white stars that seem to sparkle on the cover suggest fantasy, but that of a tamer and less dangerous fantastic world.[5]

In terms of content, the series shares other elements of pulp fiction and popular literature, including the ease of identification with the protagonist, something that hooks the reader of popular fiction. Indeed, all three of the main protagonists appeal to readers: Everyone can either identify with or knows someone like brainy Hermione, faithful and funny Ron, and orphan Harry. Moreover, the books contain the wish-fulfillment of most people's need to be special—and how much more "special" can one be than to be admitted into a world filled with like-minded people who have talents above and beyond the real world? However, in terms of true pulp fiction, often characterized by "sexual stigma and titillation . . . violence, lawlessness, cruelty, irony, misinformation, sentimentality and superstition" (Hilton 13), some sort of conspiracy, and elements of luxury like those that appear in the James Bond thrillers (Palmer 113), *Harry Potter* contains only elements of the genre rather than conforming to it absolutely. Luxuries such as magical meals or the comfort of Harry's tower room complete with curtained beds for all five inhabitants appear with regularity, while Voldemort's "conspiracy" against Harry makes up the main plot of the series. Lawlessness appears not only with Sirius's escape from Azkaban—which in any case is made respectable due to his innocence—but with Voldemort's actions throughout the series, particularly in *Goblet of Fire* in his flouting of natural laws to return to a human body. From Snape's perspective, Harry's continual breaking of school rules also could be viewed as lawlessness, though (at least so far) this is a relatively benign example. Real or threatened cruelty and violence also appear regularly, with Harry's treatment at the hands of the Dursleys, along with the Cruciatus Curse that causes indescribable pain, Professor Moody's humiliation of Draco Malfoy by turning him into a ferret and bouncing him through the corridor, Wormtail's cutting off of his own hand to resurrect Voldemort, and the murder of Cedric Diggory.

These elements of violence, while characteristic of pulp fiction, simultaneously evoke both ghost and horror stories. The traditional ghost story portrays something that should be dead invading the world of the living, which happens in *Harry Potter* with Peeves the poltergeist or ghosts Nearly Headless Nick and the Bloody Baron. In addition, the atmosphere tends to be frightening but also realistic enough that the terrors are quite believable, and this is accomplished through the use of gothic elements, many of which appear throughout the series. For example, Hogwarts possesses dungeons (where Snape's Potions classes take place), subterranean passages (the tunnels through which Harry passes to find the Sorcerer's Stone and the Chamber of Secrets), and secret entrances (the various hidden routes to Hogsmeade). In addition, other sorts of supernatural elements appear, including vampires (*Sorcerer's Stone*) and werewolves (*Prisoner of Azkaban*), along with mysterious disappearances, such as Hermione's (*Prisoner of Azkaban*) or Bertha Jorkins's (*Goblet of Fire*). Rowling shifts the plot convention of suffering at the hands of the cruel villain usually reserved for the beautiful heroine onto Harry. Elements of horror also appear throughout the series, though they are particularly strong in *Chamber of Secrets* and *Goblet of Fire*, with the threatened attack of the giant spiders, the Jekyll and Hyde parameter, and the whispered " . . . *rip* . . . *tear* . . . *kill* . . ." (*Chamber* 137) Harry hears in the former, and the entire "Flesh, Blood, and Bone" chapter dealing with the resurrection of Voldemort in the latter (chapter 32).

Two other genres commonly associated with pulp literature and that appear throughout the *Harry Potter* series include mystery and detective fiction. A major element in both is the appeal of solving a problem, whether in relation to a violent crime (usually murder), a disappearance of some sort (a theft of a valuable item), or a hidden identity (the true heir to an estate is revealed). The pattern in both genres is also similar: a secret about the crime is first hidden and then revealed, usually through the discovery of the villain's identity by a detective figure who reveals the secret and reconstructs what happened. This detective figure is generally an outsider of some sort—someone who is not a member of "regular" society—and thus not only holds different values than the norm but also can see the problem differently and more clearly than other people. He/she is able to discover the solution and solve the mystery by interpreting a variety of physical and psychological signs and, at times (like the prototypical detective, Sherlock Holmes), by thinking like the villain. The main mystery throughout the series pertains to Harry and Voldemort, raising such questions as who is Harry Potter? Who is Voldemort? Why does he want to kill Harry? Why does he keep failing? What form will their ultimate confrontation take, and what will be the end result? Specific mysteries also appear in each book: *Sorcerer's Stone* creates a mystery around the stone and its significance, as well as around what happened eleven years before the

Potter's deaths (this one has not yet been resolved); *Chamber of Secrets* constructs a traditional detective story with the petrification incidents as well as the mystery of the horrific whispers Harry hears; *Prisoner of Azkaban* deals with the identity of Sirius Black as well as the antagonism between Scabbers (Ron's rat) and Crookshanks (Hermione's cat); *Goblet of Fire* (the most complex narrative so far) entails mysteries including the Riddle family's cause of death, the identity of the person who placed Harry's name in the Goblet of Fire, and the odd behavior of Ludo Bagman and Mr. Crouch, the Minister of Magic. In addition, a number of generic aspects of mystery appear throughout the series, including the exoneration (and sometimes physical rescue) of the innocent, which is particularly strong in *Chamber of Secrets*; the combination of fantastic plot elements with a realistic narrative; and the use of the audience's prejudices, which works quite well in relation to both Rowling's creation of the Dursleys and her assumption that most readers will be as offended by Draco Malfoy's anti-Muggle sentiments as are Harry, Ron, and Hermione.

A subgenre of mystery is detective fiction, which—in contrast to crime fiction—focuses on the solution to a crime rather than on either the crime itself or the criminal (Alewyn 64). Such a distinction supports the contention that although *Harry Potter* is detective fiction, it is not crime fiction (at least not yet). The protagonists act as detectives in a number of ways: In *Sorcerer's Stone* they research the provenance of the Stone and prevent Voldemort from obtaining it; in *Chamber of Secrets* they discover the identity and motive of Tom Riddle, who is petrifying a number of people in the castle; in *Prisoner of Azkaban*, Ron and Hermione help Harry elude, capture, and free Sirius Black; in *Goblet of Fire*, Harry acts as "sleuth" in completing the three tasks of the Triwizard Tournament, thwarts Voldemort's attempts to kill him again, and discovers that Voldemort has not only regained human form but also is amassing support to control the world (Zipes 179). Of all the novels, *Chamber of Secrets* is the one that best conforms to the traditional elements of detective fiction. Detective stories begin with the discovery of the crime, which is followed by other events that impede progress toward resolution; here, this appears in the first and subsequent discoveries of the petrified victims. Various false and true clues appear throughout the narrative, such as Hagrid's mistaken belief that the spiders led by Aragog will be helpful, or the mirror that Hermione drops just before being petrified. Delaying tactics slow down the action in order to build suspense, as with Ron, Hermione, and Harry's attempts to reveal

Malfoy's part in the crime (he is not directly involved), while blocking figures and suspects also interfere: Filtch, Mrs. Norris, Peeves, and even Snape (albeit inadvertently) all act as blocking figures, while Hagrid is arrested as a false suspect. Finally, the taciturn "Great Detective" is assisted in his detective work by a garrulous assistant and a cast of "grotesques" or odd characters (Porter 330). While Harry is not especially taciturn, nor are Ron and Hermione particularly garrulous, the grotesque character appears with the ghost of Moaning Myrtle. Moreover, Harry is willing to risk everything to catch the petrifier and thus not only clear his name but prevent further danger to his fellow Hogwarts residents—thus further establishing his heroic role in the series.

Another connection to popular or pulp fiction appears in the *Harry Potter* books' generic identity as series books,[6] particularly in terms of shelf appeal, where series readers will read the cover design or logo for reassurance that the book belongs to a particular series. This suggests a certain desire for predictability that series books provide with similar plot structures and style. Here Rowling delivers. Her writing style does not vary with each installment, and the structure of the plot remains the same: Each book takes place over the duration of one school year and begins with Harry unhappy at home with the Dursleys; he is then rescued or escapes to the magical world of Hogwarts, where he and his friends Ron and Hermione solve a mystery involving Voldemort or one of his followers; after surviving an encounter with Voldemort or his representative, which adds another clue to the ongoing mystery of Voldemort and develops the escalating conflict between good and evil, Harry returns home for another summer with the Dursleys. This repeated structure reassures readers of a happy ending while allowing them to experience the vicarious enjoyment of adventure, drama, and danger.

Series books also tend to include the same groups of characters, and as the *Harry Potter* series progresses, readers reencounter old friends as well as old enemies. In addition to the central characters of Harry, Ron, and Hermione, each installment features Headmaster Dumbledore, bumbling yet well-meaning Hagrid, daunting Professor McGonagall, inoffensive Professors Sprout and Flitwick, fellow Gryffindors Neville Longbottom, Dean Thomas, and Seamus Finnigan, the Weasley family, Harry's horrible cousin, Dudley, along with Uncle Vernon and Aunt Petunia, and foes Draco Malfoy, Crabbe and Goyle, menacing Professor Snape, and the archvillain, Voldemort (who takes different forms throughout). Rowling also adds new and significant characters in each book, including a different Defense-Against-the-Dark-Arts teacher each year, along with Ginny Weasley (*Chamber of Secrets*), Sirius Black (*Prisoner of Azkaban*), and Viktor Krum (*Goblet of Fire*). Rowling's characterization is one of her strongest points: her characters are, almost without exception, extremely realistic and convincing, due to her economic yet effective description. Perhaps the best example appears in her introduction of Hagrid, Hogwarts' caretaker and later Care-of-Magical-Creatures professor:

> He was almost twice as tall as a normal man and at least five times as wide. He looked simply too big to be allowed, and so *wild*—long tangles of bushy black hair and beard hid most of his face, he had hands the size of trash can lids, and his feet in their leather boots were like baby dolphins. In his vast, muscular arms he was holding a bundle of blankets. (*Sorcerer's Stone* 14)

Hagrid's tender nature is revealed when he bids baby Harry farewell: After giving him "what must have been a very scratchy, whiskery kiss" he howls and sobs with grief (*Sorcerer's Stone* 15). Such strength of characterization provides verisimilitude, another of the pleasures of reading series fiction, with its sense of providing answers to the question of what "really" happened to characters who have become like close friends or mortal enemies to readers.

The strongest appeal of series fiction lies in this sense of resolution, or at least in "a series of profoundly satisfying narrative or thematic closures" (Watson 7). This is absolutely true for the *Harry Potter* series, for each book—or installment, since Rowling maintains she is really writing a seven-part novel—achieves a certain closure, either thematically or in terms of plot or both. At the end of *Sorcerer's Stone*, the stone has been withheld from Voldemort and destroyed, and Harry has been able to see his parents, or at least their photographs; at the end of *Chamber of Secrets*, Tom Riddle and his diary have been vanquished and Harry's alliance with Gryffindor rather than Slytherin has been confirmed. *Prisoner of Azkaban* concludes with no less than the saving of Sirius Black's and Buckbeak's lives, and Harry's discovery of a sympathetic guardian. The ending of *Goblet of Fire* is the most intriguing of the series to date: while it concludes with Harry once again surviving a direct attack from Voldemort, it also begins a new order of alliance within the wizard world, with much stronger lines being drawn between the sides of good and evil than have appeared before. Such an ending not only creates curiosity about what is going to happen next but also reinforces the series' thematic integrity.

One of the potential problems of a literary series in which the characters grow and mature as the books progress is that, at least in a successful series, they must do so without losing any of their initial appeal. Since the middle of the twentieth century, long after the glorification of innocent childhood by such poets as Wordsworth and Blake or novelists like Frances Hodgson Burnett and L. M. Montgomery, the growth from childhood to adulthood has been regarded as a loss rather than a happy progression. As Watson suggests, "it is a bold series-writer who proceeds beyond this point, for to do so must challenge the great western cultural assumption that the *potential* adulthood of the young is more charismatic than *achieved* adulthood" (206). This is particularly true for the *Harry Potter* books, whose protagonists start out at age eleven and—given the planned seven-part structure—will mature to age seventeen. However, Rowling has avoided the potential problems by making the series a typical bildungsroman (novel of formation) or *erziehungsroman* (novel of education). This genre focuses on the physical, intellectual, moral, and spiritual development of the protagonist from childhood to adulthood, charting various situations and crises which lead to the protagonist's maturity and recognition of his/her identity and place in the world. At the opening of *Sorcerer's Stone*, Harry is quite literally a child—a baby, in fact—with no knowledge of the world or his special powers; as the first few chapters progress, he starts to become aware not only of his orphan status and resulting poor lot in life (who in their right mind would want to be stuck with the Dursleys?) but also that odd things seem to happen around him. As the series develops, Harry experiences a number of events that lead to his growth, change, and maturation: He learns that he is a wizard, and that he is already famous for having vanquished Voldemort (though he has no idea how he managed to do so); he leaves the world of Muggles for Hogwarts to begin his formal education, and he adapts to the many challenges of this new environment; he makes friends as well as enemies; he encounters evil in a variety of forms and each time manages to triumph over it; he starts to contemplate his future after he graduates from Hogwarts and becomes a fully fledged adult wizard; by the end of *Goblet of Fire*, he has even started to feel the pangs of adolescence, with his first attraction to girls.[7]

The *Harry Potter* series also can be considered bildungsroman in the way it embodies three motifs common to the genre: the loss of the father and the search for a surrogate parent, the realization of conflict between the gentlemanly ideals of the past and the struggle in the present for survival and identity, and the search for and discovery of love (Gohlman 249). *Sorcerer's Stone* opens with the death of Harry's parents, and as the series progresses, the effects of this loss appear not only in his occasional pang of wondering what his parents were like—to the extent where he is willing to risk being caught by Filch just to catch a glimpse of them in the Mirror of Erised—but also in his fierce defense of both his parents when they are criticized by the Dursleys, Aunt Marge (whom he inflates like a balloon), Draco Malfoy, and Snape. His delight when he realizes that Sirius Black is innocent of his crimes and thus can be a true godfather to him, and his love for and protection of Sirius in *Goblet of Fire* signifies at least partial closure for this first stage. The second motif, Harry's realization of the conflict between the ideals of the past and the reality of the present, appears not only in the discord between Harry's life with the Dursleys and his life at Hogwarts, but also in the tensions starting to appear at the end of *Goblet of Fire* between the old and new orders within the wizard world. The last motif, the search for and discovery of love, can be interpreted in a number of ways, including the love for family, the love for a romantic partner, and the love for humanity as a whole. So far, only the first has appeared in any depth in the series, with the emphasis on Lily Potter's love for her son as one of the factors that saved Harry from the worst of Lord Voldemort's wrath. However, as Harry's feelings of attraction grow for Cho Chang, the seeker for Ravenclaw's Quidditch team, this second type of love is likely to be developed. The third, the love for humanity as a whole, is something that has appeared so far only with the character of Dumbledore, whose devotion to protecting all of the world—Muggle and wizard—from Voldemort suggests such a love. This strand connects with the potential problem of characters in series fiction losing their charismatic appeal as they grow older, and suggests that this is not a necessary outcome: while Dumbledore has started out as a mature adult figure, and is growing older as the series progresses, he is becoming more charismatic as the narrative develops. This also holds true for both Sirius Black and Severus Snape, as both become more, rather than less, interesting as the series develops.

Genres such as series books and bildungsroman overlap very closely with school stories, another of the formative genres in the *Harry Potter* books. Given their subject matter of a seven-year period of education at the premier (and possibly only) school for wizards in Britain, what better place to chart those formative adolescent years than something akin to a British public school?[8] While some critics have suggested that the traditional school story has been dead—or at the very least passé—for the last several decades,[9] *Harry Potter* signifies a return to the traditional Victorian boarding school or public school story, but with the element of fantasy added. Hogwarts follows the general organization of a British public school in that students are assigned houses—Gryffindor, Ravenclaw, Hufflepuff, and Slytherin—and take all of their meals and classes with their fellow housemates, as well as sleep in dormitories belonging to these houses and spend free time in their house common rooms. The school system of rewards and punishments is built around the houses, which compete each year for the greatest number of points in order to win the School Cup. These house divisions have the effect of promoting both house and school spirit, which can be seen very clearly in the scene when Gryffindor wins the Quidditch match in *Prisoner of Azkaban*, as well as encouraging excellence both in and out of the classroom: House points are awarded for winning at Quidditch, for good or insightful answers to professors' questions during class, or for other behavior that demonstrates the traditional values of chivalry, fair play, or courage—as when Neville is awarded the winning ten points for having had the courage to stand up to his friends (*Sorcerer's Stone*). Points are deducted from houses for breaking school rules (Fred and George Weasley are regular offenders here), disorderly conduct, incorrect answers in class, or showing disrespect to a teacher. Like Rugby or other British public schools during the Victorian age, either in fact or fiction, Hogwarts also has selection criteria, but rather than accepting students from particular social or economic spheres, the criterion to be accepted at Hogwarts is simply that students must be wizards—whether they are from Muggle or non-Muggle backgrounds is irrelevant.

In terms of structure, the series contains a few of the basic elements of the generic school story pattern, though in a way that revises rather than conforms to the norm, where a boy enters school feeling somewhat nervous but also ambitious, suffers from loneliness and the discipline of both his schoolmasters and the school's games, gradually makes a few friends and starts to flourish and even rebel, eventually "learns duty, self-reliance, responsibility and loyalty as a prefect," and finally leaves school for the real world with regret, but permanently formed with his school's code of conduct and seal (Richards 6). Certainly Harry starts out at Hogwarts feeling nervous, but his reasons are not the usual ones: Instead of being the typically invisible new boy, he is known throughout the wizard world for his encounter with Voldemort, and he is instantly recognizable because of the scar on his forehead. His ambition is to become less, rather than more, visible, and yet concurrently to live up to his reputation, as well as to remain in Hogwarts so that he no longer has to deal with the Dursleys. Nor does he initially suffer from loneliness: He and Ron become friends on the Hogwarts Express long before they arrive at the school, and Harry is greeted by Hagrid the moment he gets off the train. Like Hermione, he welcomes the discipline of his classes (except for Potions, taught by Snape), and he revels in his natural talent for Quidditch. The seeds for his rebellion have been sown in him, courtesy of the Dursleys, long before he arrived at school, and in many ways his self-reliance results from their poor treatment of him rather than from any lessons he learns at Hogwarts. However, his experiences at school do teach him about the concepts of duty, responsibility, and loyalty, though much of this results from his learning about the history of the wizard world and his place in it in relation to Voldemort. Since the series has not yet concluded, the rest of the sequence is left up to speculation—but it is difficult to imagine Harry as a prefect, especially given the teasing that he and Ron indulge in toward Percy about his prefect status.

The *Harry Potter* books do conform to the generic conventions of school stories in that they depict "schooldays as they should be" complete with practical jokes, sports, mischief, studying, "and Dickensian Christmas hols" (Richards 12), but again with the added ingredient of fantasy. Fred and George Weasley provide much fodder for humor with their continued eye for mischief, plenty of attention is given to regular Quidditch practices and matches, and studying takes on a completely new dimension when students must do homework for such classes as Potions, Transfiguration, Herbology, Charms, Care of Magical Creatures, Divination, and Defense Against the Dark Arts. The depth of description devoted to the classes is a minor departure from the tendency that traditional school stories have of ignoring the academic part of schooling, but here the details add to the enjoyment of the books because of the intriguing areas of study. Christmas holidays, however, are very much in keeping with the genre's traditions: When Harry, Ron, and (in *Prisoner of Azkaban*) Hermione remain at Hogwarts over Christmas, they enjoy sumptuous meals, snowball fights, no studying, greater freedom than usual to wander around the school, and the sight of their professors and teachers becoming more relaxed and therefore more human—at least for the duration of the break. The teachers at Hogwarts also share a number of characteristics with teachers in traditional school stories, and many of them serve as role models for proper behavior, with Professor McGonagall as the ultimate example of propriety as well as discipline: "It's one o'clock in the morning. *Explain yourselves*" (*Sorcerer's Stone* 243). In contrast, Professor Snape acts as an anti–role model, with his favoritism of Draco Malfoy and the Slytherins and his grudge against Harry. Most important, Dumbledore embodies the typical attributes of the school story headmaster by representing "all that is real—virtue, merriment, and humanity" (Quigly 36). In several ways, he approaches the prototypical fictional (and factual) public school headmaster, Dr. Thomas Arnold (1795–1842), head of Rugby School from 1828 and immortalized in *Tom Brown's Schooldays*. Arnold was renowned for his kindness as well as his charismatic leadership, and for his influence in making the English public school "a place to train character" (Richards 3). Similarly, Dumbledore is kind, charismatic, and very powerful: He is not afraid to use Voldemort's name, and many wizards believe that Voldemort is afraid of him. Moreover, he appears to be extremely knowledgeable about all aspects of the world—both in and out of Hogwarts—and he also exhibits a highly moral character.

The schools in school stories often represent microcosms of the larger world. In this isolated environment, children act in different ways than they would if they were living under the constraints of their parents' rules and regulations, and they also construct their own social order and culture. Certainly this is true for the world at Hogwarts, particularly in terms of its society. While the students must answer to Dumbledore, their professors, and their housemasters, they have far more freedom than they would enjoy in the outside world: for example, Hogwarts has no apparent curfew, and students can remain in their house common room studying or socializing as late as they please. In addition, since the children at Hogwarts seem, almost without exception, to be happy to have been selected as students, they usually attend most of their classes without complaint and pay attention in class—though the incentive to do so may be helped along by the knowledge that they could be turned into toads if they fail to pay attention. As in all societies, they also deal with the usual issues of friendships and social hierarchies. Harry spurns Malfoy's advice to help him choose the "right sort" of associations (*Sorcerer's Stone*) and befriends Ron Weasley; later, he, Ron, and Hermione sort out their initial differences and become fast friends after their encounter with the mountain troll. The initial tension between Harry and Draco Malfoy continues to build throughout the series, with their rivalry appearing not only in their classes but also in the dining hall, on the Quidditch field, and anywhere else the two are forced to meet. While Harry finds Malfoy a constant irritation, he is but a symptom of the larger evil that Harry faces in his continuing battle with Voldemort.

The emphasis placed on Quidditch, the ultimate sport for wizards, that appears in the *Harry Potter* series illustrates its generic identity as a sports story. Indeed, as Nicholas Tucker suggests, "Hogwarts pays almost as much attention to success at Quidditch as *Tom Brown's Schooldays* does to winning on the rugger field" (225). Traditionally, sports activities in school and school stories not only were regarded as a means of directing aggression and energy that students might feel toward each other into something less unsettling or dangerous, but also were intended to teach such team values as loyalty, courage, leadership, and the ability to be a good loser. Certainly their participation in Quidditch matches allows Harry and Malfoy to battle out some of their aggressions, but the game also functions as a major part of Harry's education. As the youngest house Quidditch player in a century, Harry quickly earns a name for himself as a Seeker and—like many a child—he fantasizes about being good enough someday to "play for England" and represent his country internationally. As team Seeker, his role is to chase after the Golden Snitch and catch it to win the game; he must be quick, both in terms of his wits and in terms of coordination, level-headed, and not be shaken when he doesn't immediately succeed. The game helps Harry keep his mind off his fellow students' hostility when they shun him for being able to speak Parseltongue (*Chamber of Secrets*), and he longs for the escape into the sport when he is trying to solve the second clue for the Triwizard Tournament (*Goblet of Fire*). Moreover, the physical skills he learns eventually pay off when he uses his proficiency at precision flying to avoid the Hungarian Horntail dragon and retrieve the golden egg during the tournament. For other students, however, winning becomes more important than the values that Quidditch ideally should teach. The Slytherin team is portrayed throughout as being sore losers who are willing to go to any lengths to win a game, including personal fouls on Harry and disguising themselves as dementors to break his concentration (*Prisoner of Azkaban*). Even Oliver Wood, the Gryffindor team's captain, cannot stop obsessing over game strategy before their telling match against Slytherin, and he is so devastated when the team loses a match to Hufflepuff that he cannot bear to visit Harry in the hospital wing after he falls off his broom (*Prisoner of Azkaban*). Both reactions serve to highlight Harry's healthier philosophy: While he certainly would prefer to win, he is not nearly as angry as the Slytherins or as devastated as Wood when his team loses. Instead, he takes pleasure in being recognized as a good Quidditch player, which takes some of the focus away from his connection with Voldemort.

The significance of the sports story genre also appears in the detailed description of the game and its rules. Terminology such as Beaters, Chasers, and Keepers, along with Bludgers and Quaffles, and the vivid descriptions of flying and minute details pertaining to Harry's original Nimbus Two Thousand broom and his new Firebolt keep readers interested and intrigued. Good sports stories of the modern era bring readers right into the game, and Rowling succeeds in doing so, despite the fact that this particular game is one readers will be able to play only in their imaginations. She does this not only through her detailed descriptions of Harry's experiences while training and playing but also through Lee Jordan's commentary during matches:

> And she's really belting along up there, a neat pass to Alicia Spinnet, a good find of Oliver Wood's, last year only a reserve—back to Johnson and—no, the Slytherins have taken the Quaffle, Slytherin Captain Marcus Flint gains the Quaffle and off he goes—Flint flying like an eagle up there—he's going to sc- no, stopped by an excellent move by Gryffindor Keeper Wood and the Gryffindors take the Quaffle—that's Chaser Katie Bell of Gryffindor there, nice dive around Flint, off up the field and— OUCH—that must have hurt, hit in the back of the head by a Bludger—Quaffle taken by the Slytherins—that's Adrian Pucey speeding off toward the goal posts, but he's blocked by a second Bludger—sent his way by Fred or George Weasley, can't tell which—nice play by the Gryffindor Beater, anyway, and Johnson back in possession of the Quaffle, a clear field ahead and off she goes—she's really flying—dodges a speeding Bludger—the goal posts are ahead—come on, now, Angelina—Keeper Bletchley dives—misses—GRYFFINDORS SCORE! (*Sorcerer's Stone* 186)

By placing readers in the position of being spectators, Rowling makes the fantastic elements of a game played by players flying on broomsticks and chasing a magically enchanted object with wings seem more convincing and believable.[10]

The ability to combine fantasy and reality is one of Rowling's greatest strengths, and she makes it effortless for readers to invoke their willing suspension of disbelief. It helps that the *Harry Potter* books take place in the real world, some of which is quite aware of the wizard world. Hogwarts is implied to exist in the England of today, but it is protected from the Muggle world by spells or enchantments (Hermione voices theories about just how this might be done in *Goblet of Fire*). In many ways, the series is steeped in reality: Students attend classes, do homework, and experience the same sorts of rivalries and tensions that they might experience at any British public school. The fantasy appears in the details, with owl post and live photographs appearing as the children receive mail or collect trading cards that come in packages of candy, and students encountering hippogriffs, blast-ended skrewts, and flobberworms during their Care of Magical Creatures classes. The exactness of this detail appears in almost all elements of the wizard world, which comes complete with its own financial system (seventeen silver sickles to a galleon and twenty-nine knuts to a sickle); its own candy and other treats, including chocolate frogs, butterbeer, jelly slugs, and Bertie Bott's Every Flavor Beans; its own political system, complete with departments such as the Misuse of Muggle Artifacts Office, where Ron's father works; its own transportation system, with the Knight Bus for stranded wizards; and its own education system, with not only Hogwarts in England but also Beauxbatons and Durmstrang in Europe. Magic is a part of the students' everyday lives, as they learn about the history of the wizard world along with specific spells to create light (*lumos*), levitate objects (*wingardium leviosa*), deflate Boggarts (*riddikulus*), and charms for defense like the Patronus charm Harry learns against dementors (*expecto patronum*). In addition to magic, other traditional fairy tale elements appear throughout the novels, including dragons, unicorns, trolls, and giants (not only Hagrid but also Madame Maxime in *Goblet of Fire*), and settings such as castles, huts, towers, and woods.[11]

Other generic fantasy elements that appear include a strong sense of place, along with both originality and discipline in handling materials.[12] The settings are intriguing and believable, from the Dursleys' home in the Muggle world to Diagon Alley with its interesting shops (Eeylops Owl Emporium or Flourish and Blotts, the local bookshop); Hogwarts School with its turrets, long and drafty corridors, cozy common rooms, and 142 staircases; Hagrid's cottage filled with a cheerful muddle of animals and assorted possessions; and the wizard settlement of Hogsmeade, complete with the Shrieking Shack where Professor Lupin used to take refuge during his worst throes of werewolfhood. In addition to the original details discussed earlier, Rowling demonstrates other sorts of original thinking, particularly in the scenes where Harry gets his wand from Mr. Ollivander (*Sorcerer's Stone* 83–85) and the initial Sorting Hat episode (*Sorcerer's Stone* 116–22). Her invention of Platform 9¾, the wizarding game of Quidditch, Floo Powder, the pocket sneakoscope, and howlers have contributed to the beginning of the *Harry Potter* series' mythic status, as well as to its immense popularity. Moreover, Rowling realizes that good fantasy tends to question the prevailing world-picture by asking just how fantastic our notions of reality are, and creating alternatives to what we think of as the real world. While Rowling is not suggesting that inventions such as Hogwarts are real, they do suggest a way of defining ourselves through our own wishes and desires.

Fantasy usually involves a quest of some sort, which ties it to traditional forms of both adventure and quest romance. Certainly the books contain all of the typical elements of the adventure tale. In addition to blending the familiar with the unexpected, thus offering readers comfort and excitement concurrently, adventure tales focus on a noble-natured hero who is removed from the comforts of home and the controls of normal society and forced to face innumerable dangers. Due to his intelligence, courageous spirit, resourcefulness, and self-reliance, the typical adventure hero overcomes the odds and wins the battle against his adversaries. While Harry is quite happy to be removed from his extremely uncomfortable domicile with the Dursleys, Hogwarts quickly becomes his second—and beloved—home, and from there he faces and conquers such fantastic dangers as three-headed dogs, fire-breathing dragons, deadly serpents, and dementors who suck out souls along with happy memories. In addition, the adventure hero is usually accompanied on his adventures by a faithful companion, and he receives aid from a helper figure who possesses more information than he does. Here, both Ron and Hermione fill the role of faithful companions, while Dumbledore and Hagrid appear to be the primary helper figures. Adventure plots tend to be fast-paced, heavy on dialogue and description, and maintain a buoyant and optimistic tone throughout, even though the hero at times may be tempted to give in to despair, and the books fit this description exactly as well. The climax of the adventure story usually occurs during the final battle against the most powerful opponent, and it generally arises "from the theme of honor pre-

served against the dangers of intrigue, betrayal and the clash of loyalties"
(Fisher 109). This can be seen in Harry's repeated encounters with
Voldemort or his representatives, and Harry's reliance on the memory of
his parents and their love for him giving him the strength or protection
necessary to survive those encounters. Adventure tales conclude with the
triumphant return of the hero to his true home, where he is rewarded by
discovering his proper worth and/or identity. Since the series has not yet
ended, the resolution is still unresolved—but it seems fair to expect that
the pattern will continue.

This pattern also contains generic elements of quest romance and
myth, particularly powerful genres because they incorporate so many others within them. The pattern of quest romance consists of three stages:
agon or conflict (the perilous journey and preliminary minor conflicts),
pathos or death-struggle (the crucial struggle in which either the hero or
his foe, or both, must die), and *anagnorisis* or discovery (the recognition of
the hero). In the first stage of his quest, Harry makes his perilous journey
to Hogwarts, is trained in some of the basic precepts of wizardry, and
meets the "old wise man . . . often a magician who affects the action he
watches over" (Frye 195)—clearly represented by Dumbledore. He finds
faithful companions in Ron and Hermione, and enemies in Malfoy and
his followers. Characters who elude the moral antithesis of either villainy
or heroism tend to be spirits of nature and helper figures, and they are represented by Hagrid, the centaurs in the Forbidden Forest, and (curiously)
Dobby the house-elf. Animals, too, have balances and counterparts:
Hedwig, Crookshanks, and Fawkes the Phoenix are matched by Nagini,
Scabbers, and the Basilisk. During the second stage of his quest—which
is still continuing, as the series has not yet concluded—Harry goes forth
into his great contest, which consists of repeated encounters with
Voldemort. On this journey he has already met a number of challenges,
and, if the pattern stays true, he will face not only despair but also death;
although by the end of *Goblet of Fire* he has already faced the latter, given
his survival, it seems likely that his penultimate encounter with the possibility of death is yet to come. The third stage, *anagnorisis* (or recognition
of the hero), has not yet occurred, although some of the elements to make
this possible have been set in place. For instance, Harry's birth and first
year of life with his parents is still shrouded in mystery, along with his lin-
eage on his father's side. However, he has encountered the figures of false
parents who appear to seek his death—or at least the death of his wizardly

heritage—with the Dursleys. The true father or father-figure, often represented by a wise old man or teacher, has appeared with the figure of Sirius Black. The only missing element is the heroine, who may be developed in the form of Cho Chang, or perhaps is yet to appear.

Certainly Harry encompasses all of the traditional characteristics of the hero, being associated (either literally or metaphorically) with spring (or rebirth), dawn, order, fertility, vigor, and youth; in this way, he provides the perfect counterpart for his enemy, Voldemort, who is the archetypal foe, associated with winter (or death), darkness, confusion, sterility, moribund life, and old age. By the end of *Goblet of Fire*, Harry is approaching the romantic hero's characteristic of being analogous to the deliverer or mythical Messiah, just as Voldemort is akin to the Satanic destroyer. The nearer the quest romance approaches to myth, "the more attributes of divinity will cling to the hero and the more the enemy will take on demonic mythical qualities" (Frye 187), and this is true to a certain extent of both Harry and Voldemort. In some senses, Harry has already taken on divine attributes, starting off as "the boy who lived" and then surviving increasingly serious attempts on his life. It is even truer of Voldemort, who by the end of *Goblet of Fire* has quite literally risen from the dead to become a malevolent figure who is larger than life. How Rowling portrays the imminent battle between these two forces of good and evil will determine the series' status as myth. It is already moving in that direction, both in terms of direct references and allusions[13] and in creating its own mythic elements such as the Mirror of Erised and the Devil's Snare (*Sorcerer's Stone*), the significance of Parseltongue (*Chamber of Secrets*), the Whomping Willow (*Prisoner of Azkaban*), and the Pensieve (*Goblet of Fire*).[14] A more interesting question is whether the series ultimately will progress into epic, a genre whose narrative chronicles the heroic character's achievements through an important part of history. The extent to which Rowling invokes and then develops such epic themes as the origins of life, the consequences of divine anger, the true nature of good and evil, and the concept of immortality will reveal whether the series is great literature on an epic scale, or simply *mythos* in the best sense of the word: an entertaining story.[15]

Reading *Harry Potter* through the various lenses inherent within this sort of multigenre approach leads to the realization that genre, rather than being a mere classification tool, has taken on significance as a communication system. Because of their conscious or unconscious awareness of the various genres fused in the books, readers gain the delight of recognition as they read something that feels familiar in form: they know the conventions of the game or the story before they begin, and thus they are looking for the tags, or signs, of fantasy, or pulp fiction, or the school story, or detective fiction. As they read the story (or progress through the game), they not only find these tags but also start to anticipate how Rowling will include others specific to the genre they are reading. However, Rowling takes the game one step further: as new tags of each genre appear, they reflect links to other genres as well. In doing so, they change the meaning of the tags that have preceded them, which in turn modifies the initial genre to which they belonged—and the cycle starts all over again. By fusing the genres in this way, Rowling has created something new: a generic mosaic made up of numerous individual pieces combined in a way that allows them to keep their original shape while constantly changing their significance. The way in which these pieces operate varies and changes depending on the generic tags being interpreted at any given time by any particular reader.

When speaking of genre, questions of hierarchy almost inevitably seem to come into play—what's on top? However, reading the *Harry Potter* series as generic mosaic makes this question irrelevant, at least in terms of genre. In a picture that is constantly changing and rearranging its pieces, no single genre can claim top place in the hierarchy; instead, the continual interplay among the tags and thus the genres becomes most significant, as this interplay is what creates the multiple meanings of the whole. The perpetual shifting of the mosaic's pieces encourages readers to reread the text as they succumb to the very human temptation of trying to find the "real" meaning of the series. In the end, the delight that millions of readers are discovering in *Harry Potter* is the sense of wonder that results from their repeated experience of "knowing the place for the first time."

Notes

My thanks go to the College of Humanities and Social & Behavioral Sciences at Central Michigan University for the 2001 Summer Faculty Scholars award that supported this project. I would also like to thank Professor Richard Seiter and Dr. William Spruiell for reading drafts of this chapter, and Dr. Elizabeth Heilman for inviting me to contribute to *Harry Potter's World*.

1. The first book alone has already been translated into over twenty-five languages, including French, German, Italian, Dutch, Greek, Finnish, Danish, Spanish, and Swedish. The first four books in the projected seven-volume series have already set world records for numbers

sold—some twenty million copies have sold worldwide—and the first book in the series, *Harry Potter and the Sorcerer's Stone*, spent forty-two weeks on the *New York Times* Bestseller List for adult fiction, marking the first time a work of children's literature has ever appeared on the list. The character of Harry Potter appeared on the covers of *Time* magazine on 20 September 1999 and *Newsweek* during the summer of 2000, while on 7 July 2000 children throughout North America and Europe begged their parents to allow them to attend the midnight launch of the fourth book, *Harry Potter and the Goblet of Fire* (officially published on 8 July 2000).

2. The term genre is usually invoked when referring to works sharing a similar form or style. Until the eighteenth century, the major generic classifications were lyric, epic or narrative, and dramatic, and critics tended to insist on each genre remaining "pure" and not mixed with other genres; moreover, genres were assumed to be hierarchically arranged, with epic and tragedy at the top and other (or "minor") genres at the bottom. Over the last fifty years it has become more critically acceptable to consider works in relation to a variety of generic traditions and conventions. Generic distinctions based on content are no longer exclusive, nor are they set in stone: indeed, Alastair Fowler notes that "every literary work changes the genres it relates to" (23). This is particularly appropriate when considering the ways in which Rowling combines genres, which may eventually lead to changes in the way we perceive genre as a whole.

3. British and Canadian title: *Harry Potter and the Philosopher's Stone.*

4. The cover of the American edition of *Chamber of Secrets* shows Harry grasping the tail-feathers of a red and gold phoenix as the two float past the entrance to the Chamber of Secrets, while the cover of the British edition portrays Harry, Ron, and Hedwig the owl in a flying blue car against the background of a calm blue sky. Here, the cover for the American version seems to indicate a substantially more adventurous and perhaps threatening story, in contrast to the reassurance of the happy faces and calm colors of the British edition. Both the British and American editions of *Prisoner of Azkaban* portray Harry and Hermione riding a hippogriff, but the British edition portrays the characters looking more serious than does the American version, which shows Harry, Hermione, and the hippogriff smiling and looking excited.

5. The appearance of different editions—books with the exact same content but different covers, prices, and placement in bookstores—for child and adult audiences in Britain also suggests the way in which marketing affects generic expectations. While the first editions of all the books (both British and American editions) possess dust jackets that depict children in various adventurous poses, the first three books in the series were later marketed separately in Britain and Canada for adults: in addition to omitting illustrations of the child protagonists, the adult editions are approximately £1.50 (or $3.00) more expensive than the children's versions. The fourth book in the series also has an "adult" edition, priced at £6.99 ($14.00) instead of the children's edition's price of £5.59, but the cover illustration for both editions is exactly the same. While this might suggest that the series has become so popular that adults are not concerned about being "caught" reading a children's book, it also could reflect the increasing maturity of the series' content and themes.

6. For the purposes of this discussion, I will focus on the conventions of literary series written by the same author, rather than what Watson refers to as publishers' format-series written by authors given publishers' house names, such as *The Bobbsey Twins, Tom Swift, Nancy Drew,* and *The Hardy Boys* series.

7. The series does not share any of the traditional elements of generic romance fiction, except with the implied reasons for the antagonism between Ron and Hermione in *Goblet of Fire.* It might be closer to the genre now referred to as young adult literature, but only in the most general of ways, and in the same way that it can be considered children's literature: both genres have, at various times, been defined as being literature read by people who fall into a

particular age group (usually 0–14 for children's literature, and 12–20 for young adult literature). However, if YA literature is characterized by the typical problem novel—something that involves a first-person narrator experiencing issues ranging from drug or alcohol abuse, sex, pregnancy, problems with parents or the divorce of parents—then the first four novels in the series, at least, do not correspond with this genre in a strict way.

8. The tradition of school tales goes back at least as far as the eighteenth century in tales by Sarah Fielding and Maria Edgeworth, but the genre reached its zenith during the nineteenth century with Harriet Martineau's *The Crofton Boys* (1841) and Thomas Hughes' *Tom Brown's Schooldays* (1857). The latter not only defined many of the conventions of both the nineteenth century British public school and the genre—including uniforms, sports as a means of releasing surplus energy, prefects as the elite headmasters' assistants, and school songs—but also emphasized the importance of such values as loyalty, chivalry, and the place of sports in the school curriculum.

9. Critics including Richards, Quigley, and Townsend have commented on the death of the genre since the 1960s.

10. This verisimilitude has been encouraged with Rowling's publication of *Quidditch Through the Ages*, which considers not only the evolution of the flying broomstick, but also the place of such ancient games as the German "Stichstock," Irish "Aingingein," and Scottish "Creaothceann" in the development of Quidditch, along with chapters on "Anti-Muggle Precautions," the players' roles, and the various penalties incurred from fouls. After providing an overview of Quidditch teams in Britain and Ireland, as well as throughout the rest of the world, the book concludes with a brief chapter focusing on Quidditch today. The existence of such a book furthers the significance of the sports story genre as a part of the series; written in such a convincing style, such a work encourages readers to focus on the place of sport in Harry Potter's world.

11. Fairy-tale motifs appear throughout the series, such as the Cinderella motif of Harry's home situation before he is aware of his wizardry, as well as the changeling motif.

12. Eleanor Cameron's article on High Fantasy has influenced much of my thinking about fantasy and its components. While in many ways Rowling's work does not measure up completely to my interpretation of Cameron's criteria, it certainly contains a number of elements that make it good, if not "High" fantasy.

13. Rowling incorporates numerous references to various mythologies including Greek and Roman (Apollo, Zeus, Athena/Minerva, Orpheus, Daedalus, Janus, Helen and Menelaus, Medusa, and Cerberus are but a few), Arthurian (in terms of the sword in the stone and the grail myths), Celtic, Christian, and West Indian. She also includes implicit references to other well-known authors and works including Lewis Carroll's *Alice's Adventures Through the Looking Glass*, Charles Dickens's *Oliver Twist*, Ursula Le Guin's *Earthsea* books, and Homer's *The Odyssey*.

14. Rowling has also published *Fantastic Beasts & Where to Find Them*, an encyclopedia of mythical beasts found in Harry Potter's world, including runespoors, quintapeds, nifflers, grindylows, and chizpurfles.

15. While I'm content to reserve judgment until the last book of the series is published, one of my reservations about Rowling's style is that, at least so far, her writing has lacked the sheer elegance of language that appears in other great epics of children's literature, such as Tolkien's *Lord of the Rings* or Philip Pullman's *His Dark Materials* series.

References

Alewyn, Richard. "The Origin of the Detective Novel." In *The Poetics of Murder: Detective Fiction and Literary Theory*. Ed. Glenn W. Most and William W. Stowe. New York: Harcourt Brace Jovanovich, 1983. 62–78.

Cameron, Eleanor. "High Fantasy: *A Wizard of Earthsea*." In *Crosscurrents of Criticism: Horn Book Essays 1968–1977*. Ed. Paul Heins. Boston: The Horn Book, 1977. 333–41.

Fisher, Margery. *The Bright Face of Danger: An Exploration of the Adventure Story*. Boston: The Horn Book, 1986.

Fowler, Alastair. *Kinds of Literature: An Introduction to the Theory of Genres and Modes*. Cambridge, Massachusetts: Harvard UP, 1982.

Frye, Northrup. *Anatomy of Criticism: Four Essays*. Princeton: Princeton UP, 1957.

Gohlman, Susan Ashley. *Starting Over: The Task of the Protagonist in the Contemporary Bildungsroman*. New York: Garland, 1990.

Hilton, Mary. "'The Blowing Dust': Popular Culture and Popular Books for Children." In *The Prose and the Passion: Children and Their Reading*. Ed. Morag Styles, Eve Bearne, and Victor Watson. London: Cassell, 1994. 9–19.

Palmer, Jerry. *Thrillers: Genesis and Structure of a Popular Genre*. New York: St. Martin's P, 1979.

Porter, Dennis. "Backward Construction and the Art of Suspense." In *The Poetics of Murder: Detective Fiction and Literary Theory*. Ed. Glenn W. Most and William W. Stowe. New York: Harcourt Brace Jovanovich, 1983. 327–40.

Quigly, Isabel. *The Heirs of Tom Brown: The English School Story*. Oxford: Oxford UP, 1984.

Richards, Jeffrey. "The School Story." In *Stories and Society: Children's Literature in Its Social Context*. Ed. Dennis Butts. London: Macmillan, 1992. 1–21.

Rowling, J. K. *Fantastic Beasts and Where to Find Them*. London: Bloomsbury, 2001.

———. *Harry Potter and the Chamber of Secrets*. Illus. Mary Grandpré. New York: Scholastic P, 1998.

———. *Harry Potter and the Chamber of Secrets*. London: Bloomsbury, 1998.

———. *Harry Potter and the Goblet of Fire*. London: Bloomsbury, 2000.

———. *Harry Potter and the Goblet of Fire*. Illus. Mary Grandpré. New York: Scholastic P, 2000.

———. *Harry Potter and the Philosopher's Stone*. London: Bloomsbury, 1997.

———. *Harry Potter and the Prisoner of Azkaban*. Illus. Mary Grandpré. New York: Scholastic P, 1999.

———. *Harry Potter and the Prisoner of Azkaban*. London: Bloomsbury, 1999.

———. *Harry Potter and the Sorcerer's Stone*. 1997. Illus. Mary Grandpré. New York: Scholastic P, 1998.

———. *Quidditch Through the Ages*. By Kenilworthy Whisp. London: Bloomsbury, 2001.

Scott, Alison M. "They Came from the Newsstand: Pulp Magazines and Vintage Paperbacks in the Popular Culture Library." In *Pioneers, Passionate Ladies, and Private Eyes: Dime Novels, Series Books, and Paperbacks*. Ed. Larry E. Sullivan and Lydia Cushman Schurman. New York: Haworth P, 1996. 39–46.

Townsend, John Rowe. *Written for Children: An Outline of English-Language Children's Literature*. 1965. 6th ed. London: Bodley Head, 1990.

Tucker, Nicholas. "The Rise and Rise of Harry Potter." *Children's Literature in Education* 30:4 (December 1999): 221–34.

Watson, Victor. *Reading Series Fiction: From Arthur Ransome to Gene Kemp*. London: Routledge, 2000.

Zipes, Jack. "The Phenomenon of Harry Potter, or Why All the Talk?" *The Troublesome Success of Children's Literature from Slovenly Peter to Harry Potter*. New York: Routledge, 2001. 170–90.

Chapter Nine

Wizardly Challenges to and Affirmations of the Initiation Paradigm in *Harry Potter*

Deborah De Rosa

> She can't keep writing about what a tragic little hero I am, it'll get boring.
> —J. K. Rowling, *Goblet of Fire*

When Harry Potter critiques Rita Skeeter's pesky journalism, he states, "She can't keep writing about what a tragic little hero I am, it'll get boring" (*Goblet of Fire* 390). But until Hermione Granger turns Skeeter into a beetle, Skeeter writes untruths that prevent Harry's story from getting "boring." But the question remains: How does J. K. Rowling keep it from getting "boring" considering that with the publication of *Harry Potter and the Goblet of Fire* (2000), she has written over 1,819 pages about this tragic little hero? Perhaps the answer rests in the fact that Rowling has identified quintessential truths about the human (in particular, the adolescent) experience and has presented them in the form of a modified bildungsroman. In *The Hero with a Thousand Faces* (1949), Joseph Campbell documents a recurrent pattern of literary initiations. According to his analysis of universal myths, the hero typically goes on a quest during which he encounters a mentor who assists him with a series of trials. The hero usually survives the arduous trials and returns home with an awareness of a new world order and a boon that he shares with his community (30, 35–40). The traditional journey into the "heart of darkness" typically consumes the bulk of most narratives, but Rowling prevents "boredom" by upsetting expected elements in the initiation paradigm. By opening each novel with Harry's departure from the less-than-ideal life with the Dursleys, Rowling emphasizes that Harry's experiences at Hogwarts School, although filled with mystery and apparent danger, represent a return to a safer environment in which Harry can experience, to a degree, the physical and psychological state of carefree childhood. Simultaneously,

Hogwarts provides Harry with the challenges that come with maturation. Enveloped in an environment that provides such physical and psychological nurture, Harry slowly grapples with his life-altering lessons about personal identity (his silenced family history) and complex social issues (class, race, and community).

Recognizing that "[n]o cohesive forms of instruction or initiation into the adult world exist in [Western] culture except certain academic expectations" (Sullwold 116; see also Bernstein 135–158), Rowling establishes the series' emphasis on maturation and initiation. *Harry Potter and the Sorcerer's Stone*'s first chapter establishes the events that transpire on the day that Voldemort murders James and Lily Potter, but the narrative subsequently shifts to the period immediately preceding the "celebrations" of Harry's and Dudley's eleventh birthdays and their entrance into "secondary school," the British equivalent of middle school. Harry's aunt and uncle will send their son, Dudley, to "Uncle Vernon's old private school, Smeltings," but they had planned to send Harry to Stonewall High, "the local public school" (*Sorcerer's Stone*, 32) until Minerva McGonagall's letter announces Harry's acceptance to Hogwarts School of Witchcraft and Wizardry, a highly unusual preparatory school. To mark their ensuing adulthood, attendance at Smeltings, Stonewall, and Hogwarts requires dress codes symbolic of this shift from childhood to adolescence. Dudley flaunts his new status as he models his uniform (a maroon tailcoat, orange knickerbockers, a flat straw hat, and a knobbly stick [*Sorcerer's Stone*, 32]), that establishes him as a "young man." His parents' reaction to seeing Dudley in this uniform emphasizes the symbolic link between new attire and a new epoch. Rowling writes, "Uncle Veron said gruffly that this was the proudest moment in his life [and] Aunt Petunia burst into tears and said she couldn't believe it was her Ickle Dudleykins, he looked so handsome and grown-up" (*Sorcerer's Stone*, 32). Harry too must don clothing appropriate for his new status; however, his relatives do not express such enthusiasm or pride for Harry's imminent transition. Rather, in preparation for Harry's attendance at Stonewall High, Aunt Petunia dyes Dudley's "hand-me-downs" to resemble the necessary gray uniform, whose color alone carries adult connotations. Thankfully, Harry's admittance to Hogwarts requires that he adopt a dress code consisting of a wizard's robe, a pointed hat, a cloak, and wand (the "wizardly" knobbly stick) to affirm his new identity and to foreshadow the power and status he will possess as an adult.

While attending Hogwarts theoretically prepares Harry for his final transition into adulthood, it simultaneously challenges expected initiation paradigms since, in significant ways, it functions as a restoration of childhood innocence. According to Harold Scheckter, "the first step in the transformation of the male adolescent into an adult—and this is universal—is to separate him 'from his previous environment, the world of women and children'—to sever his domestic ties" (69). This severance typically has distressing connotations because the child must leave a safe home (Foster 79, 82, 87, 91) to enter an unknown and often threatening environment that no longer shields the initiate from life's harsh realities. By having Harry leave the Dursleys to live at Hogwarts and/or with the Weasley family, Rowling inverts the traditional paradigm as she introduces Harry to the domestic safety and childhood nurture that life with the Dursleys precluded. Upon learning that he would leave Privet Drive, Harry states, "He didn't know what he was going to—but it had to be better than what he was leaving behind" (*Sorcerer's Stone*, 98). Once at Hogwarts, Harry never clicks his heels in a desire to return "home." One could argue that, considering the repeated threats from Lord Voldemort, living at Hogwarts endangers Harry more than it protects him; however, Rowling repeatedly alludes to Hogwarts's safety. She writes, "Gringotts [the bank] was the safest place in the world for something you wanted to hide—except perhaps Hogwarts" (*Sorcerer's Stone*, 162). Furthermore, even as danger slithers into Hogwarts under various guises, Albus Dumbledore's presence ensures each student's safety (*Sorcerer's Stone*, 222, 260; *Chamber*, 264–265; *Prisoner*, 68, 162, 166; *Goblet*, 312). Lord Voldemort too realizes that he can only harm Harry by transporting him away from the "well protected" Hogwarts (*Goblet*, 10). Enveloped in this air of security, Harry gains a new level of innocence, evident when he states: "The castle felt more like home than Privet Drive ever had" (*Sorcerer's Stone*, 170), and "It was the only place [where] he had ever been happy" (*Goblet*, 339). Part of Harry Potter's initiation, therefore, involves identifying an environment in which he may flourish and regain the sense of safety and nurture that he *should* have known in his childhood home.

For Harry, leaving "home" comes as a reprieve rather than as a moment of traumatic separation because of the neglect and abuse the Dursleys inflict upon him. When Hagrid leaves the orphaned infant on the doorstep of 4 Privet Drive, he incorrectly believes that he saves Harry from the horror of living with the supposedly evil Sirius Black (*Prisoner of*

Azkaban, 206–207); instead, he guarantees that Harry will spend his childhood in an atmosphere of hostility and neglect. Rowling underscores the deprivation that Harry experiences by contrasting it to the excessive abundance the Dursleys shower upon Dudley. When Dudley's "face fell" because he counted only thirty-six birthday gifts, "two less than last year," his mother averts Dudley's expected tantrum *not* by teaching him a lesson in gratitude but by promising her "popkin" two additional gifts (*Sorcerer's Stone*, 21). Similarly, Mr. Dursley discounts the consequences of overproviding for his son; rather he states, "Little tyke wants his money's worth, just like his father" (*Sorcerer's Stone*, 22). In contrast, Harry spends "almost ten years, ten miserable years" (*Sorcerer's Stone*, 29) at Privet Drive because Aunt Petunia and Uncle Vernon neglect their wizard-nephew by "withholding necessary food, clothing, shelter, and educational opportunities" (O'Brien 9). Harry wears taped-together glasses and Dudley's large, cast-off clothes. Although they give Dudley thirty-eight gifts for his birthday, they give Harry a hanger, if anything. Until the letter-deluge from Hogwarts causes Uncle Vernon to fear wizardly repercussions for his negligence, he relegates Harry to the dark cupboard under the staircase (*Sorcerer's Stone*, 19, 37). Fortunately, Harry's entrance into a wizardly world counters this neglect. Harry purchases well-fitting clothes with his inheritance; he mingles in the Gryffindor common room without Dudley's bullying; and he sleeps in a comfortable four-poster bed in a dormitory room that he shares with supportive peers. Moreover, he encounters nurturing adults who acknowledge him: Mrs. Weasley knits Harry a traditional "Weasley sweater" each Christmas and sends him sweets (a box of fudge, a plum cake, and mince pies); Hagrid gives Harry an owl and a flute (*Sorcerer's Stone*, 81, 200); Professor McGonagall buys him a Nimbus 2000 (*Sorcerer's Stone*, 164); and Sirius Black sends him a state-of-the-art Firebolt Racing Broom (*Prisoner of Azkaban*, 51, 433), a signed letter permitting him to go to Hogsmeade (*Prisoner of Azkaban*, 433), and a knot-untying penknife (*Goblet of Fire*, 410). Harry receives these gifts not because he demands them but because the givers warmly acknowledge his existence. By providing access to such basic needs and the possibility for healthy domestic ties, Harry enters a renewed state of innocence.

Rowling also manipulates the traditional initiation paradigm by "playing with her food" imagery. When Stephen Foster and Meredith Little, co-founders of Rites of Passage, Inc., developed a formal initiation ritual for modern high-school students, they incorporated fasting into the program because of its centrality to the initiation ritual. According to Foster and Little, the experience of physical deprivation empowers the initiate (97). Rowling again reverses the paradigm by showing that Harry experiences hunger as a child and physical nurturance during his rite-of-passage. The Dursleys do little to satisfy Harry's physical hunger. In contrast to Dudley, "who was so large his bottom drooped over either side of the kitchen chair" (*Chamber of Secrets*, 2), Harry is "small and skinny for his age" (*Sorcerer's Stone*, 20). Harry must often cook for the Dursleys, yet he reaps little nourishment from his efforts. He realizes that "[t]he Dursleys had never exactly starved [him], but he'd never been allowed to eat as much as he liked" (*Sorcerer's Stone*, 125) and thus he admits to sneaking into the kitchen for food (*Chamber of Secrets*, 29). Rowling extends the notion of this non-nurturing environment in *Harry Potter and the Chamber of Secrets* when Aunt Petunia banishes Harry to his room with "two slices of bread and a lump of cheese" before the dinner party at which she serves roast pork, pudding, whipped cream, and sugared violets (10). Furthermore, after the Dobby-instigated dinner fiasco, Harry literally finds himself a prisoner fed through a cat-flap: Aunt Petunia

> push[ed] a bowl of canned soup onto the room. Harry, whose insides were aching with hunger, jumped off his bed and seized it. The soup was cold, but he drank half of it in one gulp. Then he crossed the room to Hedwig's cage and tipped the soggy vegetables at the bottom of the bowl into her empty food tray. She ruffled her feathers and gave him a look of deep disgust. (22)

The Dursleys also deprive *Harry* of food when the Smeltings nurse demands that *Dudley* go on a diet: "Aunt Petunia seemed to feel that the best way to keep up Dudley's morale was to make sure that he did, at least, get more [carrots or larger grapefruits] to eat than Harry" (*Goblet of Fire*, 28).

Leaving the Dursleys ends the Dursley-imposed periods of "fasting" because Harry encounters adults who nurture him literally and psychologically. When Hagrid appears at the cottage to which the Durlseys retreat to escape the letter-deluge, he immediately gives Harry, "who was so hungry," a chocolate birthday cake and sausages (*Sorcerer's Stone*, 48, 49). Hagrid continues to physically nurture Harry throughout the series. He offers Harry a hamburger after their first trip to Diagon Alley (*Sorcerer's Stone*, 86) and repeatedly offers Harry and his friends tea, rock candy, fruitcake, treacle fudge, beef casserole, and other treats (often humorously inedible) when they visit his cabin at Hogwarts. Likewise, under

Dumbledore's care, all Hogwarts students receive more than adequate nourishment during the magical, free-flowing and floating banquets (*Sorcerer's Stone*, 203–204; *Chamber of Secrets*, 83, 86; *Prisoner of Azkaban*, 93–94, 430; *Goblet of Fire*, 180–81, 267–68, 364, 410). Similarly, aware that the Dursleys "were starving him," Mrs. Weasley (a surrogate mother) nourishes Harry to excess when she "tried to force him to eat a fourth helping at every meal" and even "conjured up a sumptuous dinner that included all of Harry's favorite things" (*Chamber of Secrets*, 42, 65). Nor does punishment mean going to bed hungry. Professor McGonagall punishes Ron and Harry for flying Mr. Weasley's car into the Whomping Willow, but she does not deprive them of a meal; rather, "[a] large plate of sandwiches, two silver goblets, and a jug of iced pumpkin juice appeared with a pop [of her magic wand]" (*Chamber of Secrets*, 83). Once again, the departure from the childhood "home" effects a period of physical nurture rather than a time of fasting and deprivation.

The typical initiate not only experiences physical deprivation in new and dangerous environments but he also encounters challenging physical trials that lead to intellectual and/or emotional growth. According to Joseph Campbell, "The original departure into the land of trials represent[s] only the beginning of the long and really perilous path of initiatory conquests and moments of illumination" (109). Although Harry experiences several dangerous trials during each encounter with Lord Voldemort and his cohorts, he also experiences physical trials (in the form of abuse and punishment) while living with his relatives during what should be his preinitiation stage. In "Symbols of Initiation in *Adventures of Huckleberry Finn*," Harold Schechter points out that many tribes in general, and Melanesian and Yamana tribes in particular, subject the initiate to physical violence (70). The Dursleys' treatment of Harry has parallels to primitive initiation. For instance, when Harry pretends to cast a spell that would ignite the Dursleys' hedge, Dudley runs to tell his mother, who severely punishes Harry:

> While Dudley lolled around watching and eating ice cream, Harry cleaned windows, washed the car, mowed the lawn, trimmed the flowerbeds, pruned and watered the roses, and repainted the garden bench. The sun blazed overhead, burning the back of his neck. (*Chamber of Secrets*, 10)

Rowling clearly contends that imposing such an unreasonable number of chores on a child amounts to abuse. She extends the image in another scene. When Harry inadvertently ruins the Dursley-Mason dinner party (because he tries to prevent Dobby from destroying the pudding), Uncle Vernon threatens to "flay [Harry] within an inch of his life" and literally treats him as a prisoner: he "paid a man to fit bars on Harry's window," fed Harry through a cat flap, and only "let [him] use the bathroom in the morning and evening" (*Chamber of Secrets*, 20, 21–22). This abuse reflects the dangers an initiate might encounter; however, this treatment never leads to moments of "illumination" for Harry. If Uncle Vernon and Aunt Petunia truly believed that physical abuse possessed beneficial character-forming potential, they would have showered such acts upon Dudley. Instead, these *permissive-indulgent* parents who "are overly tolerant of their children's misbehavior" (Stringer 26) allow Dudley to escape all punishment. Yet these same overindulgent parents take an *authoritarian* (Stringer 26) approach with their nephew, who can do no right in their eyes. Harry exposes both the abuse and his sense of powerlessness when he learns of his wizardly powers:

> A wizard? Him? How could he possibly be? He'd spent his life being clouted by Dudley, and bullied by Aunt Petunia and Uncle Vernon; if he was really a wizard, why hadn't they been turned into warty toads every time they'd tried to lock him in his cupboard? If he'd once defeated the greatest sorcerer in the world, how come Dudley had always been able to kick him around like a football? (*Sorcerer's Stone*, 57)

Harry assumes that his powers should have protected him from abuse, but this is not the case. Nor does the abuse lead to any deeper enlightenment about himself or his position in the world. Thus, by casting Harry as one who experiences the perils of initiation without its positive end results, Rowling again changes the paradigm of the initiate by showing how Harry does not spend his childhood in carefree bliss; instead, he suffers abuse before his initiations.

Harry's journey away from 4 Privet Drive and to Hogwarts is, ironically, a journey toward physical safety. The extensive physical abuse Harry experiences at the Dursleys differs significantly from the nonharmful punishment he witnesses and/or receives while with the Weasleys or at Hogwarts. Rowling affirms the need for nonexcessive punishment and the preservation of a degree of innocence when she casts Professor McGonagall reprimanding "Professor Moody" for transforming Draco Malfoy into a ferret (even though he deserves it). McGonagall states, "we *never* use Transfiguration as a punishment! . . . We give detentions. . . . Or speak to the offender's Head of House" (*Goblet of Fire*, 206). McGonagall's dictate permeates the non-Dursley chapters as adults intentionally spare adolescents from unnecessary physical trials. When Fred, George, and Ron fly their father's car without permission (in their efforts to rescue Harry), Mrs. Weasley admonishes the boys by revealing that their behavior endangers not only themselves but also the family (in case a Muggle reports seeing a flying car). To teach responsibility to family, she makes her sons "de-gnome the garden," an exercise as tedious and endless (not to mention funny) as pulling Muggle dandelions (*Chamber of Secrets*, 30, 33, 35) and yet it does not physically harm the boys. Evidently, de-gnoming the garden does not teach Ron a lesson because he (with Harry as passenger) later flies the car to Hogwarts and then crashes it into the Whomping Willow. Yet, once again, the punishment Ron receives does not amount to abuse. First, he suffers a few moments of public humiliation when he opens Mrs. Weasley's appropriately furious Howler (a talking telegram) that blends a severe reprimand with an expression of concern (*Chamber of Secrets*, 88). Second, he and Harry must complete Professor McGonagall's punishment: Ron must polish the trophies and Harry must help Lockhart answer his fan mail (*Chamber of Secrets*, 119). The punishments that Harry witnesses and/or receives while with the Weasleys or at Hogwarts are (besides being humorous) reasonable (as opposed to the Dursley's excessive demands) and justifiable (the boys actually misbehave), which suggests that Harry can temporarily return to the innocence of childhood before he must experience the trials associated with adulthood.

The final instance of Rowling's revision to the initiation paradigm emerges in her inversion of the period when the initiate experiences psychological well-being (typical to childhood) verses psychological trauma (typical to most initiation rituals). Harry experiences psychological abuse when Dudley verbally bullies Harry, when Uncle Vernon and Aunt Petunia repeatedly call him abnormal, and when they demand his "invisibility" (*Sorcerer's Stone*, 31; *Chamber of Secrets*, 6–7). However, the most brutal emotional abuse comes from Aunt Marge's crude and fierce remarks. During dinner, Aunt Marge tells Harry, whom she believes attends St. Brutus's Secure Center for Incurably Criminal Boys, that "[I]f there's something rotten on the *inside*, there's nothing anyone can do about it. . . . It's one of the basic rules of breeding. . . . You see it all the time with dogs. If there's something wrong with the bitch, there'll be something wrong with the pup —" (*Prisoner of Azkaban*, 25). She insults Harry's parents by stating that his mother, Lily, "was a bad egg. They turn up in the best families. Then she ran off with a wastrel and here's the result right in front of us'" (*Prisoner of Azkaban*, 28). She also states that James Potter was "[a] no-account, good-for-nothing, lazy scrounger . . . " (*Prisoner of Azkaban*, 28). Aunt Marge's verbal attacks upon Harry's personality and his parents represent the epitome of her conscious efforts to accentuate Harry's pariah status and to destroy any sense of childhood innocence.

Rowling forcefully establishes that, having been deprived of psychological nurture while living with the Dursleys, Harry must first experience psychological nurture if he is to succeed at the later trials that will truly test his ability to transition into an adult world. Rowling offers a model of such nurture through the Weasleys and several father-figures whom he encounters at Hogwarts. Mr. and Mrs. Weasley represent the series' model parents who have nurtured their children's emotional health, evident from their good-natured, caring, and autonomous dispositions. Ron, Fred, and George exhibit a healthy rivalry with their perfect-Prefect brother, Percy, and the twins lovingly tease their mother and the others. Not surprisingly, the Weasleys try to foster Harry's psychological health when they: (1) remember him on his birthday and at Christmas, (2) try to reduce the length of his summer stays with the Dursleys, (3) take great efforts to prevent him from getting lost while using Flo powder (*Chamber of Secrets*, 47–48, 55–56), (4) debate whether or not to tell him about the supposed threats from Sirius Black (*Prisoner of Azkaban*, 65), and (5) come to take the place reserved for his family during the opening of the Triwizards Tournament (*Goblet of Fire*, 615). Harry's belief that "[w]hat [he] found most unusual about life at Ron's . . . wasn't the talking mirror or the clanking ghoul: It was the fact that everybody there seemed to like him" (*Chamber of Secrets*, 42) affirms his sense of psychological well-being while he lives with these individuals.

Moreover, at Hogwarts, Harry finds several father-figures who nurture his psychological well-being. Hagrid and Dumbledore (in contrast to Uncle Vernon) repeatedly praise Harry, protect him from difficult information that they believe he is not ready to process, and help him remember his parents through stories, pictures, and magical encounters. Harry clearly values these individuals; however, he finds the greatest emotional comfort when reunited with his godfather, Sirius Black. In *Goblet of Fire*, when Harry needs to confide in someone about his aching scar, he turns to Sirius Black because "[w]hat he really wanted (and it felt almost shameful to admit it to himself) was someone like—someone like a parent: an adult wizard whose advice he could ask without feeling stupid, someone who cared about him, who had had experience with Dark Magic" (*Goblet of Fire*, 22). This movement toward familial relationships and psychological nurture also challenges the paradigm, which posits that the individual move away from familial safety and toward mental challenges.

Rowling's recurrent challenges to the time-honored initiation paradigm reveal a deliberate attempt to immerse her protagonist, at least temporarily, in the physical and psychological carefree state of childhood. Ironically, this renewed safety and nurturance prepares Harry for the intellectual, personal, and interpersonal challenges that will alter his worldview. As such, Rowling turns the initiation paradigm right side up in order to illustrate Harry's growth and maturation through her discussions of the academic setting, Harry's struggles with individuation, his encounters with his parents, and the process by which Harry comes to recognize the continuum between self and other.

Rowling's choice of an explicit "initiatory" setting, Hogwarts School, and the trope of the academic year call attention to the process of transformation. Secondary school requires familiarization with a new environment and different codes of behavior. On the most basic level, Hogwarts students resemble high school freshmen, who "must negotiate new physical settings while they integrate themselves into new social systems and take greater responsibility for their social and academic lives" (Schiller 217). Rowling's young wizards must adjust to their new environment and move between classrooms, a much harder process at Hogwarts than at the average secondary school because

> [t]here were a hundred and forty-two staircases at Hogwarts: wide, sweeping ones; narrow rickety ones; some that led somewhere different on a Friday; some with a vanishing step halfway up that you had to remember to jump. Then there were doors that wouldn't open unless you asked politely, or tickled them in exactly the right place, and doors that weren't really doors at all, but solid walls just pretending. It was also very hard to remember where anything was, because it all seemed to move around a lot. (*Sorcerer's Stone*, 131–32)

Furthermore, not only do young wizards lose "the safety and security of the self-contained elementary school" (Knowles 21), but they must also adjust to having subject-specific teachers, to juggling many more challenging (and in this case, interesting, if not strange) subjects, and to completing intricate (and unusual) assignments and final exams. Although Hogwarts offers the young wizards many opportunities for having fun (the banquets with unending food, the Halloween parties, and the Quidditch tournaments), academics take precedence. The young wizards begin each academic year with the song that establishes not only their devotion to the school but also to attaining knowledge:

> *Hogwarts, Hogwarts, Hoggy Warty Hogwarts*
> Teach us something please,
> Whether we be old and bald
> Or young with knobby knees,
> Our heads could do with filling
> With some interesting stuff,
> For now they're bare and full of air,
> Dead flies and bits of fluff,
> So teach us things worth knowing,
> Bring back what we've forgot,
> Just do your best, we'll do the rest,
> And learn until our brains all rot. (*Sorcerer's Stone*, 128)

Notwithstanding the song's humorous tone, Hogwarts students seriously prepare to learn "the things worth knowing." In actuality, Rowling suggests that the critical thinking and life skills the students learn in their subject areas and in their daily interactions help them to face and solve the problems inherent with understanding "the things worth knowing," one's self as well as one's place in the familial and social moral world.

The core question Harry faces as an adolescent and as a Hogwarts student is, "Who am I?" According to Edith Sullwold, the process of individuation requires that "[t]he adolescent begins the separation from childhood, and from the image of himself which has been determined primarily by his particular family. He moves into an in-between time which presents him or her with many adult possibilities, as yet unknown and unexplored" (118). For Harry, individuation begins when the letters that arrive on the days preceding his eleventh birthday foreshadow the change in identity from an unwanted and disempowered nephew to a potentially powerful wizard (*Sorcerer's Stone*, 53). Harry had always suspected that he possessed peculiar abilities; however, his initial conversations with Hagrid reveal his oblivion about his true identity. Hagrid states, "'Yeh don' know what yeh *are*?'" (*Sorcerer's Stone*, 50) and "Harry Potter not knowin' his own story when every kid in our world knows his name!" (*Sorcerer's Stone*, 53). In a later conversation with Hagrid on their return from Diagon Alley, Harry expresses frustration with his new, unknown self when he says, "I'm famous and I can't even remember what I'm famous for. I don't know what happened when Vol-, sorry—I mean, the night my parents died" (86). Since the Dursleys deny Harry's true identity, he must attend Hogwarts to realize his true self. At school, Harry can transcend his status as an "invisible" and scrawny victim of the Dursleys' bullying, just as high school allows "[m]iddle school 'nerds' successfully [to] raise their social status [and] to redefine themselves as 'normals'" (Schiller 218). Given this opportunity and his inherent wizardly power, Harry could re-create himself as a powerful and oppressive, Dudley-like figure who lords over the peers who idolize him. Instead, Harry gauges his footing along with his peers to find his place among them, not above them so that "no one could say he was just a famous name any more" (*Sorcerer's Stone*, 225).

Although attention to external behavior serves as a valid way to shape one's identity, Harry must discern whether he is fundamentally courageous and good or manipulative and evil. Harry's confusion about his wizardly identity begins immediately with the sorting ceremony. The Sorting Hat wants to classify him as a Slytherin, "those cunning folk [who] use any means / To achieve their ends" (*Sorcerer's Stone*, 118), but Harry "thinks aloud" and expresses his preference for joining the Gryffindors, "the brave at heart, / [whose] daring, nerve, and chivalry / Set Gryffindors apart" (*Sorcerer's Stone*, 118). Nevertheless, Harry's affiliation with Gryffindors does not resolve his struggle because he has recurrent nightmares about being a Slytherin (*Sorcerer's Stone*, 130); he has the ability to hear voices (*Chamber of Secrets*, 120, 137–38; *Prisoner of Azkaban*, 179–240), to speak Parseltongue (*Chamber of Secrets*, 195–96), as well as speak to ghosts (*Goblet of Fire*, 666–68); and he owns a wand with a "phoenix feather . . . from the same bird that had supplied the core of Lord Voldemort's" (*Sorcerer's Stone*, 82, 85; *Goblet of Fire*, 310). These circumstances spur his identity confusion. Ultimately, Dumbledore calms Harry's fear of actually being the Slytherin heir when he helps Harry realize that, although Lord Voldemort infused him with some Slytherin characteristics during the attempted murder, Harry possesses his mother's gift of goodness as well as the moral principles that make him a noble Gryffindor like his father.

Harry's slow realization (i.e., initiation into the reality) that he has inherited his parents' good qualities does not, however, immediately resolve the difficulty associated with the process of self-definition. During the natural process of identity formation, adolescents encounter a crucial hurdle: differentiating themselves from their parent(s). Unfortunately, Harry's orphan status complicates his identity formation. The typical adolescent (like Ron, George, or Fred Weasley) struggles to liberate himself from the parental web of influence through a long period of rebellion; however, the orphan's identity quest differs. Sharon Stringer argues that "[y]oung adult literature includes many stories of parents who left home. For some protagonists, parental absence triggers an identity search and separation from family. Until they reconnect to this missing parent, orphans may feel as if an important part of themselves is buried" (7–8). Consequently, Harry undergoes a process of identity formation fraught with conflict because his search for the truth about his parents brings him closer to them, which in turn complicates his ability to create an identity separate from them.

Guided by several sympathetic mentors who facilitate various magical "reunions," Harry undergoes a difficult grieving process that "reconnects" him with his parents. Having grown up believing that his parents died in a car crash (*Sorcerer's Stone*, 20, 29), Harry first learns the truth about his parents' murder from Hagrid, a surrogate father-figure. In tears, Hagrid praises James and Lilly's refusal to join Lord Voldemort on the Dark Side, but he acknowledges that they suffered as a result. Harry's painful silence as he listens to this narrative suggests a new connection with his parents (*Sorcerer's Stone*, 55–56). Similarly, Dumbledore's narrative of Lily Potter's self-sacrifice for her son effects a very important "reunion" with his mother. Dumbledore tells Harry:

> Your mother died to save you. If there's one thing Voldemort cannot understand, it is love. He didn't realize that love as powerful as your mother's for you leaves its own mark. Not a scar, no visible sign . . . to have been loved so deeply, even though the person who loved us is gone, will give us some protection forever. It is in your very skin. Quirrell, full of hatred, greed, ambition, sharing his soul with Voldemort, could not touch you for this reason. It was agony to touch a person marked by something so good.
>
> Dumbledore now became very interested in a bird out on a windowsill, which gave Harry time to dry his eyes on the sheet. (*Sorcerer's Stone*, 299)

Harry's grief allows him to understand his mother's love as it produces the grief that draws him closer to her. His behavior suggests that he very much desires parental love and approval, not the separation that typically occurs at this stage of adolescent development.

Rowling subtly creates three scenes that reveal the depths of Harry's loss and his desire to reunite with his parents at an age when he should separate from them. First, that Harry "felt very strange" (*Sorcerer's Stone*, 202) when he reads the message included with his father's invisibility cloak suggests newly awakened and unresolved grief. He longs to experience the cloak (i.e., his father) without Ron: "his father's cloak—he felt that this time—the first time—he wanted to use it alone" (*Sorcerer's Stone*, 205). Second, Harry "couldn't speak" when Hagrid gives him the photo album in which "[s]miling and waving at him from every page were his mother and father" (*Sorcerer's Stone*, 304). However, the scene that most forcefully illustrates Harry's desire to reconnect with his parents occurs when Dumbledore allows Harry to stumble upon the Mirror of Erised in order to come face-to-face with his family:

> Harry was looking at his family, for the first time in his life.
>
> The Potters smiled and waved at Harry and he *stared hungrily back* at them, his *hands pressed* flat against the glass as though he was hoping to fall right through it and *reach* them. He had a powerful kind of ache inside him, *half joy, half terrible sadness*. (*Sorcerer's Stone*, 209, my emphasis)

This bittersweet magical "reunion" heightens the reality of his parents' deaths and escalates Harry's longing for them, evident from his comportment and emotional responses as well as his subsequent nightmares, which represent common behavioral and cognitive manifestations of grief (Balk 39). Harry copes with this new and unresolved grief by escaping into it. On the third visit to the mirror, Harry risks losing himself in his grief until Dumbledore helps him understand that the mirror "shows us nothing more or less than the deepest, most desperate desire of our hearts. . . . However, this mirror will give us neither knowledge or [sic] truth. . . . It does not do to dwell on dreams and forget to live, remember that" (*Sorcerer's Stone*, 213–14). As a mentor, Dumbledore knowingly challenges Harry to realize that he cannot (ironically) live in a fantasy world and that returning to a child-like state of parental dependence threatens his development.

Just as Rowling introduces unresolved grief as a potential threat to her hero's full initiation, she knowingly depicts how mourning can lead to maturation and individuation. According to Phyllis Silverman, "Children will revisit the meaning of their parent's death many times over their lifetime. They will experience the loss in different ways at various stages and phases of their lives. . . . Their accommodation and adaptation is a dynamic, ongoing process" (217). Harry's grief neither magically vanishes on the last pages of *The Sorcerer's Stone* nor do the "reunions" magically awaken the typical adolescent desire to renounce his/her parents. Instead, Rowling reawakens Harry's grief with each new piece of information about his parents at moments when: Professor Dumbledore tells him about the Patronus (*Prisoner of Azkaban*, 407); when the dementors cause him to hear his parents' screams (*Goblet of Fire*, 217; *Prisoner of Azkaban*, 179, 240); Sirius reveals Peter Pettigrew's murderous betrayal (*Prisoner of Azkaban*, 356); "Professor Moody" demonstrates the curse Lord Voldemort used to kill his parents (*Goblet of Fire*, 216–17); and he speaks directly to their ghosts (*Goblet of Fire*, 666–68). Again, Dumbledore must intervene as a mentor to help Harry achieve new insight. He defends Harry's acquisition of difficult information when he states, "Understanding is the first step to acceptance, and only with acceptance can there be recovery" (*Goblet of Fire*, 680). Through this process of knowing and accepting, Harry slowly achieves a deeper bond with his parents. In his discussion of children's grieving processes, James Worden argues that "[t]he task facing the bereaved is not to give up the relationship with the deceased, but to find a new and appropriate place for the dead in their emotional lives—one that enables them to go on living effectively in the world" (15–16). Harry's ability to "construct the deceased" (Worden, 27) through his recollection of his parents' heroism and self-sacrifice not only facilitates a new emotional well-being but also saves him during each battle against Lord Voldermort (*Chamber of Secrets*, 316; *Prisoner of Azkaban*, 375–76; *Goblet of Fire*, 666–68), which in turn forges a more mature understanding of self, a stronger connection to family, and a deeper commitment to others.

Harry's struggle to discern the Slytherin and Gryffindor parts of himself and his desire to reunite with and differentiate himself from his parents epitomizes the contrast between the adolescent-child who revels in a self-centered universe and the adolescent-adult who recognizes the connection and continuum between self and other. Rowling may have created Dudley to illustrate the adolescent-child whose failure to mature emotionally limits his social development. Aunt Petunia and Uncle Vernon's decision to satisfy their son's every greedy desire produces a young man who lacks an age-appropriate level of "emotional autonomy" (Stringer 23), which accounts for his frequent temper tantrums and fits of violent rage against his neighbors, cousin, and even his parents. Conversely, Rowling foreshadows Harry's capacity for selflessness through her depictions of how he comes to understand Dobby, worry about Ginny and the petrified students, feel empathy for Neville and Hagrid's "orphaned" status, and feel partly responsible for Cedric Diggory's death. However, Rowling's more interesting and extended explorations of this initiate's shift from egocentrism to other-centeredness appears in how her protagonist responds to financial concerns. Aunt Marge reminds Harry that, while he lives with the Dursleys, he "is a burden on [his] decent, hardworking relatives" (*Prisoner of Azkaban*, 29), but Harry's status as "burden" changes when he and Hagrid journey to the underground vault at Gringotts Wizarding Bank to access part of his inheritance. Rowling imparts this financial windfall with the implication not only of the new independence it permits but also of the maturity it inspires. Not surprisingly, this eleven-year-old at first responds rather immaturely (but gleefully) to his newfound wealth. Rowling humorously describes Harry's first nonessential spending spree as follows: "He had never had any money for candy with the Dursleys, and now that he had pockets rattling with gold and silver he was ready to buy as many Mars Bars as he could carry—but the woman didn't have Mars Bars," a Muggle confection. So, "[n]ot wanting to miss [the candy that wizards eat], he got some of everything . . . " (*Sorcerer's Stone*, 101). Had Harry adopted Dudley's immature and self-centered mindset, he would have consumed the mountain of candy alone; however, it does not take Harry long to use his financial security to help others, in this case to "supplement" Ron's dry corned beef sandwich with some Chocolate Frogs and Bertie Bott's Every Flavor Beans (*Sorcerer's Stone*, 101–104).

In the "adult world," conscious selflessness amounts to more than sharing candy; it means subordinating potentially egotistical desires to the community's needs. Harry's time with the Weasleys may allow for a return to childhood innocence, but his interaction with this family also tests him. Rowling constructs the Weasleys, Harry's surrogate family, as the smallest microcosm of community. Harry's ability to respond empathetically and generously to this community's financial plight suggests a positive step toward crossing the threshold into mature adulthood. For example, when Ron Weasley shamefacedly acknowledges that he and his siblings must go to Hogwarts with used wizard robes, wands, books, and animals, Harry tries to decrease Ron's embarrassment. Rowling writes, "Harry didn't think there was anything wrong with not being able to afford an owl. After all, he'd never had any money in his life until a month ago, and he told Ron so, all about having to wear Dudley's old clothes and never getting proper birthday presents" (*Sorcerer's Stone,* 100). He also shows compassion when George tells him of the family's additional financial burden upon Ginny's admittance to Hogwarts (*Chamber of Secrets,* 46); when he sees that the Weasley vault has only "a very small pile of silver Sickles . . . and just one gold Galleon" (*Chamber of Secrets,* 57); and when Draco Malfoy and his father publicly insult the family's financial state (*Chamber of Secrets,* 61–62). Harry's feelings of compassion arouse his mature desire to help his "family" rather than to parade his wealth over them. Harry "would willingly have split all the money in his Gringotts vault with the Weasleys, but he knows they would never take it" (*Prisoner of Azkaban,* 156), so he shares his wealth in less conspicuous ways: he cheerfully shares the candy with Ron, he gives Ginny the set of books Lockhart had given him (*Chamber of Secrets,* 61), and he gives Fred and George his thousand Galleons prize money from the Triwizard's Tournament (*Goblet of Fire,* 733). Thus, rather than replicating the immature and greedy behavior he witnesses at the Dursleys, Harry's selfless generosity epitomizes what Sullwold calls "another essential aspect of adolescent transition, the entry into a larger sense of community" (114).

Rowling uses the peer group as another microcosm (though larger than the family) to test Harry's progression toward a healthy and responsible relationship to community. Upon leaving the Muggle world via the Hogwarts Express, Harry literally and figuratively enters a world that advocates a fairer code of social relations (especially considering the battle against oppressive darker forces), evident from its emphasis on learning to strike a balance between self and the nonfamilial community. Although Hogwarts admits some less-than-perfect individuals, like Draco Malfoy, the school socializes its students about the dynamics necessary for negotiating their place in the community. Almost immediately upon their arrival at Hogwarts, new students undergo—in the presence of the faculty and student community—an initiation ritual that stresses the interdependence between self and other. As Professor McGonagall explains,

> The Sorting is a very important ceremony because, while you are here, your house will be something like your family within Hogwarts. You will have classes with the rest of your house, sleep in your house dormitory, and spend free time in your house commons room. (*Sorcerer's Stone,* 114)

As each new student sits on the stool, the Sorting Hat looks "within" the individual and decides which smaller community, or house, best suits his or her character. Immediately after the sorting, the new student joins fellow cheering house members, which affirms the individual's entrance into the community. According to Knowles, the creation of such houses in middle school environments fosters "stable, close, mutually respectful relationships with adults and peers [and] are considered fundamental for intellectual development and personal growth" (49).

Membership in a "house" also initiates Harry and his peers into a relationship that assesses whether they, like typical middle school students, can learn to "[a]ssume the responsibilities of citizenship in a pluralistic society" (Knowles 50). As Rowling suggests, each student's behavior in his or her house impacts that group's standing. Professor McGonagall explains that "[while] you are at Hogwarts, your triumphs will earn your house points, while any rule breaking will lose your house points" (*Sorcerer's Stone*, 114). According to Robert Havinghurst's theory of development "the principal lessons to be learned in this state will be social and emotional, where students learn to work together on common interests and to place the pursuit of a common goal over one's personal interest" (qtd. in Allen 58–59). For Harry, this means realizing that acting blindly or foolhardily can endanger the group, a philosophy not given any consideration the self-centered universe at 4 Privet Drive. If the pressure to elevate other over self does not come naturally from within, it can often come from peer pressure socialization (Allen 55, 57). For example, when Harry and Ron plan to meet Malfoy for the Wizard's Duel, Hermione scolds them in stating: "you *mustn't* go wandering around the school at night, think of the points you'll lose Gryffindor if you're caught, and you're bound to be. It's really very selfish of you" (*Sorcerer's Stone*, 154). Consequently, when Malfoy informs the teachers that Harry, Hermione (having forgotten her earlier reproof), and Neville have wandered the school grounds at night to deliver Norbert (Hagrid's dragon) to the cliff, Professor McGonagall gives each student detention as well as a 150-point house penalty. As a result, they "put Gryffindor in last place. In one night, they'd ruined any chance Gryffindor had had for the house cup" (*Sorcerer's Stone*, 244). As such, Rowling argues that full maturation means learning to see oneself in relation to others.

One of the most important trials that Harry undergoes to test whether or not he can succeed in attaining a higher maturity level by extending the circle of influence beyond the egotistical center appears most forcefully in the debate over racial purity. As Harry learns about this taboo, he must ultimately learn to act to benefit not only self, family, or his "house" but also all Hogwarts students and faculty. Harry's changing response concerning the issue of racial purity exemplifies a slow, three-phase shift from innocence and noninvolvement to self-centeredness, communal awareness, and intervention. The process by which Harry comes to understand the issue of "pure bloods" is in itself an initiation; however, only in the end does Rowling include the literal journey and return so typical of Campbells initiation paradigm.

In the first phase, Harry appears in a state of child-like innocence. During an interchange with Malfoy at Madam Malkim's Robes for All Occasions, Harry first hears of the conflict over "pure bloods"; however, he clearly does not understand its implications (*Sorcerer's Stone,* 78). One year later, Harry learns more about the conflict when Ron fervently explains why Hermione should feel insulted when Malfoy calls her a "filthy little Mudblood" (*Chamber of Secrets,* 112). Ron states:

> It's about the most insulting thing [Malfoy] could think of. . . . Mudblood's a really foul name for someone who is Muggle-born—you know, non-magic parents. There are some wizards—like Malfoy's family—who think they're better than everyone else because they're what people call pure-blood. . . . I mean, the rest of us know it does-n't make any difference at all. Look at Neville Longbottom—he's pure-blood and he can hardly stand a cauldron the right way up . . .
>
> It's a disgusting thing to call someone. . . . dirty blood, see. Common blood. It's ridiculous. Most wizards these days are half-blood anyway. If we hadn't married Muggles we'd've died out. (*Chamber of Secrets,* 115–16)

One could argue that Harry does not respond to this discussion because "Hagrid's treacle fudge had cemented his jaws together" (*Chamber of Secrets,* 116), but then why does he, unlike his peers, not ask questions about the Chamber of Secrets when Professor Binns (the history teacher) rather reluctantly establishes that the distinction between pure and Muggle-blood started with a disagreement between the Slytherins and Gryffindors (*Chamber of Secrets,* 150–51)? Perhaps Rowling repeats the image of Harry's silence to illustrate the slow process of attaining the fun-damental knowledge that theoretically ends his innocence and thereby pushes him into the next stage of racial consciousness.

In the second stage, Harry acts out the childhood egotistical phase when he believes himself at the center of the conflict over the Chamber of Secrets and the "pure blood" debate. Tom Riddle clearly establishes that Harry is not the focus of his desire for revenge. Only when Harry tries to identify Slytherin's heir does Riddle modify his plan. Riddle states, "Haven't I already told you. . . that killing Mudbloods doesn't matter to me anymore?" (Chamber 312). Yet, until this point, Harry situates himself at the center of the conflict. After Professor Binns' lecture, Harry suspects that he is Slytherin's heir (*Chamber of Secrets*, 153) and he repeatedly defends himself when his peers accuse him of the petrifications, especially after realizing he can speak Parseltongue (*Chamber of Secrets*, 194–96, 199, 200, 204, 209). With his ego at stake, discovering the truth (especially when he finds Tom Riddle's diary) becomes paramount. He must prove to others and to himself that he is not the evil heir.

Once he understands the seriousness of Malfoy's insult and he realizes that he is not at the center of the conflict, Harry enters the third phase, namely, the literal journey underground to uncover the truth that will restore the community. In an exchange with Harry, Dobby highlights this adolescent's ability to put other before self: "'Harry Potter risks his own life for his friends!' moaned Dobby in a kind of miserable ecstasy. 'So noble! So valiant. But he must save himself, he must, Harry Potter must not—'" (*Chamber of Secrets*, 179). Harry, however, ignores Dobby's recommendation for self-preservation. After Hermione's petrification (257), Ginny's abduction (293), Hagrid's second imprisonment (281, 311), and Lockhart's attempted escape from responsibility, Harry realizes the need to act: "If only there was something they could do. Anything" (*Chamber of Secrets*, 295). At this moment, Rowling adopts the typical initiation paradigm. In an effort to save his "girl" friends and prove Hagrid's innocence, Harry journeys down plumbing pipes and offers himself in death for the benefit of his community. According to Joseph Campbell's model, initiation comes to a close when the initiate realizes a higher truth that transcends self and he "*re-emerges from the kingdom of dread (return, resurrection). The boon that he brings restores the world . . .*" (246). After he "kills" Tom Riddle, Harry returns from his journey with a new worldview and a "boon": safety for all Muggle-born wizards, including Justin Finch-Fletchley, Hermione Granger (a pure Muggle), the Ravenclaw's Prefect, and Colin Creevy, whose father is a milkman. By securing such safety, Harry asserts that racial purity is not essential for membership in a community.

Rowling's adoption of and adaptations to the initiation paradigm underlie the strategy she uses to keep readers from growing bored with the tragic little hero. In *Harry Potter*, Rowling has created an extended narrative about the tragedy of lost childhood, the possibility of transcending a horrific past, and the heroics needed to achieve a balanced view of the self and the world one inhabits. Granted, young readers do not ponder how Rowling adopts and adapts initiation paradigms (but older readers do). Perhaps, therefore, what draws them to the novels are the parallels they see in Harry and their own development. With publication dates set at one-year intervals, Harry and his reading public (especially those who read the series as they appear in bookstores) begin each "school year" (novel) one year older, and hopefully one year wiser. Furthermore, readers can leave their secure "homes" and journey with Harry as he struggles to learn about himself, his position in the world, and the world about him. On this journey together, young readers and their heroic protagonist can face the dark, difficult trials necessary to survive in an adult world, whether wizardly or Muggle, and gain new insights that they can then share with their community.

References

Allen, Harvey A. *Teaching and Learning in the Middle School*. New York: Macmillan, 1993.

Balk, David E. "Adolescents, Grief, and Loss." In *Living with Grief: Children, Adolescents, and Loss*. Ed. Kenneth Doka. Washington: Hospice Foundation of America, 2000. 33–49.

Bernstein, Jerome S. "The Decline of Masculine Rites of Passage in Our Culture: The Impact on Masculine Individuation." In *Betwixt and Between: Patterns of Masculine and Feminine Initiation*. Ed. Louise Carus Mahdi, Steven Foster, and Meredith Little. La Salle: Open Court, 1987. 135–58.

Campbell, Joseph. *The Hero with a Thousand Faces*. Princeton: Princeton UP, 1972.

Foster, Steven, and Meredith Little. "The Vision Quest: Passing from Childhood to Adulthood." In *Betwixt and Between: Patterns of Masculine and Feminine Initiation*. Ed. Louise Carus Mahdi, Steven Foster, and Meredith Little. La Salle: Open Court, 1987. 79–110.

Jorgensen, E. Clay. *Child Abuse: A Practical Guide for Those Who Help Others*. New York: Continuum, 1990.

Knowles, Trudy, and Dave Brown. *What Every Middle School Teacher Should Know*. Portsmouth: Heinemann, 2000.

O'Brien, Shirley. *Child Abuse: A Crying Shame*. Provo: Brigham Young UP, 1980.

Rowling, J. K. *Harry Potter and the Chamber of Secrets*. New York: Scholastic P, 1999.

———. *Harry Potter and the Goblet of Fire*. New York: Scholastic P, 2000.

———. *Harry Potter and the Prisoner of Azkaban*. New York: Scholastic P, 1999.

———. *Harry Potter and the Sorcerer's Stone*. New York: Scholastic P, 1997.

Schechter, Harold. "Symbols of Initiation in *Adventures of Huckleberry Finn*." In *Betwixt and Between: Patterns of Masculine and Feminine Initiation*. Ed. Louise Carus Mahdi, Steven Foster, and Meredith Little. La Salle: Open Court, 1987. 67–78.

Schiller, Kathryn S. "Effects of Feeder Patterns on Students' Transition to High School." *Sociology of Education* 72.4 (Oct. 1999): 216–33.

Silverman, Phyllis. "When Parents Die." In *Living with Grief: Children, Adolescents, and Loss.* Ed. Kenneth Doka. Washington: Hospice Foundation of America, 2000. 215–28.

Stringer, Sharon A. *Conflict and Connection: The Psychology of Young Adult Literature.* Portsmouth: Heinemann, 1997.

Sullwold, Edith. "The Ritual-Maker within at Adolescence." In *Betwixt and Between: Patterns of Masculine and Feminine Initiation.* Ed. Louise Carus Mahdi, Steven Foster, and Meredith Little. La Salle: Open Court, 1987. 111–31.

Worden, James William. *Children and Grief: When a Parent Dies.* New York: Guilford P, 1996.

Part IV

Critical and Sociological Perspectives

Chapter Ten

Comedy, Conflict, and Community: Home and Family in *Harry Potter*

John Kornfeld and Laurie Prothro

When baseball commissioner A. Bartlett Giamatti (1989) wrote about baseball as a metaphor for life, he pointed out that in life, just as in baseball, you leave home, then spend all the game trying to get back home—back to a place where you know what the score is, you know where you stand, you are safe. This transformational journey—which all young people must take to discover who they are and where they fit in the world, to create their own version of home out of the strangeness they encounter when they are "away"—forms the basis of young adult, coming-of-age literature. And unless they leave, they cannot know what it is they seek. As Rochman and McCampbell (1997, p. vii) write, "We leave home to find home."

The concept of home is inextricably entangled with that of family—individuals who together "create worlds of their own, with particular kinds of boundaries separating them from the larger world" (Handel, 1994, p. xxiv). Ideally, within these worlds, members offer one another security, support, and other assets that can become "protective factors" (Gilgun, 1999) for young people leaving home and struggling with the inevitable challenges of life. But family is not always (or only) a team clustered in the dugout, urging you on with hope and faith as you set out on your quest, waiting to welcome you with wild cheers when you return home, safe. The various cross-relationships among individuals within a family group can be welcoming or isolating; for the young adult feeling alone in the world, images of home and family can provide sustenance, or a motivation to escape. We see the effects of such family dynamics in young adult novels as the protagonists move forward purposefully in their quests. And even if the family is a harmonious, loving community, the journey demands separation from it, a "necessary abyss" (Rochman, 1993, p. 13) as a young person comes of age. Ultimately, however, it is the protective factors that young people can draw on during their journey toward self-discovery and meaning in the world; and in the *Harry Potter* series, we see what can happen when the family unit both succeeds and fails to provide them.

Family Dynamics in the Non-Hogwarts World

Like so many protagonists in coming-of-age novels, Harry Potter is essentially alone in the world. His real parents, we learn, were killed when he was an infant and, because his aunt and uncle are his only relatives, they have become Harry's unwilling guardians. The first family we meet in the Rowling series, then, are the Dursleys:

> "You must be Harry's family!" said Mrs. Weasley.
>
> "In a manner of speaking," said Uncle Vernon. "Hurry up, boy, we haven't got all day." He walked away. (Rowling, 1997, p. 309)

Abusive and cruel, the Dursleys treat Harry "like a dog that had rolled in something smelly" (Rowling, 1998, p. 5). They exclude him from family activities, lock him in his cupboard for prolonged periods of time, and, worst of all, withhold from Harry the truth about his parents and himself. The Dursleys remind us of Aunt Sponge and Aunt Spiker, the malignant guardians in Roald Dahl's *James and the Giant Peach* (1961/1988) who routinely abuse and imprison James Trotter after his parents' sudden deaths (they were eaten by a rhinoceros that had escaped from the London zoo) when he was four years old. Yet, as horrible as Trotter's and Potter's guardians may be, it is difficult to take them terribly seriously. As one-dimensional characters, their treatment of the boys reads more like farce than tragedy. Early in the story, Dahl (1961/1988, p. 40) unceremoniously disposes of James's aunts in comic book fashion by rolling a giant peach over them: "Aunt Sponge and Aunt Spiker lay ironed out upon the grass as flat and thin and lifeless as a couple of paper dolls cut out of a picture book." The Dursley family members suffer equally cartoonish (although less dire) fates: Dudley first sprouts a tail (*Sorcerer's Stone*), then later a four-foot-long tongue (*Goblet of Fire*), and his Aunt Marge balloons to an enormous size and floats to the ceiling (*Prisoner of Azkaban*). How can we fail to laugh at characters who send Harry a toothpick (*Chamber of Secrets*) and a tissue (*Goblet of Fire*) as Christmas gifts? Even Harry himself doesn't take the Dursleys particularly seriously. When they are preparing for the visit of a potential client and Dudley acts out his sycophantish speech, Harry "ducked under the table so they wouldn't see him laughing" (Rowling, 1998, p. 6).

Rowling devotes considerable attention in each book to family dynamics in the non-Hogwarts world. Much of that attention revolves around the antics of the Dursleys and another family, the Weasleys—a wizarding family whose son Ron becomes Harry's best friend at Hogwarts. The scenes at both Harry's and Ron's homes read like theater of the absurd, reducing family life to slapstick comedy. Unfortunately, by relying on stereotypical family roles and relationships to give us a few laughs, Rowling risks reifying family roles and relationships in the minds of her young readers, creating instead a troubling vision of home and family.

Consider, for example, the roles that members of each family play. The fathers both serve as the breadwinners for the household, whereas the mothers stay at home and take care of house and family. As the titular heads of household, the fathers must take on responsibilities that include maintaining discipline in the family ("You wait until your father gets home," Mrs. Weasley warns her children [Rowling, 1998, p. 33]), but each fails hilariously. Blustering, brutish Mr. Dursley bullies other family members in an effort to control all that goes on in the house (intercepting Harry's mail [*Sorcerer's Stone*], directing his family's every word and action when the potential client comes for dinner [*Chamber of Secrets*]), but he always ends up thwarted. Mr. Weasley, on the other hand, is no match for his fiery wife, who badgers and intimidates him into taking on his required leadership role:

> "Your sons flew that car to Harry's house and back last night!" shouted Mrs. Weasley. "What have you to say about that, eh?"
>
> "Did you really?" said Mr. Weasley eagerly. "Did it go all right? I—I mean," he faltered as sparks flew from Mrs. Weasley's eyes, "that—that was very wrong, boys— very wrong indeed. . . . " (Rowling, 1998, p. 39)

Alongside the provider fathers we have the nurturing mothers whose role involves cooking, cleaning, and caring for the children. Responsible for the children's proper upbringing, they dote on those who conform, or at least pretend to (Dudley in the Dursley household, Percy in the Weasley family), and admonish the children who challenge the status quo (Harry in the Dursley family and the twins in the Weasley family). Particularly disturbing is the lack of respect that Mrs. Weasley receives from her children. For example, the sweaters that she knits for Harry and her children are a standing joke throughout the series, eliciting derision rather than appreciation for the care and love that they represent.

Along with overseeing the daily functioning of the two households, the parents' prime directive seems to be to fit in and make no waves in their respective societies. The Dursleys, "proud to say that they were perfectly normal, thank you very much" (Rowling, 1997, p. 1), do everything they can to keep secret Harry's "abnormality," even going so far as to pretend that he attends St. Brutus's Secure Center for Incurably Criminal Boys: they would prefer that he be thought a criminal rather than a wizard. Similarly, Arthur Weasley has to hide his fascination with and affection for Muggles and Muggle artifacts in order to maintain his position in the Ministry of Magic bureaucracy.

The children's role in the family makes "fitting in" somewhat problematic. Girls are no problem (in fact, among the nine children in the two households, there is only one daughter, and she is so shy and passive that she is practically invisible); but boys, as the cliché goes, will be boys. Dudley and Harry, each in his own way, totally ignore the Dursleys' rules, sneaking behind the adults' backs whenever they feel like it; and the Weasley twins' schemes and antics drive their mother crazy. These boys constantly commit transgressions that threaten the family's image in the community: "You could have *died*, you could have been *seen*, you could have lost your father his *job*—" (Rowling, 1998, p. 33). Of all the boys, only Percy obeys adults and follows their rules, but he is supercilious and insufferable—the object of ridicule rather than respect—and it is no surprise that he turns into a mindless, self-important bureaucrat when he gets a job at the Ministry of Magic.

All of these family dynamics read more like situation comedy than anything else. In the Dursley house, Uncle Vernon goes to increasingly ridiculous (and futile) extremes in his role as head and protector of the family to prevent Harry from getting mail from Hogwarts, ultimately rowing the family in a violent storm to a broken-down shack on a remote island. Meanwhile, Molly Weasley, like Samantha in the old television show *Bewitched*, keeps her family and house in order through cute and funny magical means—making the dishes wash themselves in the sink and using enchanted clocks to keep track of her children's schedules and her husband's whereabouts. As in most situation comedies, the struggle between parents and sons is constant. Compared to their clever, mischievous sons, the parents seem dull-witted and obtuse. The Dursley and

Weasley parents are often unaware of their sons' pranks (and they also are totally oblivious to the deeper struggles that their children undergo in the magical world); they barely manage to contain the damage the kids create and maintain their tenuous image of normalcy in their community. The sons embody the cultural phenomenon that Steinberg and Kincheloe (1998) call "young males with an attitude"—"smart-ass kids" depicted in popular movies who run circles around their clueless parents and garner audience sympathy. The mildly adversarial parent/son relationships in Rowling's non-Hogwarts world seem designed primarily for the humor they engender; but they also perpetuate the more disturbing cultural image of the "maverick hero" adolescent male "entitled to misbehave," while the females in the family are "relegated to minor character status" (Steinberg & Kincheloe, 1998).

These stereotypical roles are not unique to the Dursleys and Weasleys: we see echoes of the same roles throughout the *Harry Potter* series. Domineering fathers head the Crouch and Malfoy families (in fact, the Malfoy family seems like a magical world version of the Dursleys), while nurturing mothers in the Crouch and Potter families literally die to save their sons. But we rarely observe these wizarding families in action; we learn about their dynamics mostly through hearsay. The Dursleys and the Weasleys are the only families we get to know well and, in book after book, these two families from Rowling's non-Hogwarts world are comical, conventional, superficial, predictable—and totally misrepresentative of the diversity of family structures in contemporary society.

From the Mundane to the Magical

Fortunately, when the protagonists (and the readers) enter the magical world, the characters, events, families, and relationships do take on depth and dimension. The difference between the Muggle and magical worlds is as striking as the difference between the black-and-white plains of Kansas and the technicolor world of Oz. Muggle football pales if compared with the pace and competition of Quidditch; no Muggle photograph competes with the kinetic excitement of a magical picture; and any Muggle prison guard would seem positively benevolent compared to the terrifying dementors of Azkaban. The contrast between the Muggle and magical worlds recalls Plato's allegory of the cave, in which the prisoners see only their pale shadows that the fire casts on the wall. Unable to turn around and see the objects themselves in the sunlight, the prisoners "in every way believe that the truth is nothing other than the shadows of those artifacts" (Plato, 1997, p. 1133). Similarly, Muggles remain unaware of the magical world all around them. As the Knight Bus conductor explains, "Them! . . . Don' listen properly, do they? Don' look properly either. Never notice nuffink, they don'" (Rowling, 1999, p. 36).[1]

This inability to recognize (or refusal to acknowledge) magic in the world is common in British children's fantasy literature. In C. S. Lewis's Narnia chronicles, Susan can no longer get into Narnia when she starts caring about "nylons and lipstick and invitations" (Lewis, 1956/1988, p. 128); in J. M. Barrie's *Peter Pan* (1911/1987), Wendy can no longer fly with Peter when the real world becomes more important than the magical world. This division between believers and nonbelievers highlights the disparity between the "real" and magical worlds. In *Peter Pan*, the dull and one-dimensional world of the Darlings is juxtaposed with the gloriously exciting magical world of Neverland; in E. Nesbit's *The House of Arden* (1908/1958), the children leave their "ordinary life . . . where nothing particularly thrilling had ever happened" (Nesbit, 1908/1958, p. 58) when they inherit a castle with a magical mole-like creature who sends them on all sorts of exciting time travels. In these and other British books of magic, it seems that a major purpose of the "real" world is to show how much more real the magical world is: a place where all important events take place, where someone alienated and alone might find a home. As Cart (2001, p. 1546) suggests, this alternative world can offer "reassurance that magic could intrude into a recognizably 'real' world whose ugly vicissitudes might otherwise have been intolerable." In L. M. Boston's *The Children of Green Knowe* (1954/1983), the young protagonist Tolly's mother is dead; he hardly knows his stepmother or father, who live in Burma, and until his great-grandmother invites him to spend the summer with her, he has been stuck during holidays at his boarding school with the headmistress. He longs for "a family like other people" (p. 3), and when he arrives at Green Knowe, a mysterious castle-like mansion full of magic, "he felt with all his heart that he was at home" (p. 18). Harry, too, like Tolly and James in *James and the Giant Peach*, yearns to escape the real world, because only in the world of magic does the vision of home and family take on any meaning or permanence.

Home and Family at Hogwarts

In the magical world of Hogwarts, the notions of home and family are far more complex and multidimensional than in the "real" world. Family connections and loyalties are bound not by birth and genetics, but by more enduring factors; the roles family members assume are determined less by age and gender than by actions and relationships forged among individuals.

When he first arrives at Hogwarts, Harry learns that he will join one of four houses. As Professor McGonagall explains, "Your house will be something like your family within Hogwarts . . . each [with] its own noble history" (Rowling, 1997, p. 114). These houses provide more than just a physical demarcation among the four groups of students. As the Sorting Hat explains, the members of each house share certain key personality traits and perspectives—Gryffindors are brave, Hufflepuffs loyal and hardworking, and so on. Hess and Handel (1994) write that a "family theme" characterizes the unique worldview of every family. At Hogwarts, members of each house, connected by common attributes that they bring to Hogwarts, as well as by the history of the house to which they belong, unite around their family theme,

> a pattern of feeling, motives, fantasies, and conventionalized understandings grouped about some locus of concern which has a particular form in the personalities of the individual members. The pattern comprises some fundamental view of reality and some way or ways of dealing with it. In the family themes are to be found the family's implicit direction, its notion of "who we are" and "what we do about it." (Hess & Handel, 1994, pp. 10–11)

More important to family, though, than this collective sense of history, purpose, and worldview is the trust, loyalty, and attachment that can evolve from this shared perspective. Harry, Hermione, and Ron exhibit these qualities in their interactions throughout most of the series. Their commitment to one another begins to emerge in the first book when Harry and Ron risk their lives to save Hermione from a troll, and then Hermione lies to Professor McGonagall to save Harry and Ron from punishment. Rowling writes (Rowling, 1997, p. 179), "There are some things you can't share without ending up liking each other, and knocking out a twelve-foot mountain troll is one of them"; but what is perhaps more significant about the encounter is that each of the three friends, in turn, recognizes each other's needs and sublimates his or her own immediate interests and needs in order to help that person. This is the essence of Noddings's (1992) notion of caring, in which an individual is "seized by the needs of another" (Noddings, 1992, p. 16) and, for a time, becomes the carer.

Except during a few notable quarrels, Harry, Hermione, and Ron care for one another throughout the *Harry Potter* series. Their association is a sort of family unit within the larger extended family of Gryffindor. They share family rituals such as eating together and opening presents together on Christmas day. And no matter what the danger, no matter what obligations may hinder them, each can count on the others to provide the "protective factors" that Gilgun (1999) says are key to resilient families. Presumably, such relationships exist among other student groups as well, both in Gryffindor and in other houses. Moreover, we learn that years ago Sirius Black, Remus Lupin, Peter Pettigrew, and Harry's father, James Potter, enjoyed such a relationship until Peter betrayed the Potters. The three surviving members' strange encounter in the Shrieking Shack after years of separation (*Prisoner of Azkaban*), with each knowing the others so well, has the feel of a somewhat strained family reunion.

In moving from the Muggle to the magical world—by coming to Hogwarts—Harry also moves emotionally from a place of isolation and loneliness to a sense of community and belonging. After one year at Hogwarts, Harry knows what home can mean, and back at the Dursleys for the summer holidays, he longs for it:

> He missed Hogwarts so much it was like having a constant stomachache. He missed the castle, with its secret passageways and ghosts, his classes (though perhaps not Snape, the Potions master), the mail arriving by owl, eating banquets in the Great Hall, sleeping in his four-poster bed in the tower dormitory, visiting the gamekeeper, Hagrid, in his cabin next to the Forbidden Forest in the grounds, and, especially, Quidditch, the most popular sport in the wizarding world. (Rowling, 1998, p. 3)

Clearly, home for Harry represents connection: friendship ("He'd never had friends before Hogwarts" [Rowling, 1998 p. 234]); shared meals; the bonding of a team sport; even a specific place within the community of Gryffindor respected by others as his own individual, private space. For the first time in his life, Harry knows what it means to belong.

But Harry's sense of belonging does not mean that relationships at Hogwarts are entirely harmonious. In fact, Hogwarts is rife with disagreements, mistrust, and intrigue. While members of each house generally support one another and espouse similar worldviews, competition among houses fuels deceit, anger, and conflict. The world of Hogwarts in some ways recalls the classic sociological dichotomy of *Gemeinschaft* and *Gesellschaft* (Tönnies, 1887/1957). According to Tönnies, social entities can be characterized by two antithetical concepts, community and society. *Gemeinschaft* (community) consists of people bound together by physical proximity and intellectual affinity[2]:

> They speak together and think along similar lines. . . . There is understanding between people who love each other. Those who love and understand each other remain and dwell together and organize their common life. A mixed or complex form of common determinative will, which has become as natural as language itself and which consists of a multitude of feelings of understanding which are measured by its norm, we call concord (*Eintracht*) or family spirit. (Tönnies, 1887/1957, p. 48)

In direct opposition to *Gemeinschaft* is the notion of *Gesellschaft* (society):

> In the *Gemeinschaft* [individuals] remain essentially united in spite of all separating factors, whereas in the *Gesellschaft* they are essentially separated in spite of all uniting factors. . . . Their spheres of activity and power are sharply separated, so that everybody refuses to everyone else contact with and admittance to his sphere; i.e., intrusions are regarded as hostile acts. (Tönnies, 1887/1957, p. 65)

In the classic vision of *Gesellschaft*, the individual is essentially alone: there is no Gryffindor-type microcosm to support him or her. For Harry, there are a few occasions when he feels that, even at Hogwarts, he is completely alone in a hostile world: in *Chamber of Secrets* when his classmates believe that he has been attacking students, and in *Goblet of Fire* when even his closest friend believes that he secretly put his name into the goblet. For the most part, though, in the world of Hogwarts the alienation that characterizes the *Gesellschaft* occurs among houses rather than individuals. This estrangement is particularly disturbing because teachers and the headmaster himself cultivate and encourage it.

From the day that students arrive at Hogwarts, they learn that competition among houses is a time-honored tradition and that at the end of each year the house with the most points will win the house cup. Rather than merely motivating students to do their very best in school, these "family feuds" undermine any chance of camaraderie among houses and intensifies their antipathy toward one another. Thus, for example, to an outsider, members of Slytherin are not merely cunning, they are devious; rather than respecting Hufflepuffs for their stolid dependability, "everyone says Hufflepuff are a lot o' duffers" (Rowling, 1997, p. 80). The secret location of each house's common room and sleeping quarters fosters a sense of security and community among house members, but it also magnifies the houses' sense of separateness from one another: they are sanctuaries in an otherwise perilous environment.

The most troubling instance in which competition undermines community and cooperation is the Triwizard Tournament (*Goblet of Fire*), in which one champion from each of three wizarding schools competes (although, as it turns out, Hogwarts fields two champions: Harry from Gryffindor and Cedric Diggory from Hufflepuff). Headmaster Dumbledore explains that a major purpose of this tournament is to foster good will among the different schools. But instead of encouraging communication, the competition merely feeds animosity and mistrust among the students from each school. In fact, as Professor Moody tells Harry (Rowling, 2000, p. 343), "Cheating's a traditional part of the Triwizard Tournament and always has been." Worse, even, is the way Harry and Cedric are pitted against each other. Amazingly, the two of them actually manage to transcend the competitive atmosphere and help one another solve clues to accomplish the required tasks. In an exhilarating moment of friendship and cooperation, the two decide to grasp the Triwizard Cup simultaneously and share the victory. The immediate result of this rare instance of interhouse cooperation is that Cedric is murdered, suggesting the disquieting notion that there is little value in working together to extend one's family beyond its usual boundaries.

Clearly, Rowling does not wish to represent Hogwarts as a utopia. Her portrayal of community and society in Hogwarts is a plausible characterization of the way people live and learn and work together. Still, the competition in Hogwarts causes alienation, conflict, and dissolution of potential understanding within the Hogwarts community. Yet Rowling, like her characters, never questions or challenges this aspect of community interaction, instead accepting it as an integral part of life.

The Family Covenant

In spite of her uncritical acceptance of destructive competition and her stereotypical representation of families in the non-Hogwarts world, Rowling still offers a compelling vision of the vital role that home and family play in the lives of young people coming of age. Harry's growing bond with Hermione and Ron, as well as his membership in the *Gemeinschaft* of Gryffindor, allows him to break away physically and emotionally from the prison of the Dursley household. He moves from passive to active resistance, effecting a daring escape from his locked bedroom in the Weasley's magical flying car (*Chamber of Secrets*), and later blowing up Aunt Marge and storming out of the Dursley house (*Prisoner of Azkaban*). By the fourth book, Harry is absolutely rebellious: "Gone were the days when he had been forced to take every single one of the Dursleys' stupid rules" (Rowling, 2000, p. 33).

We applaud Harry's increasing resistance to the Dursleys' authority. From the day the Dursleys grudgingly took Harry into their home, they abused him, lied to him, and ignored his needs; they denied him those essential protective factors that caring family members provide one another. Leibowitz (1978) writes that family memberships are defined by publicly acknowledged contractual agreements, usually marriage contracts and the like. But for Rowling, the contract that holds a family together involves much more than a legal obligation; it is an inviolable covenant among family members to provide care and support for one another, whatever the cost. In breaking that covenant, the Dursleys relinquished any right to Harry's loyalty or obedience, and they compelled him to seek home and family elsewhere.

When family members in Rowling's magical world break this covenant, the consequences are serious and permanent. Pettigrew betrayed the trust of his friends James and Sirius, causing the deaths of James and Lily Potter and Sirius's unjust imprisonment, and dooming himself to a life of service to Voldemort. Mr. Crouch "should have spent a bit more time at home with his family, shouldn't he? Ought to have left the office early once in a while . . . gotten to know his own son" (Rowling, 2000, p. 528). Instead, when the young Crouch got in trouble with the Ministry of Magic, the elder Crouch put personal ambition over the welfare of his own son and sent him to Azkaban. As a result of these actions, Crouch's family is destroyed, and his son leaves home to find a new family—with Voldemort serving as surrogate father: "I will be his dearest, his closest supporter . . . closer than a son" (Rowling, 2000, p. 678).

Voldemort's descent into evil, like Crouch's, provides an object lesson in the destructive consequences of a father's broken covenant with his family. Voldemort's father deserts his pregnant wife before Voldemort's birth, thus consigning him to grow up in an orphanage when his mother dies in childbirth. Like the younger Crouch, Voldemort later kills his father and seeks a new family—the Death Eaters, whom he refers to as "my *true* family" (Rowling, 2000, p. 646). Interestingly, while his Muggle father's desertion leads to Voldemort's murderous obsession with the purity of wizard family bloodlines, true family connections for Voldemort, as for Rowling, are more about trust, loyalty, and unity of purpose than they are about blood connections.

Fortunately, along with these illustrations of broken family covenants, Rowling furnishes us with numerous examples of parents and guardians who have provided the support their children needed. The Weasley family may get caught up in frequent family squabbles, but when the children need help, they can count on parents and siblings alike to be there (even the usually aloof Percy rushes to help Ron when Harry is dragging him out of the lake in the Champions' second task). In a very different family, Harry's huge friend Hagrid, the product of a giantess mother and wizard father, has overcome his mother's desertion and the consequent breakup of his family, thanks to the steadfast support of his diminutive father.

Harry himself has benefited from the support of parents and loved ones. Unbeknownst to Harry, Dumbledore's magic has protected him from Voldemort throughout his life at the Dursleys. Sirius Black, after his escape from Azkaban, risks recapture in order to help Harry, thereby "fulfilling [his] duty as a godfather" (Rowling, 2000, p. 522). And Harry's parents even reach from beyond the grave to give him the advice and protection he needs to escape the clutches of Voldemort and the Death Eaters in the *Goblet of Fire*. Perhaps most important for Harry is the protection that his mother gave him just before Voldemort killed her. The scar on his forehead serves as an emblem not only of Voldemort's failure to kill him but also of his mother's love, which saved him from Voldemort's death curse. Without all this support, who knows what kind of new family Harry might have sought when he escaped the abusive environment of the Dursley household? Perhaps he might have been drawn to the evil Draco Malfoy, who initially offers his friendship to Harry (*Sorcerer's Stone*). Perhaps, like Crouch and Voldemort, he would have committed an act considerably more heinous than enlarging his detestable Aunt Marge. Instead, fortified with his absent family's love, Harry escapes the Dursley home to seek a home that embodies the qualities of the family he lost when his parents were killed.

Leaving Home to Find Home

The protective factors that a family offers its members are key to holding that family together and supporting its young people when they go off on their own. In the *Harry Potter* series, we see not only what can happen when the family breaks this covenant but also how home and family can sustain young adults trying to find their place in the world.

The scar on Harry's forehead reminds us of his mother's love; but at the same time it acts as a brand, forever marking Harry as different from the rest of the students, so that despite his growing sense of connection at Hogwarts, he remains an outsider. When Hogwarts residents are mysteriously attacked (*Chamber of Secrets*), many of the students suspect Harry, and he experiences once again the feeling of alienation that dominated his years with the Dursleys. Later, when Dumbledore draws Harry's name from the Goblet of Fire and no one believes he didn't put his name in, his sense of isolation returns: "It was lonely with dislike pouring in on him from all sides" (Rowling, 2000, p. 296). Even when he is representing Hogwarts in the Triwizard Tournament, he feels "as separate from the crowd as though they were a different species" (Rowling, 2000, p. 349). The Invisibility Cloak, which he dons to go places that have been forbidden to him, epitomizes this sense of isolation.

This idea of being an outsider in your own home appears repeatedly in both classic and contemporary young adult coming-of-age literature. In Nancy Farmer's *A Girl Named Disaster* (1996), Nhamo feels like an outsider in the home she has shared with her relatives ever since her father had run away and her mother had been killed by a leopard. At one point, she sees all her relatives gathered around the fire together. "The [women] sat comfortably together, like kernels on a mealie cob. There was no space where Nhamo might fit herself in, so she waited patiently in the doorway" (Farmer, 1996, p. 13). Similarly, in Monica Hughes's *The Keeper of the Isis Light* (1981), sixteen-year-old Olwen Pendennis has lived alone on the planet Isis all her life with a robot Guardian. But when settlers from Earth come, she learns that the Guardian has genetically altered her to keep her alive in the Isis atmosphere. The settlers are repulsed by her lizard-like skin, and she becomes an alien in her own home. In another science fiction novel, H. M. Hoover's *This Time of Darkness* (1980), one of the young protagonists is literally an Outsider, accidentally trapped in a huge underground city devoid of all nurturing connections.

For all these characters, including Harry, this sense of alienation eventually gives them the resolve to leave what had been familiar and seemingly safe, in order to find home. Harry still seeks the family that he lost when he was an infant (he even plays the position of "Seeker" on the Gryffindor Quidditch team), and he gets closer to that goal only when he leaves behind the protection of his Hogwarts family. At the same time as isolating him, his Invisibility Cloak actually brings him closer to his father: "His father's . . . this had been his father's. He let the material flow over his hands, smoother than silk, light as air" (Rowling, 1997, p. 205). And the very first time he uses the cloak, alone, he stumbles upon the Mirror of Erised and sees his dead mother and father waving and smiling at him: "Harry was looking at his family, for the first time in his life" (Rowling, 1997, p. 209). Three years later, when he has been forcibly transported hundreds of miles away (*Goblet of Fire*), his parents' images emerge from Voldemort's wand and guide him back to the safety of Hogwarts. Perhaps the most poignant moment in the series thus far is the almost mystical encounter Harry has with his father all alone way out on the edge of the lake:

> "Come on!" he muttered, staring about. "Where are you? Dad, come on—" . . .
>
> And then it hit him—he understood. He hadn't seen his father—he had seen himself. . . .
>
> Harry flung himself out from behind the bush and pulled out his wand.
>
> "EXPECTO PATRONUM!" he yelled.
>
> And out of the end of his wand burst, not a shapeless cloud of mist, but a blinding, dazzling, silver animal . . .
>
> The Patronus turned. It was cantering back toward Harry across the still surface of the water. It wasn't a horse. It wasn't a unicorn, either. It was a stag. It was shining brightly as the moon above . . . it was coming back to him. . . .
>
> It stopped on the bank. Its hooves made no mark on the soft ground as it stared at Harry with its large, silver eyes. Slowly, it bowed its antlered head. And Harry realized . . .
>
> "Prongs," he whispered.
>
> But as his trembling fingertips stretched toward the creature, it vanished.
>
> (Rowling, 1999, pp. 411–12)

By conjuring a Patronus in the animal form that his father could assume when he was alive, Harry comes tantalizingly close to achieving his quest to find his true family: As Dumbledore tells him, "Harry, in a way, you did see your father last night. . . . You found him inside yourself" (Rowling, 1999, p. 428).

Harry's solitary search for his true family is a search for his own identity; his quest for home and family is the journey we all take trying to find our place in the world, and coming-of-age literature can help young people in their quests. They can move, as Harry does, "from innocence (and ignorance) to the truth about themselves and the world" (Rochman, 1993, p. 32) only by breaking free of home and creating their own. In Rodman Philbrick's *The Last Book in the Universe* (2000), Spaz leaves what is to him familiar and relatively safe to go to his sick sister, who represents all he has ever known of love or family connection. It is a terrifying journey through alien territory, but he undertakes it out of love, and he ultimately finds hope for a new and better home. Similarly, in Cynthia Voigt's *A Solitary Blue* (1983), Jeff leaves the emotionless home he shares with his father in search of the home where he feels "wrapped in love" (Voigt, 1983, p. 40) by his mother. But when her promises prove false, he realizes what his father has provided—a safe haven from the destructive manipulation of his mother—and returns to make a better home with his father. There are no set formulas for finding home; like Harry, the characters in these and countless other books (and the young people reading them) must find their own way. Although they feel isolated and alone, both Spaz and Jeff, like Harry, find help and support along the way.

Without the protective factors that the infant Harry received from his parents, he might not have instinctively rejected Malfoy's overtures of friendship and instead connected with Hermione and Ron and their ethos of caring. He needed first to make a home in Hogwarts from which to break away, "to go the long way around, to stray and separate in the hope of finding completeness in reunion, freedom in reintegration with those left behind" (Giamatti, 1989, p. 93). The home and family that Harry finds at Hogwarts gives him the strength to stray and separate as he undertakes his ultimate quest: to find his parents and thereby find his place in the world.

Notes

1. Of course, we learn in the next *Harry Potter* book that Muggle ignorance regarding the magical world is not entirely a result of Muggle obtuseness. The magical world has established a complex bureaucracy to ensure that Muggles do not learn about the existence of witches and wizards. Like the prisoners in Plato's cave, their Muggle heads are kept pointing away from the light.

2. In addition to the importance of neighborhood and friendship, Tönnies's *Gemeinschaft* also involves "closeness of blood relationship" (Tönnies, 1887/1957, p. 48) among some adults and their children. In Hogwarts, we see occasional examples of blood connections within communities (parents and siblings belonging to the same house), but, for the most part, *Gemeinschaft* at Hogwarts is defined more by physical and intellectual proximity than by blood relationships.

References

Barrie, J. M. *Peter Pan.* 1911. New York: Henry Holt, 1987.

Boston, L. M. *The Children of Green Knowe.* 1954. New York: Harcourt Brace, 1983.

Cart, M. "Fantasy Is Flourishing." *Booklist* 97.16 (2001): 1546.

Dahl, R. *James and the Giant Peach.* 1961. New York: Puffin Books, 1988.

Farmer, N. *A Girl Named Disaster.* New York: Orchard Books, 1996.

Giamatti, A. B. *Take Time for Paradise: Americans and Their Games.* New York: Summit Books, 1989.

Gilgun, J. F. "Mapping Resilience as Process among Adults with Childhood Adversities." In *The Dynamics of Resilient Families.* Ed. H. I. McCubbin, E. A. Thompson, A. I. Thompson, and J. A. Futrell. Thousand Oaks: Sage Publications, 1999. 41–70.

Handel, G. Introduction to the first edition, 1967. In *The Psychosocial Interior of the Family.* Ed. G. Handel and G. G. Whitchurch. New York: Aldine de Gruyter, 1994. xxiii–xxx.

Hess, R. D., and G. Handel. "The Family as a Psychosocial Organization." In *The Psychosocial Interior of the Family.* Ed. G. Handel and G. G. Whitchurch. New York: Aldine de Gruyter, 1994. 3–17.

Hoover, H. M. *This Time of Darkness.* New York: Viking Press, 1980.

Hughes, M. *The Keeper of the Isis Light.* New York: Atheneum, 1981.

Leibowitz, L. *Females, Males, Families: A Biosocial Approach.* Belmont: Wadsworth Publishing, 1978.

Lewis, C. S. *The Last Battle.* 1956. London: Lions, 1988.

Nesbit, E. *The House of Arden.* 1908. London: Ernest Benn, 1958.

Noddings, N. *The Challenge to Care in Schools.* New York: Teachers College P, 1992.

Philbrick, R. *The Last Book in the Universe.* New York: Blue Sky P, 2000.

Plato. *Complete works.* Ed. J. M. Cooper. Indianapolis: Hackett Publishing, 1997.

Rochman, H. *Against Borders: Promoting Books for a Multicultural World.* Chicago: American Library Association, 1993.

Rochman, H., and D. Z. McCampbell. "Introduction." In *Leaving Home: Stories.* Ed. H. Rochman and D. Z. McCampbell. New York: HarperCollins, 1997. vii.

Rowling, J. K. (1997). *Harry Potter and the Sorcerer's Stone.* New York: Scholastic P, 1997.

———. *Harry Potter and the Chamber of Secrets.* New York: Scholastic P, 1998.

———. *Harry Potter and the Prisoner of Azkaban.* New York: Scholastic P, 1999.

———. *Harry Potter and the Goblet of Fire.* New York: Scholastic P, 2000.

Steinberg, S. R., and J. L. Kincheloe. "Privileged and Getting Away with It: The Cultural Studies of White, Middle-Class Youth." *Studies in the Literary Imagination* 31.1 (1998): 103–26.

Tönnies, F. *Community and society.* 1987. Trans. and ed. C. P. Loomis. East Lansing: Michigan State UP, 1957.

Voigt, C. *A Solitary Blue.* New York: Atheneum, 1983.

Chapter Eleven

The Seeker of Secrets: Images of Learning, Knowing, and Schooling

Charles Elster

Harry thought that none of the lessons he'd had so far had given him as much to think about as tea with Hagrid.

—J. K. Rowling, *Harry Potter and the Sorcerer's Stone*

One source of the popularity of the *Harry Potter* books is their multigenre appeal to a variety of audiences. Children and adults can read the books on various levels: as adventure, sports story, school story, fantasy story set in a parallel, magical world, heroic tale or psychological mystery (Elster 3). As heroic tales with realistic overtones, the *Harry Potter* books tell two parallel stories. On the personal plane, the books work as a bildungsroman, stories about a boy, Harry Potter, as he grows up, leaving home, going away to school, hoping to succeed and learn to be a wizard. This is the same story as that of any of the students at Hogwarts. But on the heroic plane, Harry's personal family story is central to the fate of the (wizard) world, as the evil arch-wizard Voldemort seeks to regain his power and Harry must thwart him.

Furthermore, the *Harry Potter* books add a dimension of psychological suspense to the heroic tale. From Harry's (and the reader's) perspective, many of the books are like paranoid nightmares (or like Alfred Hitchcock movies) in which nobody believes what you know to be true. Despite his heroic status, Harry is often suspected of criminal action. He is falsely accused of attacking his fellow students at Hogwarts in *Harry Potter and the Chamber of Secrets*, and of entering his name in the Triwizard Tournament in *Harry Potter and the Goblet of Fire*. In *Harry Potter and the Prisoner of Azkaban*, Harry learns that his godfather, Sirius Black, was falsely convicted of betraying Harry's parents to Voldemort and seeking Harry's destruction. The climax of each book results in Harry vindicating himself and his version of events. Thus, each book involves the discovery by Harry of hidden knowledge.

The *Harry Potter* books depict a complex world of knowledge and knowers. Knowledge is depicted as multilayered and multifunctional. In the actions of Harry Potter, learning is depicted as an active search for answers that are only tangentially related to classroom learning tasks. And the learner's (Harry's) active search for answers is often actively thwarted by adults who have their own interests. Teachers and other adults often hide knowledge from children rather than revealing it.

On the surface, the *Harry Potter* books depict a traditionally dichotomous view of learning: school learning, which is stodgy and bookish, and "real learning," which involves solving the big problems of life. But on second look, this dichotomy is less than adequate in defining the world of Harry Potter. Harry is depicted as an active seeker after knowledge, a participant in "inquiry based learning." And his school learning does contribute to the solution of the mysteries he works hard to solve. Furthermore, the world of Hogwarts School is one in which learning is more than the mastery of classroom subjects; it also involves the mastery of a complex social order of loyalty and competition, and of problematic teacher-student relationships. This complex social world also requires a kind of inquiry-based learning.

Harry is an interesting kind of hero. He is depicted as an active learner, seeking the solution to mysterious plots that threaten him and the whole world. But he is, in some ways, curiously passive. At the start of each book he begins passively, as Voldemort's dangerous and mysterious plots are aimed at him and the solution of the mysteries are thrust upon him. As each book progresses, he is forced into a more active role.

Like other heroes of children's classics, Harry operates more or less independently of adults. But again this generalization is inadequate, for he does have adult helpers, especially in the later two books: they include teachers of the Defense Against the Dark Arts classes (Remus Lupin in *Prisoner of Azkaban* and Mad Eye Moody in *Goblet of Fire*), as well as his mysterious godfather, Sirius Black, in *Prisoner of Azkaban* and *Goblet of Fire*, and, in a detached sort of way, the Hogwarts' headmaster Albus Dumbledore throughout the series. He also has child helpers, especially his bookish friend Hermione Granger. Together the two of them solve the mysteries, he by his courage and daring, she by her bookish learning. But despite the help he receives from others, Harry's unshared knowledge separates him from the group. He is essentially isolated in his special (heroic) position as the person destined to battle the evil Voldemort.

When he plays Quidditch, Harry Potter is the Seeker, the player whose role it is to catch the small, speedy Golden Snitch, which ends the Quidditch match. Throughout the novels, Harry is the Seeker after secret knowledge, knowledge of clues to Voldemort's dark plans. At the end of each book, Harry uncovers Voldemort's plot (catches the Snitch) and ends the game—until their rematch in the next volume.

Images of Knowledge: Learning for School and for Life

In the *Harry Potter* series, learning is represented in two aspects: school learning and life learning. On the one hand, learning takes place at Hogwarts, the wizard school Harry attends, through traditional teacher-directed coursework, in-class exercises, and comprehensive examinations, even though the content of the curriculum is magical arts. This school world resembles an English boarding school education, with its traditional components of competition and hierarchical relationships (between students and between teachers and students). Roald Dahl has depicted his own English boarding school upbringing in his memoir *Boy: Tales of Childhood* and other writings.

On the other hand, "life learning" takes place as Harry and his friends undertake the solution of various life-threatening mysteries. Here learning is learner-directed, with very little involvement of adults, and applied to critical, real-life problems. Learning is represented as a bold, heroic adventure, and success often involves breaking rules. Throughout the books, there is an ironic parallelism between the (trivial) world of classes and official school learning and the (crucial) secret world of knowledge needed for the quest to vanquish Voldemort. For example, at the climax of *Sorcerer's Stone*, Harry tells his friends Hermione and Ron what is most important in his life: not grades, but rather the struggle between good and evil in which his family story is bound up:

> Don't you understand? If Snape gets hold of the Stone, Voldemort's coming back! Haven't you heard what it was like when he was trying to take over? There won't be any Hogwarts to get expelled from! He'll flatten it, or turn it into a school for the Dark Arts! Losing points doesn't matter anymore, can't you see? D'you think he'll leave you and your family alone if Gryffindor wins the house cup? If I get caught before I can get to the Stone, well, I'll have to go back to the Dursleys and wait for Voldemort to find me there, it's only dying a bit later than I would have, because I'm

never going over to the Dark Side! I'm going through the trapdoor tonight and nothing you two say is going to stop me! Voldemort killed my parents, remember? (*Sorcerer's Stone*, 270)

Heroic Knowledge

From the perspective of Harry as superhero, classroom learning is often an annoying distraction from his true concerns. Readers can identify with this anti-school stance from a more realistic perspective: Harry's heroic exploits are exaggerated forms of any individual's "getting on in real life" for which traditional school learning is at best a partial and inadequate preparation.

Harry always has to juggle school work with heroic tasks. In *Goblet of Fire*, Harry juggles two extracurricular concerns for which classroom learning is merely interference: Harry is supposed to be solving the secret of the silver egg, which will prepare him for his second trial in the Triwizard Tournament, but he is really concerned with clues to Voldemort's current whereabouts and intentions:

> "You said you'd already worked out the egg clue!" said Hermione indignantly. "Keep your voice down!" said Harry crossly. "I just need to—sort of fine-tune it, all right?" He, Ron and Hermione were sitting at the very back of the Charms class with a table to themselves. They were supposed to be practicing the opposite of the Summoning Charm today—the Banishing Charm. Owing to the potential for nasty accidents when objects kept flying across the room, Professor Flitwick had given each student a stack of cushions on which to practice . . . "Just forget the egg for a minute, all right?" Harry hissed . . . "I'm trying to tell you about Snape and Moody. . . . " This class was an ideal cover for a private conversation, as everyone was having far too much fun to pay them any attention. (*Goblet of Fire*, 479–80)

Here the chaotic classroom provides a cover for the friends' sharing of information crucial to extracurricular concerns. At other times, the need for Harry to study his school subjects is a welcome distraction from his real problems: "Harry was almost glad that exams weren't far away. All the studying he had to do kept his mind off his misery" (*Sorcerer's Stone*, 245).

The *Harry Potter* books depict Harry's learning as heroic problem-solving, a matter of actively figuring out a problem. There are mysteries to be solved and these provide the impetus for "real" learning. Harry is a detective in the tradition of Phillip Marlowe and Nancy Drew, and the series is more clearly in the mystery genre than in the fantasy genre (May

4). In these books, knowledge is depicted as dualistically light and dark, good and evil. Dumbledore and Voldemort represent these polar opposites, light and dark. Harry's quest, like that of all heroes and detectives, is always to preserve the good and hinder the dark side.

Read as hero tales, the *Harry Potter* stories show a group of hero-comrades, like the Argonauts, Gilgamesh and Enkidu, or the Super League of superheroes, at work together to foil the evil Voldemort. Their combined talents are complementary: Harry's courage and aptitude, Hermione's book knowledge, and Ron's loyalty and potential. For example, when he is about to set off to retrieve the Sorcerer's Stone, Harry is joined by his two friends:

> "I'll use the invisibility cloak," said Harry. "It's just lucky I got it back."
>
> "But will it cover all three of us?" asked Ron.
>
> "All—all three of us?"
>
> "Oh, come off it. You don't think we'd let you go alone?"
>
> "Of course not," said Hermione briskly. "How do you think you'd get to the Stone without us? I'd better go and look through my books. There might be something useful . . . " (*Sorcerer's Stone,* 271)

This pattern of three or four heroic comrades is played out in Harry's father's generation, as revealed in *Prisoner of Azkaban.* Moony, Wormtail, Padfoot, and Prongs who bequeath the Marauder's Map to Harry, are in fact his father, James Potter, along with his comrade-animagi Sirius Black, Remus Lupin, and Peter Pettigrew. In Harry's heroic group, Neville Longbottom, the bullied underachiever, is sometimes included as a fourth member.

Real-World Learning

Harry's heroic quest for knowledge to foil Voldemort's dangerous plans is a heroic version of more realistic strata of "real-world" learning, in which people use their intelligence(s) to succeed in life's various spheres of experience. For example, the interpersonal (including romantic) learning involved with growing up is depicted as Harry and his friends become teenagers in *Goblet of Fire.* Here the out-of-school agenda has the more realistic aspect of teenage romantic aspirations. Harry must ask a girl to the Triwizard Banquet, and this realistic growing-up task becomes an added challenge that seems to dwarf the other fantastic and heroic ones (396). In addition, Harry learns not to trust people like the journalist Rita

Skeeter, who always misrepresents her subjects or the Triwizard Tournament judge, and Mr. Bagman, who offers to help Harry in the tournament. And Hermione teaches a valuable lesson by helping Harry and Ron to get over a breach in their friendship.

Another type of "real-life" learning depicted in the books is entrepreneurial knowledge. George and Fred Weasley, Ron's brothers, are the perennial school cut-ups who are also inventors and entrepreneurs of wizard joke products (in contrast to their brother Percy, the priggish former Head Boy and Ministry flunky).

> "What are Weasely Wizard Wheezes?" Harry asked as they climbed.
>
> Ron and Ginny both laughed, although Hermione didn't. "Mum found this stack of order forms when she was cleaning Fred and George's room," said Ron quietly. "Great long price lists for stuff they've invented. Joke stuff, you know. Fake wands and trick sweets, loads of stuff. It was brilliant, I never knew they'd been inventing all that. . . . And you know, they were planning to sell it at Hogwarts to make some money, and Mum went mad at them. Told them they weren't allowed to make any more of it, and burned all the order forms. She was furious at them anyway. They didn't get as many OWLs as she expected." OWLS were Ordinary Wizarding Levels, the examinations Hogwarts students took at the age of fifteen. (*Goblet of Fire*, 54–55)

As in other scenes, the children speak quietly. Here, knowledge involved in inventing and marketing products is placed in stark contrast with the school knowledge associated with doing well on standardized exams.

Gendered Learning

The depiction of knowledge and learning in the *Harry Potter* books is a gendered depiction, recycling the traditional contrast between girls, who are successful at book learning, and boys, who are successful at adventures. Hermione and Ron, Harry's two best friends, represent contrasting images of learning: Hermione is the overachieving book learner, and Ron the "normal boy" who does school work grudgingly and who enjoys jokes, sports, and flouting authority. Harry himself is at the same time a "normal boy" and the heroic boy able to use his knowledge to accomplish important tasks.

Hermione, while a dedicated student, is not as adventurous and bold as Harry. Whereas Harry is depicted as passionately bound up with his extracurricular quest to vanquish Voldemort, Hermione, at least at the beginning of the series, is the opposite:

Hermione, however, had more on her mind than the Sorcerer's Stone. She had started drawing up study schedules and color-coding all her notes. Harry and Ron wouldn't have minded, but she kept nagging them to do the same. (*Sorcerer's Stone*, 228)

Hermione does not take easily to flying, because it is a "natural" rather than schooled sort of learning:

Hermione Granger was almost as nervous about flying as Neville was. This was something you couldn't learn by heart out of a book—not that she hadn't tried. At breakfast on Thursday she bored them all stupid with flying tips she'd gotten out of a library book called *Quidditch Through the Ages*. (*Sorcerer's Stone*, 144)

Harry, the adventurous boy, has just the opposite experience when he first flies:

Blood was pounding in his ears. He mounted the broom and kicked hard against the ground and up, up he soared; air rushed through his hair, and his robes whipped out behind him—and in a rush of fierce joy he realized he'd found something he could do without being taught—this was easy, this was *wonderful*. He pulled his broomstick up a little to take it even higher, and heard screams and gasps of girls back on the ground and an admiring whoop from Ron. (*Sorcerer's Stone*, 148)

It is Harry who must actively use the knowledge provided by Hermione to solve the mysteries. In *Prisoner of Azkaban*, Hermione is given a Time Turner device (which allows its user to go back several hours in time) and she uses it to take two classes at once; Harry, on the other hand, uses it to save the Hippogriff's life and free the falsely accused Sirius Black. Hermione is aware of her own limitations in book learning, and so she becomes the helper for Harry's exploits.

"Me!" said Hermione. "Books! And cleverness! There are more important things— friendship and bravery—and—oh Harry—be *careful*!" (*Sorcerer's Stone*, 287)

Living and Learning in a Wizard School

The setting for the *Harry Potter* books is the Hogwarts School of Wizardry, a castle somewhere in the north of England. One school year provides the time frame for each book, beginning with Harry's first year at Hogwarts in *Sorcerer's Stone*. This depiction—and to some extent, satire— of English boarding school life could be one of its attractions. Those readers who know enough Latin and mythological references (that is, recipients of traditional classical educational traditions) will appreciate the Latin wordplay in the incantations or the meaning of the name of the werewolf instructor, Remus Lupin.

The boarding school culture depicted in the *Harry Potter* books includes traditional boarding school elements: uniforms, school supplies, bullying, and the joy of getting off campus for the privileged older students. It includes fierce competition among students and school hierarchies. Ron Weasleys's older brother Percy is the comically self-important Head Boy, a situation that both repels and attracts the nonacademically oriented Ron: when Ron looks into the Mirror of Erised, which reveals to the viewer his deepest wish, he sees himself as Head Boy (*Sorcerer's Stone*, 210–11).

The curriculum and instruction at Hogwarts School is of interest from the fantasy standpoint for readers interested in the creation of a traditional boarding school with a curriculum of magical studies.

> Harry found Ron at the back of the library, measuring his History of Magic homework. Professor Binns had asked for a three-foot-long composition on "The Medieval Assembly of European Wizards." [In keeping with the medieval atmosphere, students at Hogwarts write with quills on parchment.]
>
> "I don't believe it, I'm still eight inches short . . ." said Ron furiously, letting go of his parchment, which sprang back into a roll. "And Hermione's done four feet seven inches and her writing's *tiny*." (*Chamber of Secrets*, 147)

At Hogwarts, classes and examinations seem to be a combination of book learning and practical applications.

> They had practical exams as well. Professor Flitwick [teacher of Spells] called them one by one into his class to see if they could make a pineapple tap-dance across a desk. Professor McGonagall watched them turn a mouse into a snuffbox—points were given for how pretty the snuffbox was, but taken away if it had whiskers. Snape made them all nervous, breathing down their necks while they tried to remember how to make a Forgetfulness potion. (*Sorcerer's Stone*, 262)

It is up to the students to make the connections between what they learn in class and what their real concerns are. In *Chamber of Secrets*, Hermione interrupts the History of Magic teacher's boring lecture on "the International Worelock Convention of 1289" and cleverly gets him to tell the class about the mysterious Chamber of Secrets, which is rumored to lie somewhere in Hogwarts and which is somehow connected to the recent attacks within the School (149). Likewise, Hermione uses her knowledge of potions to concoct the Polyjuice Potion that will allow them to impersonate Slytherin students in order to learn if the wicked Draco Malfoy is involved in the attacks (159). But often descriptions of classes are mere scene-setting for the real action of solving the mysteries. The description of classes seems to become less prominent in the later books, particularly in *Prisoner of Azkaban*—the Hogwarts setting has been well-established and the adventure aspect of the books takes over.

Loyalty and Competition

The *Harry Potter* books show a competitive educational system in which the four residential houses—Gryffindor, Slytherin, Ravenclaw, and Hufflepuff—compete against each other to earn points for the annual house cup. The awarding and taking away of these points can come from both academic work and discipline-related actions by students. It provides the structure for the favoritism of teachers for students that results in bullying and taking points off. Competition is also portrayed in the Quidditch (sports) competition between the houses, and in the Triwizard Tournament between Hogwarts School and two foreign wizarding schools in *Goblet of Fire*.

This culture of team loyalty and competition is a serious business. When Harry loses points for Gryffindor, he is ostracized by his classmates:

> From being one of the most popular and admired people at the school, Harry was suddenly the most hated. Even Ravenclaws and Hufflepuffs turned on him, because everyone had been longing to see Slytherin lose the house cup. Everywhere Harry went, people pointed and didn't trouble to lower their voices as they insulted him. Slytherins, on the other hand, clapped as he walked past them, whistling and cheering, "Thanks Potter, we owe you one!" (*Sorcerer's Stone*, 244)

Sorting for Success

In the *Harry Potter* books there is a dialectic about whether accomplishment in learning is a matter of nature or nurture. On the one hand, Harry has highly developed magical abilities that he has presumably inherited, genetically, from his dead parents, who were accomplished wizards. On the other hand, Harry and his friends are the enemies of the Malfoy family and others who want to keep Mudbloods (children of nonwizard parents) out of Hogwarts.

As evidence of an inherited-trait view of aptitude, there are several images of magical sorting of students into instructional and social groups. For example, letters of invitation to Hogwarts arrive magically to those children qualified to enter (*Sorcerer's Stone*, 51). The Goblet of Fire magically selects those students qualified to enter as champions in the Triwizard Tournament (*Goblet of Fire*, 269–71). The magic wand used by a wizard or wizard student must be matched up carefully with its user to harmonize with a wizard's natural tendencies. When Harry is first given his wand, the storekeeper and wand expert remarks: "Well, I say your father favored it—it's really the wand that chooses the wizard, of course" (*Sorcerer's Stone*, 82). Harry's wand is very similar to Voldemort's, signalling a mysterious bond between the two arch-enemies.

Perhaps the most memorable sorting device in the series is the Sorting Hat, which sorts incoming students into their respective school houses:

> The last thing Harry saw before the hat dropped over his eyes was the hall full of people craning to get a good look at him. Next second he was looking at the black inside of the hat. He waited. "Hmm," said a small voice in his ear. "Difficult. Very difficult. Plenty of courage, I see. Not a bad mind either. There's talent, oh my goodness, yes—and a nice thirst to prove yourself, now that's interesting. . . . So where shall I put you?" (*Sorcerer's Stone*, 121)

Sorting into houses seems to equal recognition of certain natural traits. The Sorting Hat's song in *Goblet of Fire* makes these traits explicit:

> By Gryffindor, the bravest were
> Prized far above the rest;
> For Ravenclaw, the cleverest
> Would always be the best;
> For Hufflepuff, hard workers were
> Most worthy of admission;
> And power-hungry Slytherin
> Loved those of great ambition. (177)

Although Harry is sorted into Gryffindor (lion), proving his courage, there are hints that he could also belong in Slytherin (serpent), cunning, which is the house of Voldemort (their wands are very similar too). Further books in the series will very likely reveal more about Harry's connection to Voldemort and the house of Slytherin.

Teachers and Students

The *Harry Potter* books show two sorts of teacher-student relationship. On the one hand, the institutional relationship is one in which teachers instruct students in a preset curriculum, and where teachers reward and punish students, sometimes fairly, often unfairly. Students are rewarded and punished by the giving and taking of points for their respective houses, so that academic learning (and acceptable behavior) are regulated inside and outside the classroom through a system of competition between houses.

> Professor Sprout was standing behind a trestle bench in the center of the greenhouse. . . . "We'll be repotting Mandrakes today. Now, who can tell me the properties of the Mandrake?"
>
> To nobody's surprise, Hermione's hand was first into the air.
>
> "Mandrake, or Mandragora, is a powerful restorative," said Hermione, sounding as usual as though she had swallowed the textbook. "It is used to return people who have been transfigured or cursed to their original state."
>
> "Excellent. Ten points to Gryffindor," said Professor Sprout. (*Chamber of Secrets*, 91–92)

Punishment for infractions of school rules involves not only points taken away from the culprit's house but also more personal punishments, such as detentions and unpleasant tasks. This traditional student-teacher relationship is parodied most humorously in the figure of Filch, the caretaker who is empowered to punish students who dirty the school or are caught in areas they are not supposed to be in:

> "Mess and muck everywhere! I've had enough of it, I tell you! Follow me, Potter!"
>
> So Harry . . . followed Filch back downstairs, doubling the number of muddy footprints on the floor.
>
> Harry had never been inside Filch's office before; it was a place most students avoided. The room was dingy and windowless, lit by a single oil lamp dangling from the low ceiling. A faint smell of fried fish lingered about the place. Wooden filing cabinets stood around the walls; from their labels, Harry could see that they contained details of every pupil Filch had ever punished. Fred and George Weasley had an entire drawer to themselves. A highly polished collection of chains and manacles hung on the wall behind Filch's desk. It was common knowledge that he was always

begging Dumbledore to let him suspend students by their ankles from the ceiling. (*Chamber of Secrets*, 125)

On the other hand, Harry has mentoring relationships with at least five adults: the gamekeeper Hagrid, his godfather Sirius Black, two of the Defense Against the Dark Arts teachers, Lupin and Mad Eye Moody, and the school director Albus Dumbledore. Lupin, unlike other teachers, calls the students by their first names (*Prisoner of Azkaban*, 135); he invites students to his office (*Prisoner of Azkaban*, 153); and he gives Harry private tutoring in resisting the dementors (*Prisoner of Azkaban*, 188, 256 ff). Mad Eye Moody invites Neville, the most persecuted of the students, into his office and steers him toward books on herbology (*Goblet of Fire*, 219–21). One could imagine that a similar hidden mentoring network exists for Harry's arch-enemy, Draco Malfoy, for Hermione, or for other students. These unusual mentoring relationships are highlighted against the norm of formal, hierarchical teacher-student relationships.

Adults are depicted as routinely hiding knowledge from children. This situation begins with the Dursleys hiding Harry's story from him until he discovers who he is on his twelfth birthday. Later on, adults in the wizarding world hide knowledge from him. For example, in *Sorcerer's Stone*, Hagrid tries to deflect Harry's suspicion that Professor Snape is involved in Voldemort's plan to do away with Harry and steal the Sorcerer's Stone:

> "Now, don't ask me anymore," said Hagrid gruffly. "That's top secret, that is."
>
> "But Snape's trying to steal it."
>
> "Rubbish," said Hagrid again. "Snape's a Hogwarts teacher, he'd do nothin' of the sort."
>
> "So why'd he try and kill Harry?" cried Hermione. . . .
>
> "I'm telling yeh, yer wrong," said Hagrid hotly. "I don't know why Harry's broom acted like that, but Snape wound' try and kill a student! Now, listen to me, all three of yeh—yer meddlin' in things that don't concern yeh. It's dangerous. You forget that dog, an' you forget what its guardin', that's between Professor Dumbledore an' Nicolas Flamel—"
>
> "Aha!" said Harry, "so there's someone called Nicholas Flamel involved, is there?"
>
> Hagrid looked furious with himself. (*Sorcerer's Stone*, 192–93)

Other adults beside Hagrid seem to want to "protect" Harry from knowing the awful truth of Voldemort's intentions toward him. In

Prisoner of Azkaban, Harry overhears Ron's parents discussing the danger he is in:

> "makes no sense not to tell him," Mr. Weasley was saying heatedly. "Harry's got a right to know. I've tried to tell Fudge, but he insists on treating Harry like a child. He's thirteen years old and—"
>
> "Arthur the truth would terrify him!" said Mrs. Weasley shrilly. "Do you really want to send Harry back to school with that hanging over him? For heaven's sake, he's happy not knowing!" (65)

A few adults "break the rule" of silence and do share knowledge with Harry: In *Goblet of Fire*, Hagrid shows him the dragons that he will need to face in the Triwizard Tournament, and Mad Eye Moody also assists him in meeting the Triwizard challenges. In *Prisoner of Azkaban*, Professor Lupin trains him to deflect the dementors. In fact, Lupin is the exceptional adult who declaims, at the climax of *Prisoner of Azkaban*, that "they [the students] have a right to know everything!" (350). As a dark-comic aside, the divinations teacher Professor Trelawny predicts Harry's death daily, but everyone agrees that her predictions are bogus (*Prisoner of Azkaban*, 106–9).

Professor Dumbledore, the headmaster of Hogwarts School and the epitome of the powerful, good wizard, is an ambiguous figure in the *Harry Potter* books. Although he is reputed to be very powerful (Voldemort will not attack him or the school), his approach to protection seems laissez-faire or devious. He exists as the standoffish God who seems to have a plan for good people to prove they can vanquish evil. He rarely helps directly, although he occasionally appears in order to provide information, as when Harry discovers the Mirror of Erised. Dumbledore shares the secret knowledge that Harry seeks, but he does nothing to assist Harry.

> Nobody at Hogwarts now knew the truth of what had happened the night that Sirius, Buckbeak, and Pettigrew had vanished except Harry, Ron, Hermione and Professor Dumbledore. As the end of term approached, Harry heard many different theories about what had really happened, but none of them came close to the truth. (*Prisoner of Azkaban*, 428)

Harry is Adam to Dumbledore's God. Like Adam (and Prometheus) he is destined to steal (rather than be given) essential knowledge. And he avoids going to talk to Dumbledore when he suspects that Voldemort and his helpers are near.

The Seeker of Secret Knowledge

As I said earlier, Harry Potter's quest for knowledge is a goal-oriented quest. His goal is to solve mysteries and thereby foil the plans of the evil Voldemort. Adults do not often help—in fact, they often interfere with solving the mystery. For Harry, life knowledge and book knowledge come together: he puts to use school knowledge, nonschool knowledge, and magical devices to advance the cause of good magic. Harry must uncover and connect clues: for example, Harry learns that Hagrid may have brought the Sorcerer's Stone from Gringotts Bank to Hogwarts School (*Sorcerer's Stone*, 142). Harry and Hermione use the library's "restricted books" section to uncover clues about Nicholas Flamel (*Sorcerer's Stone*, 197) and about the Triwizard Tournaments challenges (*Goblet of Fire*, 485). Harry must also use the clues to act boldly when righting wrongs: the Time Turner that Hermione used to increase her studying time becomes helpful in the adventure of freeing the Hippogriff and Sirius Black (*Prisoner of Azkaban*, 395). In *Goblet of Fire*, goal-oriented learning is more formalized in the Triwizard Tournament, in which the competing champions must choose and use magical skills, such as antidragon spells and underwater spells, to overcome three challenges (358).

Of all his classes, the Defense Against the Dark Arts classes help Harry the most in his heroic quest. In *Prisoner of Azkaban*, Remus Lupin's lesson in confronting one's own fears (in the form of the Boggart) is a true life-learning lesson) (132–40), and the lessons about animagi, magicians who can transform themselves into animals, prove especially important for Harry's education (108). In *Goblet of Fire*, Mad Eye Moody gives lessons on resisting the most deadly curses, including the one that killed Harry's parents.

Important knowledge, knowledge connected to the solution of mysteries and the accomplishment of the evil-foiling quest, is depicted in the *Harry Potter* books as hidden knowledge. It is the hero's role to actively seek, uncover, and use secret knowledge despite interferences.

Harry's world is a world of secrets within a world of secrets. The setting for Harry's quest is a secret world of wizards that is hidden from Muggles (nonwizards), and wizards are capable of making Muggles forget what they've seen (memory modification spells) if they do observe wizarding activities. An important function of the Ministry of Magic, in which Ron Weasley's father works, is to hide the world of magic from the

Muggles, just as, in George Orwell's dystopic novel *1984*, it is the function of the Ministry of Truth to alter official records in order to manipulate the "reality" of the populace.

> But what does a Ministry of Magic *do*? Well, their main job is to keep it from the Muggles that there's still witches an' wizards up an' down the country. (*Sorcerer's Stone*, 65)

Within the wizarding world, there are restrictions on the use of magic, especially if it draws attention from the Muggle world (*Prisoner of Azkaban*, 26).

Within this secret world of wizarding, Harry's quests involve the discovery of knowledge that is hidden even within the wizarding world. How did the infant Harry survive Voldemort's fatal attack on his parents. What power does Harry possess that can foil Voldemort? What is the nature of the relationship between Harry and Voldemort? (They can both speak to snakes, they use very similar wands.) Harry begins the series not even knowing his own story:

> "CAR CRASH!" roared Hagrid, jumping up so angrily that the Dursleys scuttled back to their corner. "How could a car crash kill Lily an' James Potter? It's an outrage! A scandal! Harry Potter not knowin' his own story when every kid in our world knows his name!" (*Sorcerer's Stone*, 53)

Harry's true education is his discovery of his own story.

Each of the *Harry Potter* books involves a quest in which Harry and his friends must uncover secret knowledge. And in each of the books, Harry uncovers knowledge that he is afraid to share with others. In *Chamber of Secrets*, he hears a frightening, bodiless voice, which turns out to be the voice of a serpent, but he does not alert Dumbledore and others in authority, even when his reticence puts him in jeopardy of false accusations:

> "But why not join the feast afterward?" said Snape, his black eyes glittering in the candlelight. "Why go up to that corridor?"
>
> Ron and Hermione looked at Harry.
>
> "Because—because—" Harry said, his heart thumping very fast; something told him it would sound very far-fetched if he told them he had been led there by a bodiless voice no one but he could hear, "because we were tired and wanted to go to bed," he said. (*Chamber of Secrets*, 145)

When Harry encounters the huge dog (called the Grim) that portends evil in *Prisoner of Azkaban*, he does not tell his closest friends "because he knew Ron would panic and Hermione would scoff" (184). In *Goblet of Fire*, his scar burns when Voldemort is near, but he does not tell anyone until he finally gains Sirius Black as a confidant.

Harry is reluctant to reveal his knowledge for fear of not being believed. In *Chamber of Secrets*, he is made to look guilty of attacks on students, and of illegally entering the Triwizard championship (*Goblet of Fire*, 287). The books contain many images of knowledge that is revealed but not believed: the unfounded accusations against Harry; the Sneakascope, which wails whenever someone untrustworthy is near (but which is never believed) (*Prisoner of Azkaban* 77); Professor Trelawny's bogus predictions. Likewise, Mad Eye Moody, the Defense Against the Dark Arts instructor and famous captor of dark wizards, has superhuman powers of sight, able to see through an Invisibility Cloak. But, Cassandra-like, he is also not believed by many of the characters.

In addition to keeping his own secrets, Harry succeeds in his quest for knowledge by overhearing crucial conversations, sometimes with the help of the Invisibility Cloak, sometimes without. Harry overhears Ron's parents talking about the escape of Sirius Black from Azkaban Prison and the danger to Harry; Harry and his friends overhear a crucial conversation in the Three Broomsticks (*Prisoner of Azkaban*, 202 ff).

In his quest for secret knowledge, Harry learns that rule bending and cheating are expected. For example, in the Triwizard Tournament competition described in *Goblet of Fire*, the champions are given help from each other, from interested adults, and from nonhuman helpers, despite the fact that they are supposed to confront the challenges without help. Harry learns in *Prisoner of Azkaban* that his own father was also a "troublemaker," a rulebender and an unregistered animagus. Breaking rules is depicted as part of the adventurous hero's means of acquiring and using knowledge.

Harry makes use of several magical objects that allow him privileged knowledge: the Invisibility Cloak, which he uses to wander the Hogwarts corridors undetected and to eavesdrop on crucial conversations; the Marauder's Map, which shows the hidden passages and the current whereabouts of everyone in Hogwarts. Both the Invisibility Cloak and the Marauder's Map are magical tools that Harry inherits from his adventuresome, rule-bending father.

Conclusions

In his farewell speech at the annual end-of-year banquet, Professor Dumbledore presents a traditional image of school learning—learning as a passive process, the head filled with knowledge.

> "Another year gone!" Dumbledore said cheerfully. "And I must trouble you with an old man's wheezing waffle before we sink our teeth into our delicious feast. What a year it has been! Hopefully your heads are all a little fuller than they were . . . you have the whole summer ahead to get them nice and empty before next year starts. . . ." (*Sorcerer's Stone*, 304)

But we know from Dumbledore's character that he may be speaking with an ironic wink, knowing well that a more active form of learning and a darker form of knowledge lies beneath the obvious surface.

The *Harry Potter* books depict complex worlds of knowledge: unofficial, secret knowledge behind the official school curriculum; active, goal-oriented inquiry outside of traditional book learning and exams; a world of moral issues, of good versus evil behind the morally neutral world of school knowledge.

The books depict a world in which the child-hero makes his quest alone, often despite the interference of adults and their deliberate hiding of answers. And yet the child seeker is sometimes lucky to have helpers—peers, exceptional adults, magical creatures. The seeker of the knowledge that matters must do so in between work on school learning tasks. Yet he needs to know when school knowledge can be useful in his heroic quest.

Harry is essentially alone in his knowledge of Voldemort's plots. His story is in the tradition of other myths of unshared knowledge: Jonah, the biblical prophet who must prophesy the destruction of Ninevah; Cassandra, the Greek seer who foresees the future but is not believed by those who hear her. Like Jonah, Harry is a passive prophet who is chosen for his task and to some extent resists it. Like Cassandra, he must contend with a world that often does not believe him. In the same way Jonas, the hero of Lois Lowry's novel *The Giver*, is separated from the group as he becomes the Receiver of the community's painful past experiences.

In *The Giver*, Jonas is the Receiver of wisdom, of the accumulated experiences of the community. Although separated by his knowledge, Jonas is an official representative of the community. In contrast, Harry Potter, the Seeker, has no official mandate to pursue his quest for knowledge, and he must pursue his quest despite the interference and mistrust of those around him. His quest is essentially separate from the learning of those around him, just as in the game of Quidditch he is seeking a different ball from the one the other players are seeking—it is the object of his quest alone, but an object that, if found, is crucial to his team's ability to win the game.

The *Harry Potter* books contain a tension between the duality of Harry's existence—the Muggle world and the magical world, school learning and life learning, solitary seeking and the life of the community —and the transcending of this duality—the help Harry receives from friends and mentors, the connections between school learning and life learning, and between Harry's individual quest and the life of the community. This tension between duality and the transcendence of duality creates a complex representation of knowledge and learning, which contributes to the pleasures experienced by readers of the series.

References

Dahl, Roald. *Boy: Tales of Childhood*. London: Puffin, 1984.

Elster, Charles. "From the Editor: The Year of Harry Potter." *TELLing Stories* 4 (2000): 1, 3.

Lowry, Lois. *The Giver*. Boston: Houghton Mifflin, 1993.

May, Jill. "Harry Potter and All Those Other Fantasy Characters." *TELLing Stories* 4.2 (2000): 3–5.

Orwell, George. *1984*. New York: New American Library, 1951.

Rowling, J. K. *Harry Potter and the Sorcerer's Stone*. New York: Scholastic P, 1997.

———. *Harry Potter and the Chamber of Secrets*. New York: Scholastic P, 1998.

———. *Harry Potter and the Prisoner of Azkaban*. New York: Scholastic P, 1999.

———. *Harry Potter and the Goblet of Fire*. New York: Scholastic P, 2000.

Chapter Twelve

Blue Wizards and Pink Witches: Representations of Gender Identity and Power

Elizabeth E. Heilman

During the years of my late childhood and early adolescence, I yearned to be lost in literary worlds where I could experience more poignancy and power than my own life provided. I was especially attracted to reflective characters who faced challenges. I lived the experiences of Ponyboy in *The Outsiders* and Sam Gribley in *My Side of the Mountain* so acutely that they almost became my own. The fact that I was a girl and these characters were boys created a thin barrier against my fully appropriating the lessons and experience of the texts. At that age, I was frustrated with my femaleness because almost all of the intriguing and powerful characters I read about were males. I related more to Heathcliff than to Catherine in *Wuthering Heights*. I remember picking up one title after another in the library of my junior high school, looking for a book with a good strong girl. It was a rainy Friday afternoon and I'd completed another dreary week as a nearly invisible girl in a humorless school with highly attenuated social positioning and fierce academic competition. I went home with a book about a nerdy girl who gets transformed when a popular boy asks her out. This idea became a vehicle for some of my longings and dissatisfactions. But it wasn't at all what I'd been looking for.

I now have a son who is a thirsty and reflective reader as I was at his age. He seeks entertainment, but he also reads to know himself and the world on a more profound level. When I select books for him I think about the contributions they will make to his existential and cultural understanding. At first, I resisted the *Harry Potter* books simply because of the hype surrounding them. But in the spring of 2000, I bought the first book in the series, *Harry Potter and the Sorcerer's Stone* (Rowling, 1997). My son, Alex, then an eleven-year-old sixth grader, was home with a case of the flu when we began reading the book together. We would hold the book open so that we could both see the pages, and read silently together. On the first day, when I returned to him and the book after dinner, he was several chapters ahead of me. Later, when he was taking a shower, I got a hold of the book, and I began to catch up. We were transfixed.

Reading books in this way has always given me a chance to talk with my son about all sorts of ideas. For example, we have been alert to sexism in many of the texts we have shared. The *Box Car Children* series, with older brother Henry having the lion's share of adventures, while the younger sisters cook and clean, is typical of the kind of text that irritates both of us. We've noticed that the *Winnie the Pooh* books and movies, which Alex's little sisters like are dominated by male characters. Pooh, Tigger, Christopher Robin, Owl, Piglet, and Eeyore are all male. The only female is Kanga, the mother of the little boy animal, Roo. Alex's sister, MaryRose, however, insists that Roo and Piglet are girls, which is a reminder that text can be interpreted against the grain and that sexism can be struggled against through acts of interpretation.

While reading the first *Harry Potter* book, I told Alex that I really hated the way Hermione cowered in fear when faced with the troll, and that I was disappointed that she had to be rescued by the boys. While Ron and Harry successfully face a horrible twelve-foot-tall troll (Rowling, 1997, pp. 174–76), Hermione couldn't move. She was "flat against the wall in terror" (p. 175), while Harry and Ron both respond bravely and effectively. Hermione had been portrayed as a girl who knew a lot of spells, but when she needed to put that knowledge to use, she failed.

> Hermione had sunk to the floor in fright; Ron pulled out his own wand—not knowing what he was going to do. He heard himself cry out the first spell that came into his head: *Wingardium Leviosa!* The club flew suddenly our of the troll's hand. . . . (Rowling, 1998, p.176)

As we read, I was disappointed by scenes like this and by the absence of powerful females. When I was twelve and thirteen, it was very important to me to find books with strong girls. As my son and I read through all four books, it was clear to us that the *Harry Potter* books feature females in secondary positions of power and authority and replicate some of the most demeaning, yet familiar, cultural stereotypes for both males and females. Themes related to power and gender seemed to conform to a rigid set of patterns, which reflect capitalist and patriarchal gender regimes.

Is this important, since the books are fun to read and have a lot to recommend them? I think so. Gender representations, like other forms of cultural ideology, both obscure and justify oppressive practices even though interpretations of the meaning of gender can be dynamic and multiple (Connell, 1987, 1991, 1993, 1995; Messner, 1997; Pyke, 1996). Gender representations are personal ways to understand ourselves, others, and society but they are also impersonal reflections of macrolevel power relations (Bourdieu, 1977; Chafetz, 1990; Connell, 1996; Foucault 1980; Lipman-Blumen, 1984). Though both feminist and poststructuralist theories tell us that text can be read from multiple, contradictory, and even transgressive positions, it is still important for criticism to reveal dominant and hegemonic conventions.

In order to reveal dominant conventions, feminist theories of children's literature have pursued multiple levels of analysis, beginning with female representation in literature. How much narrative space is devoted to males? Like *Winnie the Pooh*, the *Harry Potter* books are dominated by male characters. Among the students named, there are twenty-nine girls and thirty-five boys. Yet, the more important characters are predominantly male. The main characters are two boys, Harry Potter and Ron Weasley, and a girl, Hermione Granger. The characters that are frightening, evil, or suspected of evil, are overwhelmingly male. These include Voldemort, Wormtail (Peter Pettigrew), and Severus Snape. Those described as Death Eaters, the evil wizards who followed Voldemort, include a married couple, Mr. and Mrs. Le Strange, and sixteen males. Within the Ministry of Magic, the seat of power, all of the ministers are male except for Bertha Jorkins, who is described as gossipy and absentminded. Most of the irritating (but not evil) grown-ups are female. These include Mrs. Figg, Professor Trelawney, and Rita Skeeter, and Aunt Petunia, who has twice the neck of the usual person, which comes in handy when she is craning her neck over fences for gossip.

Males are represented more often, but they are also depicted as wiser, braver, more powerful, and more fun than females. It is not simply who is present, but, also, how characters are portrayed and what they do that matters. Most of the girls are depicted as anti-intellectual and most keenly interested in the low-status magic of Divination Class. At the height of action, females are not typically very involved, and they are fearful and emotional. The relative powerlessness of females is most evident in the portrayal of the main character, Hermione. During the action-filled denouement of the first book (Rowling, 1997, chap. 16), Harry, Ron, and

Hermione are working together toward the Sorcerer's Stone. Hermione shrieks, screams, and speaks "nervously," reactions the boys do not have. Though Hermione's knowledge helps them along, Harry sends her back. She agrees with this decision, throws her arms around Harry, and says, "Harry—you're a great wizard you know." He says, "I'm not as good as you." And she responds, "Books and cleverness! There are more important things—friendship and bravery and—oh Harry be careful!" (p. 287). Thus, Harry's ability to make friends and be brave establishes him as the true great one.

This type of scenario occurs repeatedly. Sometimes females begin an action scene as a token presence, but something always happens to them. Hermione is primarily an enabler of Harry's and Ron's adventures, rather than an adventurer in her own right. In the middle of *Harry Potter and the Chamber of Secrets* (Rowling, 1998), she is the one who makes the important Polyjuice Potion, which works fine for Harry and Ron, leading them into further adventures, but it goes awry when Hermione uses it on herself. She accidentally turns herself into a cat, which causes her to sob and pull her robes over her head. She is hospitalized for weeks. In another plot twist, she is later immobilized by being turned into a "petrified person" yet, in her immobilized condition, she provides crucial information, which Ron "tugs and twists" out of her hand. Hermione's knowledge is important, but it is primarily used for Harry's adventures, not her own. In the fourth book, she teaches Harry how to summon his broom, which helps him triumph in the Triwizard Tournaments and escape Voldemort, but Hermione, of course, does not compete or face Voldemort herself. Similarly, Fleur, a female is "allowed" to be one of four students competing in the Triwizard Tournament, but she ends up last. During the second task, she gets tangled up in weed and cannot save her own sister. Harry has to save the sister.

In each action scene in each book, these characterizations are repeated. Hermione speaks in a "terrified voice" (Rowling, 1998, p. 336) or a petrified whisper (p. 339). Harry and Ron are never described in this way. Furthermore, though Hermione's knowledge is sometimes useful, it is Harry's "stupid" bravery that really saves the day. It is important that both Harry and Ron have knowledge when they need it, but they are not bookish like Hermione. Research on boys' school culture suggests that bookishness and academic achievement are considered feminine (Epstein, 1998; Mac an Ghaill, 1994; Paetcher, 1998). When Harry attacks the troll and rescues Hermione in *Sorcerer's Stone*, it is described as "both very brave and very stupid" (p. 176). In *Harry Potter and the Prisoner of Azkaban* (Rowling, 1999), in a scuffle with a suspected evil doer, Rowling narrates, "Perhaps it was the shock of Harry doing something so stupid, but Black didn't raise the wands in time" (p. 340). In this passage, Hermione is not helpless. She kicks Sirius Black. Yet, when females are given token power, their inequality is reinforced, their status is not enhanced. The kick is a minor effort and Black turns out to be a good guy, not a serious opponent.

Among the adults, Professor McGonagall seems to mirror Hermione as a smart female of clearly secondary status. Like Hermione, she is book smart, but not wise, powerful, or brave. Like Hermione, she is a stickler for rules and is often described as having her arms full of books and spilling them (Rowling, 1997, p. 267; Rowling, 2000, p. 205). Her characterization is reinforced by her physical description. Her hair is worn in a bun and she has beady eyes and square glasses. McGonagall's secondary status is also evident in the nature of her interactions with students. Unlike Headmaster Dumbledore, students can trick her. Ron and Harry successfully lie to her, for example, at the end of Book II. They told Professor McGonagall that they were on their way to visit Hermione in her sick bed, when, in fact, they were scheming to get into the Chamber of Secrets. It would be hard to imagine Dumbledore being fooled by these two boys. It also would be inconceivable to imagine Dumbledore responding emotionally as McGonagall did, with "a tear glistening in her beady eye" (p. 288). She is sentimental and lacks discernment.

McGonagall is also something of a mother figure, concerned that students get enough sleep and stay well. For example, "The Gryffindor party ended only when Professor McGonagall turned up in her dressing gown and hair net at one in the morning to insist that they all go to bed" (Rowling, 1999, p. 265). Professor McGonagall also makes motherly inquiries of Potter: "Are you sure you feel all right Potter?" (Rowling, 1998, p. 90). Even the female students are depicted as motherly and more gentle. Boys are told to back away from unicorns. "They prefer a woman's touch" (Rowling, 2000, p. 436). This depiction is consistent with research on the portrayal of women in children's literature. For example, Barnett (1986) found females in children's storybooks to be comforting, consoling, and providing of emotional support, whereas the males were more likely to be represented obtaining a goal or overcoming an obstacle. Tetenbaum and Pearson (1989) also found that female storybook characters were depicted as more caring and concerned about relationships than were males.

McGonagall's secondary status is evident not just in her "soft" relations with students but also in her relations with peers. She is effectively silenced by men when offering her opinion about what to do next at the dramatic climax of *Harry Potter and the Goblet of Fire* (Rowling, 2000). She is chastised by Dumbledore, who calls her by her first name: "Why are you disturbing these people? Minerva, I am surprised at you" (p. 703). We watch as Professor McGonagall's voice is drowned by Fudge's and see that Dumbledore, by contrast, can assert power: "'Listen to me, Cornelius,' said Dumbledore, taking a step toward Fudge, and once again, he seemed to radiate that indefinable sense of power"(pp. 705–6). At the conclusion of this passage, Professor McGonagall's ideas go unheeded and she is dismissed on an errand. She "nodded and left without a word." The relative powerlessness of the two most masterful women only serves to underscore female weakness.

The girls on the Quidditch team provide another example of how token inclusion reinforces inequality. Though the girls often score, scoring rarely wins the game. It is ultimately unimportant. Catching the snitch wins the game and the seekers that do this are male. In order to find the Snitch, the one female seeker Cho Chang trails Harry instead of going after it for herself (Rowling, 1999, p. 261). The girls are not involved in the most complex moments of play and never play dirty or get badly hurt. Feminist researchers in physical education (Flintoff, 1994; Hasbrook, 1999; Scraton, 1990) have observed that male students and teachers consider competitive sports to be a "naturally male" activity. This concept of naturally competitive males is reinforced by the fact that the captains are male, and their hard, rugged names, Flint and Wood, emphasize their masculinity. Even as sports team members, the girls exhibit girlish behavior by giggling at the possibility of playing with handsome new captain and seeker, Cedric Diggory. "He's that tall good looking one, isn't he?" asked Angelina. "Strong and silent," said Katie and they started to giggle again. By contrast, the boys concentrate on the implications of new leadership in the opposing team. "We mustn't relax! We must keep our focus!" shouts Wood, his eyes bulging. (Rowling, 1999, p. 169)

Quidditch is not the only context for giggling. The second two books are littered with references to giggling girls, although there is not a single reference to giggling boys. For example, "Mrs. Weasley was telling

Hermione and Ginny about a love potion she had made as a young girl. All three of them were rather giggly" (Rowling, 1999, p. 70); "Groups of giggling girls often turned up to spy on Krum" (Rowling, 2000, p. 317); "Girls giggling around Cho" (Rowling, 2000, p. 396); "Parvati will you go to the ball with me? Parvati went into a fit of giggles" (Rowling, 2000, p. 401). The females are emotional and cry readily throughout all four books. In *Sorcerer's Stone*, Hermione overhears Ron saying that she has no friends and soon after "Harry and Ron overheard Parvati Patil telling her friend Lavender that Hermione was crying in the girls' bathroom and wanted to be left alone" (Rowling, 1997, p. 172). This demonstrates both the portrayal of girls as gossipy and the portrayal of Hermione as emotional and vulnerable. At the end of the first book, Hermione is publicly recognized for "the cool use of logic in the face of fire," and she buries her face in her arms. "Harry strongly suspected she had burst into tears" (Rowling, 1997, p. 305). Lavender Brown cries when her pet rabbit, Binky, is killed by a fox (Rowling, 1999, p. 148). Pansy Parkinson is in tears after Malfoy was "attacked" by a Hippogriff (Rowling, 1999, p. 118). Sometimes female crying is described more subtly. McGonagall, regretting her treatment of Pettigrew, "sounded as though she had a sudden head cold" (Rowling, 1999, p. 207). In another example, "Mrs. Weasley kissed all of her children, then Hermione, and finally Harry. 'Do take care, won't you Harry,' she said as she straightened up, her eyes oddly bright" (Rowling, 1999, p. 72). Yet males rarely touch or cry. Acceptable male tears occur when Dumbledore has an aesthetic response to music (Rowling, 1997, p. 128) or when Wood "sobbed unrestrainedly" after winning the Quidditch game (Rowling, 1999, p. 312). Even death is an occasion for female, but not male emotional outburst. At Cedric's death it was only girls who "were screaming, sobbing hysterically" (Rowling, 2000, p. 672).

Though they are portrayed as giggly, emotional, gossipy, and anti-intellectual, many of the girls are very hazy characters. Certain traits do not seem to be authoritatively owned by any one female character, but, instead, are presented in groups. Alicia Spinnet, Angelina Johnson, and Katie Bell are typically mentioned en masse and give identical responses to situations. It seems that Rowling was using her "cut and paste" function. When girls are mentioned individually, they are often not distinct. In *Chamber of Secrets*, "Fourth year Alicia Spinnet . . . seemed to be nodding off against the wall behind her. Her fellow chasers, Katie Bell and Angelina Johnson, were yawning side by side opposite" (pp. 107–8). In

Prisoner of Azkaban, "Wood pointed at Alicia Spinnet, Angelina Johnson, Katie Bell" (p. 144). "Angelina, Alicia and Katie had come over too" (p. 110). Later, "Angelina, Alicia and Katie suddenly giggled" (p. 169) when they found out Cedric Diggory was to be the new seeker for Hufflepuff. It is not until *Goblet of Fire* that we find out Angelina is "a tall black girl" (p. 261). This late detail reads as a diversity afterthought. Other grouped female sets are the Parvati Patil, Padma Patil, and Lavendar Brown group and the Pansy Parkinson and Millicent Bulstrode set. This repeated grouping reinforces a tendency for readers to interpret females as types rather than as individuals. It also reinforces the idea of the sociological construct of the communal and friendly girl compared to the individual and competitive boy. Chodorow (1978), for example, believes that girls retain pre-oedipal attachments to their mothers and "come to define and experience themselves as continuous with others" (p. 169).

The inferior position of females is further reinforced through characterizations that highlight their insecurities and self-hatred, especially as it relates to their looks and bodies. The "Fat Lady" in the portrait at the entrance of Gryffindor Hall is an example of this. She has no personal name and is never called anything but the fat lady or a very fat woman. Her size and gender define her. She is characterized as lazy, inattentive, and gossipy, and more concerned about her appearance than her work. After her portrait (herself) is slashed, a male ghost reports:

> "Ashamed your headship sir. Doesn't want to be seen. She's a horrible mess. Saw her running through the landscape on the fourth floor, sir, saw her dodging between the trees. Crying something dreadful," he said happily. (Rowling, 1999, p. 161)

Strong negative body image messages are conveyed through the main character, Hermione. It is significant that the two "bright" females are unattractive and unsexy. Professor McGonagall is a severe-looking, tall woman who has black hair worn in a tight bun, and who wears square spectacles. Hermione is introduced in *Sorcerer's Stone* as having "a bossy sort of voice, lots of bushy brown hair, and rather large front teeth" (p. 105). In *Goblet of Fire,* when Rita Skeeter reports that Hermione is "stunningly pretty," Hermione is ridiculed: "'Stunningly pretty? Her?' Pansy Parkinson had shrieked the first time she had come face to face with Hermione after Rita's flattering newspaper article had appeared. 'What was she judging against—a chipmunk?'" (p. 316). Hermione is only presented as the attractive date of Viktor Crum after she has a form of plastic surgery. She lets her teeth remain shorter after a corrective spell (p. 405). She is transformed like Cinderella and, like many tomboys in teen novels, into a "princess." She becomes physically acceptable.

> But she didn't look like Hermione at all. She had done something with her hair; it was no longer bushy but sleek and shiny, and twisted up into an elegant knot at the back of her head. She was wearing robes made of a floaty periwinkle blue material, and she was holding herself differently somehow . . . the reduction in the size of her front teeth was more noticeable than ever. (p. 414)

The message to girls is: get a makeover. You are not okay. It is disturbing that the females that are most physically beautiful—the Veelas—are not even human. They are portrayed as male fantasy sex objects able to seduce, beguile, and confuse males. Yet, all females are influenced by superhuman standards of beauty. Only some girls who conform to a certain rigid standard of beauty can have a date. Yet, Ron and Harry, not described as good looking themselves, get dance dates with "the two best looking girls in the year" (Rowling, 2000, p. 411).

This is a dangerous and yet common message. Many females dislike their natural appearance and purchase a variety of products and perform a range of beauty regimens that can be ridiculous, painful, and even life threatening (Fallon, 1990). Women who want aesthetic cosmetic surgery have particularly low self-esteem (Hueston, Dennerstein, & Gotts, 1985). Research also indicates that many adolescent girls value their looks more than their intelligence and schoolwork (Tiggerman & Gardiner, 2000). It is particularly unfortunate that Hermione, a good student, changes her teeth to become more good looking.

Hermione is not the only female student worried about looks. Eloise Midgen tried to charm away acne and ended up taking off her nose. Moaning Myrtle, a ghost, was an ugly, outcast, pimple-afflicted girl who wouldn't have died had she not been hiding out because, as she explains, "Olive Hornby was teasing me about my glasses" (*Chamber of Secrets*, p. 299). Research shows that teenagers with acne suffer emotionally and are at higher risk of "psychological disorder" (Papadopoulos, Walker, Aitken, & Bor, 2000). Moaning Myrtle is viciously treated. Looks clearly matter. This portrayal of females, which highlights looks and reinforces low self-esteem, is politically and economically significant. In a capitalistic system, the creation of an insecure female helps to sell clothes, accessories, and various beauty products and processes. As Gilbert and Taylor (1991) explain, gender ideologies are powerful because they "work at an unconscious level through the structuring of desires, as well as at a conscious or rational level" (p. 135).

In spite of their efforts to be beautiful and accepted, females in the *Harry Potter* series are often treated with secondary status in familial and romantic relationships. Both nuclear families, the Weasleys and the Dursleys, have stay-at-home mothers and employed, head-of-the-household fathers. Harry and Ron are also in charge when placed in a dating relationship at the Yule ball and are totally disrespectful to Parvati and Padma Patil, their dates: "Harry felt as if he were a show dog being put through its paces" (*Goblet of Fire*, p. 415). Ron totally "disses" Padma: "'Aren't you going to ask me to dance at all?' Padma asked him. 'No,' said Ron, still glaring after Hermione" (*Goblet of Fire*, p. 423). Ginny is the archetypal girl and is presented as deeply passive, weak, and receptive. She has a crush on Harry, which disables her. She becomes literally mute and still. Later, she is weak enough to be fully possessed and used by the evil Lord Voldemort. As Luce Irigaray (1985) describes, women become paralyzed or hysterical because they have no means and no metaphors for expressing desire. Cho Chang is the beautiful and exotic Asian love interest of Harry and serves more as a symbolic rather than as a fully developed character. This is disturbingly suggestive of what Kim (1990) describes as race and gender hierarchies, which have objectified Asian Americans as permanent outsiders: "Asian men have been coded as having no sexuality, while Asian women have nothing else" (p. 71).

In a study of young romance readers, Willinsky and Hunniford (1993) found that because adolescent girls read in a realist manner, texts represent a dangerous seduction. Girls tend to read romance texts as preparation for the romances they foresee as part of their immediate future (pp. 91–93). Willinsky and Hunniford maintain that "[this] reading is like having your fortune read in good faith with the tingle of excitement in watching it unfold in the crystal ball" (p. 94).

Yet, both boys and girls potentially suffer from such power imbalances. In order for a theory of gender identity to be inclusive, gender identity conventions must be understood as *equally though differently alienating* for men and for women. Female archetypes tend to describe types of powerlessness, whereas dominant male archetypes tend to describe types of powerfulness. To the extent that each distort reality and circumscribe choices and free will, each is limiting, hegemonic, and alienating.

There are quite narrow and specific identities suggested for both males and females in the *Harry Potter* series. In the *Harry Potter* books, boys are stereotypically portrayed, with the strong, adventurous, independent type of male serving as a heroic expression of masculinity, whereas the weak, nonsuccessful male is mocked and sometimes despised.

As R. W. Connell (1996) reminds us, types of gender presentations "do not sit side by side like dishes in a smorgasbord; there are definite relations between them." For example, "some masculinities are more dominant than others" (p. 212). The form of masculinity that is culturally dominant in a given setting is called hegemonic masculinity. Hegemonic cultural practices are those in which ordinary people give "spontaneous consent" to the "general direction imposed on social life by the dominant fundamental group" (Gramsci, 1978, p. 12). A certain type of boy "naturally" seems better. Ordinary people do not realize the extent to which their ideas of gender are culturally created. As Connell explains, "hegemonic" signifies a position of cultural authority and leadership, not total dominance; other forms of masculinity persist alongside. The hegemonic form need not be the most common form of masculinity; it is simply the most valued (Connell, 1996, p. 211). Hegemonic masculinity is straight, strong, and domineering and it oppresses not only women but also the many men excluded from it. Even "subscribers" may find its norms unattainable (Messner, 1997, pp. 7–8).

Nearly all of the males seem to be engaged in power struggles. Yet, the reader has a very clear idea of which males are in top positions. The coolest males seem to be Harry, Dumbledore, and Bill Weasley, who works for Gringotts (the bank) in Egypt and has a ponytail. The traits of powerful males include bravery, confidence, class status, and personal charisma. Although the Weasleys are poor, Bill's status is different. He displays both cultural and financial power. Dumbledore is a leader and is interested in chamber music, which is suggestive of upper-class status. We know that even Harry has money.

Harry's status is interesting. At first he appears to be an outsider and thus is neither dominant nor powerful. He is a skinny boy with tousled hair who is trying to find his place. And yet, as the stories progress, he obtains significant status. He becomes rich and famous. He has some of the best stuff such as a top quality broom and an Invisibility Cloak. He is also a school sports star able to get a date with one of the prettiest girls in the school. I think that part of Harry's appeal comes from the fact that he is introduced to us as a skinny, orphaned outsider and yet he goes on to have success in every important venue of masculinity. Research suggests that maintaining peer status and moving from "nerd to normal" are a chief preoccupation of the young adolescent (Kinney, 1993). Harry's success is satisfying to any reader who wants power or vindication.

Yet, if Harry simply achieved status and remained unproblematically popular, there would be little narrative tension. Thus, Rowling often places Harry in situations in which other students or the wizarding world are mistrustful of Harry. He is repeatedly vindicated.

Harry's triumphs are reinforced by the fact that in the series, most males are not powerful or in positions of cultural authority and leadership. Just as token inclusion reinforces the inequality of the females, the multitude of males who are insecure, low status, and less than fully masculine reinforces the dominance of hegemonic masculinity. Percy Weasley lacks power because his Hermione-like rule following undermines his masculinity. Cedric Diggory is not a dominant male because of what appears to be his social class status. Hufflepuffs are loyal and good workers, but they are not intelligent leaders.

Being a pretty boy "thick" Hufflepuff is unmanly.

> "He's that tall good looking one isn't he?" said Angelina. "Strong and silent," said Katie. "He's only silent because he's too thick to string two words together," said Fred impatiently. (Rowling, 1999, p. 169)

Cedric displays a form of working-class masculinity. When male self-esteem is undermined by being an insubordinate and taking orders from others, men who are working class reconstruct their position as embodying true masculinity by focusing on their strength, endurance, and capacity to tolerate pain (Donaldson, 1991; Pyke, 1996). This is the sort of tough, dumb masculinity Cedric possesses.

There are numerous nondominant adult males in these books who are deeply undesirable. These include Argus Filch, Professor Flitwick, Gilderoy Lockhart, Professor Quirrell, and Peter Pettigrew or "Wormtail." Their negative portrayal serves as a textual warning. They demonstrate the consequences of failed masculinity. No boy readers would want to be like any of them. Argus Filch is the failed wizard owner of Mrs. Norris, the cat. Owning and doting on the cat makes him seem effeminate. Filch is a squib, which means that he was born of a wizarding family but cannot do magic. The frustration this failure causes contributes to his antisocial behavior and his nasty bullying of students. "Tiny little Professor Flitwick" drinks cherry syrup and soda with ice and an umbrella, decorates with live fairies, speaks in a squeaky voice, and is emotionally sensitive. For example, when he was afraid, "he let out a squeal" and then "burst into tears." Similarly, Quirrel, another weak male, faints after telling everyone that there is a troll in the castle in *Harry Potter and the Sorcerer's Stone*. This portrayal is in the same book: "'Now don't forget that nice wrist movement we've been practicing!' squeaked Professor Flitwick, perched on top of his pile of books as usual. "Swish and flick, remember, swish and flick'" (p. 171). Professor Flitwick is characterized with words and images that are connotative of crude cultural stereotypes of gay men.

Such negative portrayals reinforce the vilification of nondominant masculinity and femininity common in many school settings. Gay young people and young people who do not conform to dominant gender identities are at particular risk. They are much more likely than their peers to be the victims of violence and harassment, to drop out of school, and to think about and attempt suicide (O'Conor, 1995; Stoelb & Chiriboga, 1998). In the *Harry Potter* books numerous expression of nondominant masculinity are mocked.

Gilderoy Lockhart is characterized as a deeply conceited man whose bravado and mannerisms serve to hide his utter incompetence and fearfulness. He carries stacks of autographed pictures with him most of the time and is jealous of attention given to Harry. He has coiffed golden, wavy hair and wears curlers at night. He wears robes in a wide array of colors, including forget-me-not blue, lavender, turquoise, mauve, lurid pink, deep plum, jade green, and midnight blue. Certainly this vain, fearful, pink-robed, curler-wearing man is less than masculine, even though many of the young female students like him.

Both Quirrel and Wormtail are weak males. Their physical possession by Lord Voldemort emphasizes their lack of masculinity. Professor Quirrel is nervous, prone to fainting, pale, and often trembling. Who would suspect p-p-poor, st-stuttering Professor Quirrell of being connected with Voldemort? Quirrell became a host and a slave to the disembodied Voldemort. Peter Pettigrew, known as "Wormtail" since he can take the form of a rat, is described in his student days as that "fat, little boy" by Madame Rosmerta (Rowling, 1999, p. 207). McGonagall recalls him with the description, "Stupid boy . . . foolish boy . . . he was always hopeless at dueling . . . " (Rowling, 1999, p. 208).

McGonagall says Pettigrew "hero worshiped Black and Potter" but was "never quite in their league, talent wise" (Rowling, 1999, p. 207). His failure to compete with the dominant males leads him to be vulnerable to possession and use by the evil Voldemorte.

Among the students, Neville and the brothers, Colin and Dennis Creevy, are portrayed, in varying degrees, as "wimps." Language used to describe them reinforces their lowliness. Creevy sounds like creepy. Neville sounds like snivel. Although other boys are often hurt in Quidditch, Neville leaves in disgrace after he fell off a broom during a Quidditch lesson: "Neville, his face tear-streaked, clutching his wrist, hobbled off with Madam Hooch . . . " (Rowling, 1997, p. 147). He is viciously mocked. His unattractiveness to girls is emphasized by Pansy: "'Ooh, sticking up for Longbottom?' said Pansy Parkinson, a hard-faced Slytherin girl. 'Never thought *you'd* like fat little cry-babies, Parvati'" (Rowling, 1997, p. 147). Neville is also victimized by teachers such as Snape. During potions lessons, "Neville regularly went to pieces" (Rowling, 1999, p. 125). Snape says, "tell me boy, does anything penetrate that thick skull of yours?" Neville is described as "pink and trembling. He looked like he was on the verge of tears" (Rowling, 1999, p. 126). Neville is a poor student and a poor athlete. Even though he is occasionally given the limelight (e.g., standing up to bullies) he also makes important mistakes. He wrote down a secret password on paper and it got into the wrong hands. After this, he received a letter shrieking about how he brought shame on the whole family: "The Slytherin table exploded with laughter at the sight of him" (Rowling, 1999, 271–72). Even his family is not understanding. The misery this boy experiences is a testament to the consequences of failed masculinity.

Ron is sometimes at risk of being in this category. His lack of family money weakens his male authority. His formal robes look like a woman's dress, and his broom and other wizarding equipment are substandard. In *Goblet of Fire*, he is mocked: "People were pointing and laughing. The 'cute weeny owl'" (p. 405). Even Ron's owl, Pigwidgeon, undermines Ron's masculinity. The boys who do not measure up to the masculine ideal are consistently derided and are actively excluded from participation in school social life. This is quite similar to what occurs in many schools in Great Britain, Australia, and the United States (Epstein, 1997, 1999; Martino, 1995, 1999; Kehily & Nayak, 1997). In Rowling's books, boys establish their masculinity by avoiding behaviors common to the girls and the less masculine males. Hegemonic males do not express fear, cry, giggle, or gossip, and they are not concerned about their appearance. Hegemonic males are good at sports and have access to possessions, money, and prestige. Socialization into this type of competitive, unflinching masculinity helps to create consumers, soldiers, and corporate strivers. It also reinforces contempt rather than sympathy and public support for the downtrodden.

Implications: Disrupting Gender Stories

Though any one gender stereotype would not be significant, repeated and varied examples of demeaning stereotypes are very significant. In addition, these gender ideologies are especially powerful because the books are pleasurable and popular. Part of the pleasure comes from the "comfort" of the stereotypes. Sutherland (1985) classifies ideology in children's literature as the politics of assent (which reflects and reinscribes societal norms), the politics of advocacy, and the politics of attack. Ideology is invisible in books focusing on "assent," whereas books featuring the politics of advocacy and attack either promote or denounce particular sociocultural practices. Yet, this seems too simplistic. In the *Harry Potter* books, all three occur. Furthermore, Hollindale's (1988) observations that ideology in children's literature is not "a political policy, . . . it is a climate of belief" (p. 19) seems more accurate for the *Harry Potter* books. All books present ideology and authors do so with different levels of intention.

How do these ideologies work? Influence, art, and interpretation lie with the reader rather than the author and text. Sumara (1993/1999) points out that:

> The way in which we come to know ourselves in the literary work is not embedded in the work, but rather emerges from our own interaction with the work. It is in this interactive process, manifested in the feeling of being lost, that the reader of the novel is sometimes able to find feelings, ideas, possible worlds thats/he did not have prior to the reading. (p. 293)

The most compelling ideology comes in the form of the more subtly suggestive and pleasurable reading. Barthes (1976) describes two types of literary pleasure: *plaisir* and *jouissance*. A reader feels *plaisir* when familiar cultural and ideological situations are mirrored in literature. Readers overwhelmingly describe the *Harry Potter* books as pleasurable works in which the young reader can readily be lost. In the *Harry Potter* books, character types and the hierarchies of class, culture, and gender are very much the same as those in other popular books and movies and in real-life situations. The type of pleasure called *jouissance* "unsettles the reader, jarring him out of cultural assumptions, bringing her to the brink of the abyss" (Tobin, 1988, p. 213). If this occurs, it seems more likely to be inspired by details of fantasy. Thus, the *Harry Potter* books are ideologically conservative and are read for *plaisir*, but to some readers they could be innovative in plot complexity, language use, or visual, technological, and magical detail. Yet, even the more creative and original components do not seem *unsettling*. As Susan Sontag (1990) has asserted, "real art makes us nervous" (p. 8).

As Walkerdine (1990) explains, there is a need for gender-neutral stories that are equally appealing to gender-confining, stereotypical, and prejudicial material. Can this be? Such books would create a different kind of reading pleasure. I believe that part of the popularity of the *Harry Potter* books stems from their highly familiar depictions of gender and power. Novels that confront readers' stereotypes elicit either rejection or the unsettling pleasure of *jouissance*. Yet, all texts can be resisted, read against the grain, and deconstructed. I urge *Harry Potter* readers to think about these portrayals. Even though I am an experienced critical and feminist reader of texts, my formal examination of these books revealed much more than my initial casual reading. Children talking with each other, with parents, or with teachers should question how we achieve "common sense" ideas about femininity and masculinity and consider who is served and who is harmed through gender ideologies. Certainly books such as these help to normalize a world in which most childcare workers and secretaries are female and most world explorers, engineers, and firefighters are male. In educational settings, critical discussions about literature, culture, and gender ideology can be very productive (Davies, 1989, 1993, 1997; Lee & Beach, 2001; Peyton, 2000; Yeoman, 1999). Children can learn what Bronwyn Davies (1989) describes as the discursive practices of society. When this happens, children "are able to position themselves within those practices in multiple ways, and to develop subjectivities both in concert with and in opposition to the ways in which others choose to position them" (p. xi).

Given the enormous readership of the *Harry Potter* texts, scholarship on these works and thoughtful consideration of ways to introduce critical themes into curriculum is very important. Such critiques help readers, parents, and classroom teachers consider the ways that literary portrayals potentially reproduce and legitimize inequality, and even help create identity. When I read as a young person, I looked for ideas about how and who to be. Even if young readers are not actively seeking lessons in gender identity, they can be learned. For this reason, feminist critical pedagogy encourages educators to examine the ways in which popular texts, such as these books, function to legitimize relations of power and gender experiences (Lewis, 1997; Luke, 1997). In this way, the critical gaze, rather than the books themselves, become the focus of curriculum. These texts are particularly useful starting points for such curriculum because they embody both engaging and constricting themes and images.

References

Barnett, M. A. "Sex Bias in the Helping Behavior Presented in Children's Picture Books." *Journal of Generic Psychology* 147 (1986): 343–51.

Barthes, R. *The Pleasure of the Text* Trans. R. Miller. New York: Hill and Wang, 1976.

Bourdieu, P. *Outline of a Theory of Practice*. New York: Cambridge UP, 1977.

Chafetz, J. *Gender Equity*. Newbury Park: Sage, 1990.

Chodorow, N. *The Reproduction of Mothering*. Berkeley: U of California P, 1978.

Connell, R. W. *Gender and Power*. Stanford: Stanford UP, 1987.

———. "Live Fast and Die Young: The Construction of Masculinity among Young Working-Class Men on the Margin of the Labour Market." *Australian and New Zealand Journal of Sociology* 27 (1991): 141–71.

———. "The Big Picture: Masculinities in Recent World History." *Theory and Society* 22 (1993): 597–623.

———. *Masculinities*. Los Angeles: U of California P, 1995.

———. "Teaching the Boys: New Research on Masculinity, and Gender Strategies for Schools." *Teachers College Record* 98.2 (1996), 2086–238.

Craighead George, J. *My Side of the Mountain*. New York: Penguin, 2000.

Davies, B. *Frogs and Snails and Feminist Tales: Preschool Children and Gender.* Sydney: Allen and Unwin, 1989.

———. *Shards of Glass: Children Reading and Writing beyond Gendered Identities*. Cresskill: Hampton Press, 1993.

———. "Constructing and Deconstructing Masculinities through Critical Literacy." *Gender and Education* 9 (1997): 9–30.

Donaldson, M. *Time of Our Lives: Labour and Love in the Working Class*. Sydney: Allen and Unwin, 1991.

Epstein, D. "Boyz' Own Stories: Masculinities and Sexualities in Schools." *Gender and Education* 9.1 (1997): 105–15.

———. "Real Boys Don't Work: 'Underachievement', Masculinity and the Harassment of 'Sissies.'" In *Failing Boys: Issues in Gender and Achievement*. Ed. D. Epstein, J. Elwood, V. Hey, and J. Maws. London: Open UP, 1999. 96–108.

Fallon, A. "Culture in the Mirror: Sociocultural Determinants of Body Image." In *Images: Development, Deviance, and Body Change*. Ed. T. E. Cash and T. Prizinsky. New York: Guilford, 1990. 80–109.

Flintoff, A. "Sexism and Homophobia in Physical Education: The Challenge for Teacher Educators." *Physical Education Review* 17.2 (1994): 97–105.

Foucault, M. *Power/Knowledge: Selected Unterviews & Other Writings, 1972–77.* Ed. C. Gordon. New York: Pantheon, 1980.

Gilbert, P., and S. Taylor. *Fashioning the Feminine.* Sydney: Allen and Unwin, 1991.

Gramsci, A. *Selections from the Prison Notebooks of Antonio Gramsci.* Trans. and Ed. Q. Hoare and G. Nowell-Smith. New York: International Publishers, 1978.

Hasbrook, C. A. "Young Children's Social Constructions of Physicality and Gender." In *Inside sports.* Ed. J. Coakely and P. Donnelly. London: Routledge, 1999. 7–16.

Hinton, S. E. *The Outsiders.* New York: Puffin Books, 1997.

Hollindale, P. "Ideology and the Children's Book." *Signal* 55 (1988): 3–22.

Hueston, J., L. Dennerstein, and G. Gotts. "Psychological Aspects of Cosmetic Surgery." *Journal of Psychosomatic Obstetrics and Gynecology* 4 (1985): 335–46.

Irigaray, L. *This Sex Which Is Not One.* Trans. Catherine Porter with Carolyn Burke. Ithaca: Cornell UP, 1985.

Jones, M. "Why Harry's Hot." *Newsweek,* 17 July 2000: 52–61.

Kehily, M., and A. Nayak. "Lads and Laughter: Humour and the Production of Heterosexual Hierarchics." *Gender and Education* 9.1 (1997): 69–87.

Kim, E. H. "Such Opposite Creatures: Men and Women in Asian American Literature." *Michigan Quarterly Review* 29 (1990): 69–71.

Kinney, D. A. "From Nerds to Normals: The Recovery of Identity among Adolescents from Middle School to High School." *Sociology of Education* 66 (1993): 21–40.

Lee, G., and R. Beach. "Response to Literature as a Cultural Activity." *Reading Research Quarterly* 36.1 (2001): 64–74.

Lewis, C. "The Social Drama of Literature Discussions in a Fifth/Sixth Grade Classroom." *Research in the Teaching of English* 31 (1997): 163–204.

Lipman-Blumen, J. *Gender Roles and Power.* Englewood Cliffs: Prentice Hall, 1984.

Luke, A. "Texts and Discourse in Education: An Introduction to Critical Discourse Analysis." In *Review of Research in Education.* Vol. 21. Ed. M. Apple. Washington: American Educational Research Association, 1997. 3–48.

Mac an Ghaill, M. *The Making of Men: Masculinities, Sexualities and Schooling.* London: Open UP, 1994.

Martino, W. "Deconstructing Masculinity in the English Classroom: A Site for Reconstituting Gendered Subjectivity." *Gender and Education* 7.2 (1995): 205–20.

———. "'Cool Boys,' 'Party Animals,' 'Squids' and Poofters: Interrogating the Dynamics and Politics of Adolescent Masculinities in School." *British Journal of Sociology of Education* 20 (1999): 239–63.

Messner, M. *Politics of Masculinities: Men in Movements.* Thousand Oaks: Sage, 1997.

O'Conor, A. "Breaking the Silence: Writing about Gay, Lesbian, and Bisexual Teenagers." In *The Gay Teen: Educational Practice and Theory for Lesbian, Gay, and Bisexual Adolescents.* Ed. G. Unks. New York: Routledge, 1995. 13–15.

Paetcher, C. *Educating the Other: Gender, Power and Schooling.* London: Falmer Press, 1998.

Papadopoulos, L., C. Walker, D. Aitken, and R. Bor. "The Relationship between Body Location and Psychological Morbidity in Individuals with Acne Vulgaris." *Psychology, Health & Medicine* 5.4 (2000): 431–39.

Peyton, J. "Boy Talk: Critical Literacy and Masculinities." *Reading Research Quarterly* 35.3 (2000): 312–38.

Pyke, K. "Class-based Masculinities: The Interdependence of Gender, Class, and Interpersonal Power." *Gender & Society* 10.5 (1996): 527–50.

Rowling, J. K. *Harry Potter and the Sorcerer's Stone.* New York: Scholastic P, 1997.

———. *Harry Potter and the Chamber of Secrets*. New York: Scholastic P, 1998.

———. *Harry Potter and the Prisoner of Azkaban*. New York: Scholastic P, 1999.

———. *Harry Potter and the Goblet of Fire*. New York: Scholastic P, 2000.

Scraton, S. *Gender and Physical Education*. Geelong, Australia: Deakin UP, 1990.

Sontag, S. *Against Interpretation*. New York: Anchor Books, 1990.

Stoelb, M., and J. Chiriboga. "A Process Model for Assessing Adolescent Risk for Suicide." *Journal of Adolescence* 21 (1998): 359–70.

Sumara, D. "Of Seagulls and Glass Roses." In *Contemporary Curriculum Discourses: Twenty Years of JCT*. Ed. W. Pinar. New York: Guilford, 1993/1999. 289–311.

Sutherland, R. "Hidden Persuaders: Political Ideologies in Literature for Children." *Children's Literature in Education* 16 (1985): 143–57.

Tetenbaum, T. J. and J. Pearson. "The Voices in Children's Literature: The Impact of Gender on the Moral Decisions of Storybook Characters." *Sex Roles* 20 (1989): 381–95.

Tiggerman, M., and M. Gardiner. "I Would Rather Be Size 10 Than Have Straight A's." *Journal of Adolescence* 23.6 (2000): 645–60.

Tobin, M. "Bridging the Cultural Gap: Eighteenth-Century Narrative and Post-Modernism." *CLIO: A Journal of Literature, History, and the Philosophy of History* 17 (1988): 211–23.

Walkerdine, V. *Schoolgirl Fictions*. London: Verso, 1990.

Willinsky, J., and R. M. Hunniford. "Reading the Romance Younger: The Mirrors and Fears of a Preparatory Literature." In *Texts of Desire: Essays on Fiction, Femininity and Schooling*. Ed. L. Christian Smith. London: Falmer, 1993. 87–105.

Yeoman. "How Does It Get into My Imagination?: Elementary School Children's Intertextual Knowledge and Gendered Storylines." *Gender & Education* 11.4 (1999): 427–41.

Chapter Thirteen

Images of the Privileged Insider and Outcast Outsider

Elizabeth E. Heilman and Anne E. Gregory

As we read, we relate the things we know and experience with the story. We connect, our current knowledge of the world, and our life history with the happenings, mood, and perspective of the text. In effect, we are situating our perceptions so that they can be better utilized to construct our understandings of present, past, and future realities. This is true whenever we are attempting to attach meaning or to create an interpretation of something. So, as we read the *Harry Potter* books, we are enmeshed in this process. We are actively searching for personal meaning in words, signs, and symbols, and literary devices such as plot, genre, characterization, images, and narrative voice. Readers' interpretations are intimately tied up with all previous experiences, including experience of texts. These connections, often referred to as intertextuality (Barthes, 1977; Bloome & Egan-Robertson, 1993; Cairney, 1996; Hartman, 1995; Lemke, 1992; Still & Worton, 1990), involve us in activity that both draws on and forms our perspectives of the world.

Because text helps to form our perspectives of the world, it is important to consider what types of cultural information are being transmitted. All texts present worldviews and relationships and, thus, are ideological. When relationships among people in society and social and cultural norms are presented in text, it is important to question who benefits from the representation. When Antonio Gramsci tried to understand why ordinary working-class Italians supported fascism in the 1920s in Italy, he realized that citizens were persuaded not by force but by cultural power. In the Marxist tradition, ideology is understood as a cultural force that allows the ruling class to have power with the minimum use of force. It is more efficient and effective to control people culturally than to control them physically. It is harder to tell people that they are inferior and powerless than it is to make them believe it themselves.

Gramsci (1971) viewed the state as a hegemonic superstructure of power. Yet, hegemonic power is not located solely within the political and economic superstructure. Instead, ideology is carried out by what Althusser (1986) has termed "ideological state apparatuses." These include the religious, legal, political, social, and community institutions that people encounter every day. Yet, hegemony is also carried out by seemingly personal institutions such as peer groups, the family, and the school and through a range of freely chosen cultural forms such as music, television, and literature. As Foucault (1983) describes, power can be hard to recognize because "A relationship of power is that mode of action which does not act directly and immediately on others. Instead it acts upon their actions" (229).

In the *Harry Potter* books, Rowling has created an ideological world presenting privileged insiders and outcast outsiders across a wide range of signifiers. These include gender (discussed in chapter 12), social class, peer group affiliations, race, culture, and nationality. As such, the *Harry Potter* books legitimize numerous forms of social inequality and their related cultural norms, rituals, and traditions. Yet, there are tensions and critiques within the texts as well. Hermione worries about the rights of house elves and Harry defends Ron when he is teased for his low social class standing.

Post-Marxist cultural studies of literature attempt to recognize that literature and cultural products can simultaneously represent, reproduce, and transform cultural, political, and institutional norms. However, the presence of a moderate amount of social critique does not make the *Harry Potter* texts progressive. Literary texts containing a moderate critique of the dominant social order it can actually serve to reinforce a primarily oppressive and conservative vision. As Aviram (1998) explains:

> the text simultaneously promotes revolution, liberation, and subversion, on the one hand, and complicity, repression, and containment, on the other. This ambivalence is inevitable because literary texts work by presenting patterns of surprise against a background of the expected and familiar, thus implicitly reinforcing the background by building a structure of surprise to be seen in contrast to it. If this relation is translated into political terms, the background is the conservative force of tradition or hegemony, while the pattern of *surprise* is the force of change and the manifestation of freedom. (p. 55)

The following discussion is provided to help readers of *Harry Potter* think critically about these portrayals and how they serve to normalize who has power in school, especially among peer groups and in sports, and who has power in society, especially related to social class, race, and nationality.

The Portrayal of Social Class

Social class position is suggested by the very first line of *Harry Potter and the Sorcerer's Stone* (Rowling, 1997). "Mr. and Mrs. Dursely, of number four, Privet Drive, were proud to say that they were perfectly normal, thank you very much." Tensions are then developed in the description of Harry's living conditions at the Dursleys. Harry's bourgeois middle-class aunt and uncle considered him an oddity, a nuisance, and a burden to shoulder. Harry is not allowed to speak of or ask questions about his parents. He is required to sleep in a cupboard under the stairs, to wear broken glasses and cousin Dudley's oversized hand-me-downs. He is the target of his family's ridicule, disdain, and punishment. Through their actions, Harry is constantly reminded of his position as an outsider or interloper in their family, someone who is tolerated but not respected or loved. He is a loner.

Once Harry learns of his parentage, that he is indeed a wizard, things begin to change in terms of how he views himself and his family. During his first trip to Diagon Alley with Hagrid for school supplies, Harry learns that he possesses a small fortune when he visits Gringotts, the goblin bank. He is able to purchase necessary school supplies without the assistance of anyone else, which is a relief considering his uncle's comments about not being willing to pay for Harry's schooling at Hogwarts. The family's interactions begin to change in relation to Harry's new status as a wizard, and he is allowed to move from the cupboard to a bedroom. This change reflects the Dursley family's awareness of relative power and status positions. Family is where we initially learn our role, our position within the larger social terrain (Steinberg, Darling, Fletcher, Brown, & Dornbusch, 1995). The Dursleys growing awareness of Harry's new status enables him to transcend the position of the lowly orphan for whom they have begrudgingly taken care, to escape their constant harassment, and to begin to think of himself as a part of a society, as belonging. He has experienced success socially within the culture of the wizarding community on this one outing and this success has the potential of elevating his status within his social class.

When Harry is at Hogwarts, his relative power and status continue to be a strong theme in the series. Once at school, Harry experiences friendship and camaraderie with fellow students Ron Weasley and Hermione Granger, and he is not a loner. The legendary status that accompanies him, that he is the only person to have had an encounter with Voldemort and survive, often forces Harry into the role of hero or savior as the series continues. Harry often assumes the mantel of hero (e.g., when he waits until all the hostages were saved from the Merpeople, task two in the Triwizard Tournament, in *Goblet of Fire)*, and is subject to hero worship from adults (i.e., Gilderoy Lockhart) and students (i.e., Colin Creevey) alike. However, his legendary status works against him when he is perceived by others as attempting to gain more status for himself (e.g., when he is accused of giving out signed photographs of himself in *Chamber of Secrets*) and is left alone (e.g., when Ron felt that Harry had entered himself into the tournament without even telling him in *Goblet of Fire*).

Throughout all of the books, the Malfoys, both Draco and his father, Lucius, serve as reminders of what privilege is and what it enables one to do and say. As part of a longstanding wizarding family with wealth, Draco often makes (and is allowed to get away with) comments about the social standing and monetary holdings of other characters in the stories. He refers to Hagrid and the work that he does as that of a servant, initially referring to him as a savage who lives in a hut, gets drunk, and tries to do magic (*Sorcerer's Stone*, p. 78). He refers often to the Weasley family as being poor and having too many children. In *Chamber of Secrets*, Draco carries this to an extreme by stating that a signed photo of Harry would be worth more than the Weasleys' house. Most of the comments made by the Malfoys are offered in an effort to bully and remind others of their inferior position in relation to them. These types of comments reveal a rigid hierarchy even among the pureblooded wizarding families.

With the introduction of the house elf, Dobby, in *Chamber of Secrets*, we are able to see more of the privileging that occurs with wealth in the wizarding community. If you have wealth, you have a house elf that serves you unquestioningly, often resorting to violence against itself when it disobeys its master. Like other marginalized peoples in England and the United States, the house elves do not speak standard English. The house elf is a slave, an idea that is appalling to Hermione in *Goblet of Fire* and she attempts to organize, to work for wages, paid holidays, and freedom of house elves everywhere. However, her success is minimal as the house elves and others within the wizarding community cannot understand why the elves would want to be free. The house elves of Hogwarts, and the elf

Winky in particular, see freedom as a disgrace to their way of life. They accept their enslavement and see Hermione's efforts as a danger to their way of life.

These messages are deeply disturbing as Rowling reinscribes and normalizes the marginalized status of the immigrant or dialect speaker. It also gives credence to the erroneous view positing that oppressed people can and should be satisfied with their lot. As a member of the dominant culture, Hermione's articulation of injustice serves only to further infantalize the house elves. Rowling's portrayal of the worker population suggests that they need someone to speak for them. In fact, oppressed peoples can and do speak for themselves. Since Hermione's efforts are mocked, and the house elves do not work for their own liberation, a conservative hegemonic situation dominates.

Another instance in which social class issues are portrayed in the *Harry Potter* books comes with the appointment of Professor Lupin to the teaching staff as the Defense Against the Dark Arts instructor in *Prisoner of Azkaban*. His robes are described as unusually shabby, appearing to have "been darned in several places, and his appearance ill and fatigued." Though quite young, his light brown hair was flecked with gray and he carried "a small, battered case held together with a large quantity of neatly knotted string. The name *Professor R. J. Lupin* was stamped across one corner in peeling letters" (*Prisoner of Azkaban*, p. 74). His position as an instructor saves him from overt discrimination from the students, but he clearly has lower status because of relative poverty.

Social class, in these examples, helps to illustrate insider and outsider perceptions of the world. They provide a means by which we can begin to examine how the identity of a culture is learned and perpetuated (Bloome, 1985; Oldfather & Dahl, 1994; Taylor, 1992). They can serve as a lens through which we can begin to examine our own stories and those of others (Vavra, 2000; Nelson, 2001).

Insiders and Outsiders in Peer Groups

All new wizards are sorted into one of four houses on their first day of their first year at Hogwarts. This feat is accomplished through the use of the Sorting Hat. When placed upon the head of a young wizard or witch, it will state which house is an appropriate match for them. Each house serves as the core of an individual's peer group and this house affiliation determines class schedules and lessons, where a student is seated when dining and the location of sleeping chambers. House members have certain defining characteristics. The Gryffindors are considered daring, brave, and chivalrous; the Hufflepuffs are deemed to be just, loyal, and unfraid of toil; the Ravenclaws are of ready mind and include those of wit and learning; and the Slytherins are cunning, using any means to achieve their ends (*Sorcerer's Stone*, p. 118). Therefore, house membership establishes the way in which students are perceived by the others around them as well as the way in which they perceive themselves.

Throughout the first three narratives, each house is vying for the house cup, presented at the end of the school year. In order to attain it, points are given and deducted from houses based upon the actions of their members. This sets up an atmosphere of competition among the houses, although most of the tension exists between the Slytherin and Gryffindor houses. This is an interesting juxtaposition to consider once we learn the gender of the founding members of Hogwarts in the *Chamber of Secrets*. Of the four founding members, two were male and two were female. The two male founders were Godric Gryffindor and Salazar Slytherin, and a riff developed between them based upon who should be allowed to attend the school. This riff caused Slytherin to leave. The female founders, while siding with Gryffindor, are minimized in the recounting of the history of this interaction, an allegiance that appears to continue into the present day.

Throughout most of the four books, members of the Slytherin house are viewed suspiciously by all the members of the other households. Descriptions of the Slytherin members relate that they are often dark, unattractive, greedy, and a bit dense. Millicent Bulstrode, Crabbe, and Goyle are all described as being particularly large. Harry and Ron are easily able to draw Crabbe and Goyle out in order to get their hair for the Polyjuice Potion, in the Chamber of Secrets; and even the descriptions and distrust of Professor Snape, the Slytherin house advisor, suggest these qualities. Early in *Sorcerer's Stone*, Harry learns that most of the dark wizards have come from the Slytherin house. Little affection can be engendered for the Slytherin house and its members since Draco Malfoy and his henchmen, Crabbe and Goyle, belong to this house, and they remind Harry of his cousin, the over privileged, dull, mean-spirited Dudley and his gang.

Quidditch, the wizarding sport similar to soccer, played in the air with four balls on broomsticks, provides entrée into another form of peer group affiliation for members of Hogwarts. Each house has its own team comprised of a seeker, three chasers, two beaters, and one keeper. Membership on the Quidditch team is not afforded to just anyone. There is a competitive selection process as is common to most school sports. However, there is a rule that first-year students are not allowed to play. They are not even allowed to have broomsticks at school yet. However, when Professor McGonagall sees Harry ride a broom the first time when he is chasing after Draco Malfoy and is able to catch Neville's remembrance ball (*Sorcerer's Stone*), this rule is bent and Harry is allowed to play on the Gryffindor Quidditch team. Not only is Harry allowed to play, he is also awarded the seeker position, the most important position on the team. The seeker is the one who ultimately decides the outcome of the game, for a game is not over until the seeker has the Golden Snitch. In this role, Harry is highly successful, enabling the Gryffindor team to win most of their competitions and narrowing in on the winning of the Quidditch cup. His teammates often lift him on their shoulders at the end of games, Wood, the team captain, spends many hours with Harry helping him to strategize for upcoming matches, and he enjoys recognition from not just his peers but also from students who are older and in other houses.

This uncritical portrayal may accurately reflect the type of privilege given to star athletes in American and British schools, but, on a more disturbing level, it shows an unquestioning acceptance of an unfair policy. This type of portrayal helps to normalize unfortunate practices in American schools in which policies are enacted with little thought or inquiry made into how policy might impact the larger community of students or what students may feel or believe to be in their interest. It is often assumed that what follows from such enactments of policy benefits the greater good and is something that the larger community would itself want, when, in fact, it often does not. In many secondary schools, according privilege to certain sports players reinforces inequalities based on race, class, and gender and serves to create a large group of outsider children (Eckert, 1989; Foley, 1990; Kinney, 1993).

Another group membership that is put forth in the *Chamber of Secrets* is that of being a Parseltongue or Parselmouth, or one who is able to speak with snakes. Parselmouth is a very rare gift for one to have in the wizarding world, and one that is only associated with dark wizards. Reflecting on a family trip to the zoo, Harry recalls communicating with a boa constrictor and somehow freeing it so that it could return to Brazil (*Sorcerer's*

Stone). However, this occurs before Harry finds out that he is a wizard and he is very unaware of how he was able to do this. During a meeting of the Hogwarts dueling club the members of the school become aware of Harry's ability to speak to snakes when Malfoy conjures a snake during his duel with Harry. Professor Lockhart angers the snake by sending it flying across the room and into a wall. As the snake approaches another student, Justin Finch-Fletchley, Harry speaks to the snake and persuades it not to attack. Yet, Harry is not rewarded for this effort. The students are worried that all parseltongues might be evil and that the presence of a parseltongue harkens the return of the Slytherin's heir. Even though Harry had proven himself to be a crusader for the good, as a result of this incident Harry is once again viewed as an outcast. This scene tells us that insider and outsider groups are very tightly drawn and one who does not conform to all of the traits of an insider group can become an outsider rather quickly.

In the *Goblet of Fire*, circumstances during the Triwizard Tournament again make Harry an outcast and provides another demonstration of selective peer group membership for Harry. Not only is Harry the youngest contestant, defying the age line, but also there were to be only three contestants and Harry makes number four. Harry did not wish to participate and became involved due to magical forces beyond his control, but his peers thought that he cheated in order to be involved. His involvement in the tournament brings about opposition from the other schools participating in the event. The other schools have only one representative. Even members of Harry's own school viewed his participation as an attempt by Harry to acquire more fame. In this situation, Harry again becomes a misunderstood outcast. When Harry provides assistance to his competitor, Cedric Diggory, in the first task and is reluctant to leave the other competitors hostages in the second task, his fellow students begin to see that Harry is not solely motivated by a desire to win.

Each of these instances portray difficulties with peer group affiliation in which Harry moves from privileged insider to outcast outsider. The nuances and dynamics of peer group formation are likely to be very much on the minds of the young readers of the *Harry Potter* series. It is during adolescence that most children experience an increased orientation toward peers and peer-related activity, with adolescents spending more than 50 percent of their waking hours with friends (Heaven, 1994; Steinberg, 1993). The peer group serves as the context for sociable behavior, the exploration of social relationships, and it provides a sense of belonging for the adolescent (Heaven, 1994). Adolescents are searching for a place to belong, and when they are unable to find it they can become at risk for many other difficulties. Research indicates a clear connection between depression and low social support (Vernberg, 1990). Parker and Asher (1987) found that 25 percent of students who were rated as low on acceptance by their peers were likely to drop out of school compared to 8 percent of other children. Research on adolescents suggests that for most students, friendships and acceptance in school peer groups is a primary area of concern (Corsaro & Eder 1990; Willis 1981) and that problems such as Harry faces of fluctuating insider and outsider status are profoundly upsetting (Asher & Cole, 1990).

Harry's situation can potentially serve as means for examining peer group relations with students who read these books. Theses novels provide a means to begin a dialogue about the process of social enculturation that students engage in their own lives and share in the reading of these books (Halliday, 1994; Mariage, 2001). Such reading and discussion can potentially provide a space in which students can step outside of their personal experience and engage with others to learn new things (Altmann, 2001; Oldfather & Dahl, 1994).

Culture, Heredity, and Nationality

Differences highlighted by culture and nationality arise in *Sorcerer's Stone* upon Hagrid's arrival at the Dursleys. Muggles and wizards are described as members of different cultural groups. It is during the interchange between Hagrid and Uncle Vernon when Harry first learns of his wizarding background. It is the first time that Harry hears the word Muggle and associates it with the Dursleys, members of a cultural group who denied Harry knowledge of his wizarding ethnic background. Following his return from his initial trip to Diagon Alley with Hagrid, Harry is confronted with his uncle's desire to stamp out the notion of wizardry and witchcraft, at least when Harry is in his family's home. Harry is not allowed to utter the word magic or to mention his school or friends or anything that is related to his wizarding background when he returns to their home during the summer holidays (*Chamber of Secrets, Prisoner of Azkaban*). To compound the matter, Uncle Vernon often refers to magic as rubbish in what appears to be an attempt to minimize its importance for Harry.

Harry's Aunt Petunia holds beliefs that are similar, though they are formed from a personal account or firsthand knowledge of having magic in the family. Harry's mother, Lily, was Petunia's sister. When Lily was selected for Hogwarts, their parents were pleased with the prospect of having a witch in the family. Petunia's recounting of this appears to be tinged with a bit of jealousy, and she consistently describes Harry's parents as abnormal weirdos and connections with wizards are undesirable and socially embarrassing. One can begin to see the connection between the feelings of Harry's family and their subsequent treatment of Harry. In the eyes of the Dursleys, Harry is a member of an outcast group and this status helps to justify his mistreatment.

In addition to privileged insider and outcast outsider distinctions between wizards and Muggles, there are also distinctions made throughout the four books between Muggle-born wizards and witches and those who came from pure wizarding families. Among the wizarding families, there is a hierarchy, often based on social class and profession and related to the quality of bloodlines. The higher your social standing, the better your job, and the more power you have to make it difficult or easier for others around you. This is evidenced in Lucius Malfoy's success in coercing the other governors of Hogwarts to suspend Hagrid after the incident with Buckbeak in *Prisoner of Azkaban*. The most vocal critics of outsider Muggle-born wizards are the wealthy, insider Malfoys who believe that those from Muggle families should not be allowed to attend Hogwarts. The Malfoys view Muggle-born wizards as not being the same, pointing out that they haven't been "brought up to know our ways" (*Sorcerer's Stone*, p. 78). As a Muggle-born witch, Hermione Granger often is the object of many of these insults. In *Chamber of Secrets*, Draco Malfoy calls her a Mudblood, the most insulting thing you can call a person born to nonmagic parents, when she implies that he bought his way onto the Slytherin Quidditch team.

> "At least no one on the Gryffindor team had to buy their way in," Hermione said sharply. "They got in on pure talent."
>
> The smug look on Malfoy's face flickered.
>
> "No one asked your opinion, you filthy little Mudblood," he spat.
>
> Harry knew at once that Malfoy had said something really bad because there was an instant uproar at his words. (*Chamber of Secrets*, p. 112)

In *Goblet of Fire*, she is viewed as a second-class citizen by the Malfoys as they sit in the same box during the Quidditch World Cup.

Mr. Malfoy's eyes had returned to Hermione, who went slightly pink, but stared deter-
minedly back at him. Harry knew exactly what was making Mr. Malfoy's lip curl like
that. The Malfoys prided themselves on being purebloods; in other words, they considered anyone of Muggle descent, like Hermione, second-class. (*Goblet of Fire*, pp. 101–2)

However, it is not with the Malfoys that this desire to preserve the
race of pureblood wizards begins. It has a long history in the wizarding
community. In the *Chamber of Secrets*, in Professor Binns's recounting of
the history of the founding of Hogwarts, we learn of a dispute between the
original founders that ended in one of them leaving. The source of the dispute centers on this very concept. Salazar Slytherin felt that Hogwarts
should be a school only for those of pureblooded wizarding families, and
that those from Muggle families should be denied entrance. He did not
think that Muggle-born wizards and witches could be trusted. The other
founding members disagreed with him, and this eventually led to his
departure from the school. Thus, the core narrative drama of outsiders and
insiders, which plays out in competition among houses and also in large-
scale struggles between light and dark forces, is related to differences in
beliefs about purebloods and Mudbloods.

Muggles and Mudbloods are not the only wizard world outsiders.
Within the pureblooded wizarding family, there is the rare incidence of
someone being born who does not have magical powers. This type of person is called a Squib. Filch, the caretaker of Hogwarts, is one. The description of him and his interactions with the students belies a sense of
desperation to be like the others, to be normal. He attempts this with
Kwikspell. This is a course in magic, for those who do not have magical
powers. Inside his community, Filch is a shamed handicapped person
whose life is marked by this difference.

Within the wizarding community, other biological, racial-like distinctions are made, which include the Veelas, Giants, and Werewolves.
Although these are all human-like creatures they are portrayed as being
substandard, like the elves described earlier. The Veelas are beautiful sirens
who captivate men, making their minds completely and blissfully blank
(*Goblet of Fire*, p. 103) and capable of being controlled. They, however, turn
to ugly birdlike creatures when they lose control; causing Mr. Weasley to
say to the boys, "(that) is why you should never go for looks alone!" (*Goblet
of Fire*, p. 112). A clear implication is that beauty is the only attribute that
the Veelas possess.

Goblet of Fire describes the extent to which giants are scorned among the wizarding community. They are said to be vicious, bloodthirsty, and brutal (p. 439), which is what has caused their near extinction. They are portrayed as savages who are not very clever, for they have almost killed themselves right out of existence. They are a feared and hated group from whom the civilized people (wizards and witches) need to be protected. Yet, Hagrid, the most gentle adult in the series, is half giant. Harry isn't bothered by Hagrid's parentage, but others are. Harry "could tell that most wizards would not have said 'So what?' upon finding out that one of their friends had a giantess for a mother" (*Goblet of Fire*, p. 429).

Therefore, it comes as little surprise that even when the wizarding world wants to create alliances against evil Lord Voldemort, nobody supports Dumbledore's suggestion to send envoys to the giants and make amends. Even in times of crisis the giants remain outsiders.

> "Envoys to the giants?" Fudge shrieked, finding his tongue again. "What madness is this?"
>
> "Extend to them the hand of friendship, now, before it is too late," said Dumbledore, "or Voldemort will persuade them, as he did before, that he alone among wizards will give them their rights and their freedom!"
>
> "You—you cannot be serious!" Fudge gasped, shaking his head and retreating further from Dumbledore. "If the magical community got wind that I had approached the giants—people hate them, Dumbledore—end of my career—" (*Goblet of Fire*, p. 708)

To be a member of either the giant or the werewolf group would engender much dislike, rejection, and fear within the wizarding community. Our earliest introductions to Hagrid in *Sorcerer's Stone* seem to imply, long before we know for sure of his mixed heritage (*Goblet of Fire*), that he is very different from those of normal wizarding parentage. He is referred to as a savage (*Sorcerer's Stone*), and, as a student, was expelled from Hogwarts for misdeeds that caused harm to others (*Chamber of Secrets*). He introduces the students to dangerous creatures as their instructor in the class, Care of Magical Creatures, and these creatures cause injury to students (*Prisoner of Azkaban*). All of these instances reinforce the idea that even biracial members of outcast wizard groups engender fear and disdain. In this light, it is not surprising that both Hagrid and Madame Maxime, headmistress of Beauxbatons, choose to deny their mixed, part-giant heritage when confronted with questions. The following passage also shows how Rowling often uses nonstandard English for members of outsider groups:

"No, don' go! I've—I've never met another one before!"

"Anuzzer what, precisely?" said Madame Maxime, her tone icy.

Harry could have told Hagrid it was best not to answer; he stood there in the shadows gritting his teeth, hoping against hope he wouldn't—but it was no good.

"Another half-giant, o'course!" said Hagrid.

"'Ow dare you!" shrieked Madame Maxime. Her voice exploded throught the peaceful night air like a foghorn; behind him, Harry heard Fleur and Roger fall out of their rosebush. "I'ave nevair been more insulted in my life! 'Alf-giant? Moi? I'ave—I'ave big bones!" (*Goblet of Fire*, pp. 428–29)

Another person of mixed heritage found in the *Harry Potter* series is Fleur Delacour, who we learn is part Veela when the wands are weighed in before the Triwizard Tournament begins. This is seen as a reason for her extreme beauty, but no alarm accompanies the revelation. This appears to imply that, even among those of mixed parentage, there are some combinations that are more acceptable than others. This parallels racial hierarchies in much of Western society.

With the arrival of Professor Lupin in *Prisoner of Azkaban*, we are introduced to werewolves and the perception of them by others in the wizarding community. Werewolves are feared outcasts. Professor Snape, angry because he is again passed over for the job of Defense Against the Dark Arts instructor, attempts to bring this fact about Professor Lupin to light. When he is covering for Professor Lupin during one of his absences, he assigns the students to learn about werewolf characteristics. Snape hopes that the students will then use this information to have Lupin dismissed. The plan backfires when Lupin returns the next day, and he cancels the assignment. Although the Lupin character is the most developed of the magical creatures, little narrative space is spent on describing what it means to be a werewolf or describing the persecution he feels from within the wizarding community. Again, this suggests that it is perfectly acceptable to fear differences among people, and that there are differences that make certain people better than others. These portrayals of deep, biologically rooted difference can possibly serve to reinforce readers' notions of biological differences among races. In fact, according to genetic surveys and the analyses of DNA haplotype, race is a cultural construct with no biological importance (Templeton, 1998). As biological anthropologists Sussman and Templeton explain in an interview:

"Race is a real cultural, political and economic concept in society, but it is not a biological concept, and that unfortunately is what many people wrongfully consider to be the essence of race in humans—genetic differences," Templeton said. "The folk concept of race in America is so ingrained as being biologically based and scientific that it is difficult to make people see otherwise," said Sussman, a biological anthropologist. "We live on the one-drop racial division—if you have one drop of black or Native American blood, you are considered black or Native American, but that doesn't cover one's physical characteristics." "Templeton's paper," Sussman continued, "shows that if we were forced to divide people into groups using biological traits, we'd be in real trouble. Simple divisions are next to impossible to make scientifically, yet we have developed simplistic ways of dividing people socially." (Fitzpatrick, 2001)

Differences between privileged insiders and outcast outsiders are drawn not only on racial or biological "blood" lines but also along lines of nationality. The non-British are often treated with disdain and suspicion, and they are described with glaring cultural stereotypes. French wizards— Madame Maxime and her students—arrive in an enormous carriage resplendent in its decoration with "golden steps and cross wands on the coat of arms" (*Goblet of Fire*, p. 243). They are described as sparkly and are dressed in robes of fine silk without any cloaks. This is an indication that beauty is viewed as being more important than comfort given the chill of the October evening, and such an attitude is compounded by their representative, Fleur Delacour, a beautiful girl with long silvery-blond hair (p. 252). When anyone from Beauxbatons speaks, it is with a decidedly pronounced accent (i.e., most of the /th/ diagraphs have been replaced with the letter z, and letters are omitted to produce an aspirated sounding word, for example, hope is "ope") (pp. 244–45).

The Hungarian students are described as having builds similar to Crabbe and Goyle (i.e., stout), wearing cloaks of matted fur and immediately take up residence at the Slytherin table in the great hall. This suggests that they are impoverished, evil, and uncouth. The Hungarians arrive in a boat that is described as having a skeletal and menacing appearance. Their headmaster, Professor Karkaroff, is described as having a rather weak chin and a cold shrewd look about his eyes. This is a continuation of the characterization begun in the *Goblet of Fire* with the Quidditch world cup, in which the Bulgarian minister is given a pronounced accent when he decides to speak English (p. 115), and the members of the Bulgarian Quidditch team are described as surly and grumpy (p. 83).

These stereotypical negative representations of French and

Hungarian cultures serve to normalize nationalistic disdain among the British for other Europeans and serve to justify dominance. There is limited mention of other, nondominant cultures within the four books. Those that are referred to are mentioned in a very cursory manner. These minimal descriptions appear as an attempt to be politically correct rather than as an honest attempt to include others. Some examples of this can be seen in *Sorcerer's Stone*, when Thomas Dean is referred to as a black boy but is never mentioned again. In *Prisoner of Azkaban*, we are introduced to Cho Chang, the Asian girl seeker for the Ravenclaws and, although she appears again in *Goblet of Fire*, it is only to relate that she is a love interest of Harry. Her specific ethnicity is not described (although the name seems Chinese) and her personality is not developed. There are several peripheral characters who have culturally relevant names, like Seamus Finnigan (we assume he is Irish) and Parvati Patil (we assume she is Indian) but the books contain nothing to identify their ethnicity or provide information about them in terms of who they are and how they are culturally different from the main characters, Harry, Ron, and Hermione. It is not insignificant that these minor characters are from postcolonial nations and that China, Ireland, and India have suffered enormously under British imperialism.

Though these sorts of racist and colonial representations are fairly common in media and books for children (Whitlark, 1999; Wojcik-Andrews, 1996), they are dispiriting. Texts help readers to *create* ideas about empire, race, class, gender, and power rather than merely *reflect* relations among groups and nations in the world. As Said (1993) observes, "In time, culture comes to be associated, often aggressively, with the nation or the state; this differentiates 'us' from 'them,' almost always with some degree of xenophobia. Culture in this sense is a source of identity, and a rather combative one at that" (xiii). Texts such as these help to create ideas about others, but they also influence readers' ideas about themselves and the millions of dominant and nondominant culture children who read these books and in some way place themselves as insiders or outsiders as they read.

While no one book, fictional or factual, can answer every individual's identity questions, literature does have the potential to spark a discussion about identity or to slow readers down to take a closer look (Johnson, Giorgis, Colbert, Conner, King, & Kulesza, 2000, p. 432). Oftentimes, this is what is needed when children study literature. Literature can be useful not only from the perspective that it has the potential to create possible worlds for readers but also that it can, to some extent, represent the way things are, and thus it can be used as a tool to understand and critique social experiences. As readers interact (Rosenblatt, 1994) with a story, they are engaging in a socializing process. The story transmits cultural information socializing the reader into the ways of thinking, speaking, reading, and writing within that culture, though some of this information may not be easily inferred from the text (Ashton, 1996). This type of socialization provides a means to acquire cultural models that will serve as the starting point for how we construct our everyday theories of the world and how we will behave and act within it (Gee, 2001). Our basic assumptions about the nature of truth and reality and the origins of knowledge shape the way we see the world and ourselves as participants within it (Wright, 2000, p. 2). How we speak and what we say, in relation to various topics and occasions, helps to define us. This allows us to create our identity as a means of positioning ourselves in relation to others and their interpretations. However, it is not only through these relationships and self-perceptions that our identity and ways of knowing others is formed. This can also occur through the cultural connections, such as customs and traditions (Johnson, Giorgis, Colbert, Conner, King, & Kulesza, 2000) that we experience.

According to Gee (1989), "Discourses are ways of being in the world; they are forms of life which integrate words, acts, values, beliefs, attitudes, and social identities as well as gestures, glances, body positions, and clothes" (Gee, 1989, p. 7). They are what instruct us in our comportment and understanding of self in relation to the other members of the various communities to which we belong. As such, it should be understood that we are members of not one Discourse, but rather of many (Gee, 1989). It should be understood that Discourses can be, and often times are, used as a form of "gate" to ensure access to only the "right" people and limiting access to others. As we have outlined above, this clearly occurs in the *Harry Potter* series.

Implications for Education

Davies (2000) posits that critical literacy provides us both with ability to challenge discourses and with alternatives to the practices that are currently being enacted. It enables us to deconstruct, write, create, and reconstruct meanings for texts. In this sense, we are able to minimize the differences allowing both access to and critique of dominant forms of literacy while promoting diverse literacies among our students.

When knowledge can be socially constructed and multiple Discourses (Gee 1989, 1992) are encouraged and promoted, critical literacy will begin. Students become able to critique the culture promoted by the text, because they have seen it (Block, 1998). In the case of the *Harry Potter* books, we can analyze the promotion and perpetuation of the dominant culture and the demarcation of privileged insiders and outcast outsiders across signifiers of gender, social class, peer group affiliations, race, culture, and nationality.

Of course, teaching critical literacy involves changing perspectives of what the role of teacher involves, from one who disseminates information to one who facilitates learning in a form of apprenticeship with students. Such apprenticeship would enable students and teachers alike to constantly position and reposition one another as they construct meaning around a shared experience, for example, the reading of a story. This type of interaction would foster students' ability to discuss how and why they know things and would provide opportunities for rethinking happening within stories or life. Students can reflect on how feeling and behaving within various situations continues to evolve. (Mariage, 2001). The role of teachers would be to manage the context as the community of students constructs events on a moment-by-moment basis. In so doing, teachers act as facilitators in the construction of our student's interpretations, scaffolding the learning so that it is manageable for them to undertake (Russell, 1997).

It is within classrooms, and the Discourses that we foster and allow to flourish, that students begin to construct and reconstruct their sense of self and others as they negotiate the meanings of texts and textual elements with others (Oldfather & Dahl, 1994). The *Harry Potter* series' realistic, fantastic, and stereotypical portrayals of the relative power and privilege of insiders and outsiders offer rich opportunities for important discussions and the critical construction of self, society, and other.

References

Althusser, L. "Ideology and Ideological State Apparatuses." In *Critical Theory since 1965*. Ed. A. Hazard and L. Searle. Tallahassee: U of Florida P, 1986.

Altman, G. T. M. "The Language Machine: Psycholinguistics in Review." *British Journal of Psychology* 91 (2001): 129–71.

Asher, S. R., and J. D. Cole. *Peer Rejection in Childhood*. Cambridge: Cambridge UP, 1991.

Ashton, P. "The Concept of Activity." In *Vygotsky in the Classroom: Mediated Literacy Instruction and Assessment*. Ed. L. Dizon-Kraus. White Plains: Longman Publishers, 1996. 111–24.

Aviram, A. "Notes toward a New Formalist Criticism: Reading Literature as a Democratic Exercise." *Studies in the Literary Imagination* 31.1 (1998): 37–9.

Barthes, R. "The Death of the Author." In *Image, Music, Text*. Trans. S. Heath. New York: Hill and Wang, 1977. 142–48.

Block, A. A. "Reading children's magazines: Kinderculture and popular culture." In *Kinderculture: The Corporate Construction of Childhood*. Ed. S. R. Steinberg and J. L. Kincheloe. Boulder: Westview P, 1998.

Bloome, D. "Reading as a Social Process." *Language Arts* 62 (1985): 134–42.

Bloome, D., and A. Egan-Robertson. "The Social Construction of Intertextuality in Classroom Reading and Writing Lessons." *Reading Research Quarterly* 28 (1993): 304–33.

Cairney, T. H. "Pathways to Meaning Making: Fostering Intertextuality in the Classroom." In *Lively Discussions: Fostering Engaged Reading*. Ed. L. B. Gambrell and J. F. Almasi. Newark: International Reading Association, 1996. 170–80.

Corsaro, W., and E. Donna. "Children's Peer Cultures." *Annual Review of Sociology* 16 (1990): 197–220.

Davies, L. "The Future of Education: International Perspectives." *Educational Review* 52 (2000): 125–31.

Eckert, P. *Jocks & Burnouts: Social Categories and Identity in High School*. New York: Teachers College P, 1989.

Fitzpatrick, T. *Biological Differences among Races Do Not Exist, WU Research Shows*. Retrieved 11 December, 2000 from http://wupa.wustl.edu/record/archive/1998/10–15–98/articles/races. html.

Foley, D. E. "The Great American Football Ritual: Reproducing Race, Class, and Gender Inequality." *Sociology of Sport Journal* 7 (1990): 111–35.

Foucault, M. "The Subject and Power." In *Michel Foucault: Beyond Hermeneutics and Structuralism*. Chicago: U of Chicago P, 1983. 208–26.

Gee, J. P. "Literacy, Discourse, and Linguistics: Introduction." *Journal of Education* 171 (1989): 5–17.

———. *The Social Mind: Language, Ideology, and Social Practice*. New York: Bergin and Garvey, 1992.

———. "Reading as Situated Language: A Sociocognitive Perspective." *Journal of Adolescent & Adult Literacy* 44 (2001): 714–26.

Gramsci, A. *Selections from the Prison Notebooks of Antonio Gramsci*. Trans. E. Q. Hoare and G. N. Smith. New York: International Publishers, 1971.

Halliday, M. A. K. "The Place of Dialogue in Children's Construction of Meaning." In *Theoretical Models and Processes of Reading*. 4th ed. Ed. R. B. Ruddell, M. R. Ruddell, and H. Singer. Newark, DE: International Reading Association, 1994.

Hartman, D. K. "Eight Readers Reading: The Intertextual Links of Proficient Readers Reading Multiple Passages." *Reading Research Quarterly* 30 (1995): 520–61.

Heaven, P. C. L. *Contemporary Adolescence: A Social Psychological Approach*. Melbourne: Macmillan Education, 1994.

Johnson, N. J., C. Giorgis, C. Colbert, A. Conner, J. King, and D. Kulesza. "Children's Books: Identity." *The Reading Teacher* 53 (2000): 432–40.

Kinney, D. A. "From Nerds to Normals: The Recovery of Identity among Adolescents from Middle School to High School." *Sociology of Education* 66 (1993): 21–40.

Lemke, J. L. "Why Intertextuality?" In *Systematic Perspectives on Discourse*. Vol. 1. Ed. J. D. Benson and W. S. Graves. Norwood: Ablex Publishing, 1992.

Mariage, T. V. "Features of an Interactive Writing Discourse: Conversational Involvement, Conventional Knowledge, and Internalization in 'Morning Message.'" *Journal of Learning Disabilities* 34 (2001): 172–97.

Nelson, R. M. *Place, Vision, and Identity in Native American Literatures.* http://www.richmond. edu/~rnelson/pvi.html.

Oldfather, P., and K. Dahl. "Toward a Social Constructivist Reconceptualization of Intrinsic Motivation for Literacy Learning." *Journal of Reading Behavior* 26 (1994): 139–59.

Parker, J. G., and S. R. Asher. "Peer Relations and Later Personal Adjustment: Are Low-Accepted Children at Risk?" *Psychological Bulletin* 102 (1987): 357–89.

Rosenblatt, L. M. (1994). "The Transactional Theory of Reading and Writing." In *Theoretical Models and Processes of Reading.* 4th ed. Ed. R. B. Ruddell, M. R. Ruddell, and H. Singer. Newark: International Reading Association, 1994.

Rowling, J. K. *Harry Potter and the Sorcerer's Stone.* New York: Scholastic P, 1998.

———. *Harry Potter and the Chamber of Secrets.* New York: Scholastic P, 1999a.

———. *Harry Potter and the Prisoner of Azkaban.* New York: Scholastic P, 1999b.

———. *Harry Potter and the Goblet of Fire.* New York: Scholastic P, 2000.

Russell, D. R. "Rethinking Genre in School and Society." *Written Communication* 14 (1997): 504–55.

Said, Edward. *Orientalism.* New York: Vintage, 1979.

Steinberg, L. *Adolescence.* New York: McGraw-Hill, 1993.

Steinberg, L., N. Darling, A. C. Fletcher, B. B. Brown, and S. M. Dornbusch. "Authoritative Parenting and Adolescent Adjustment: An Ecological Journey." In *Examining Lives in Context.* Ed. P. Moen, G. Elder, and K. Luscher. Washington: American Psychological Association, 1995. 423–66.

Still, J., and M. Worton. "Introduction." In *Intertextuality: Theories and Practices.* Ed. M. Worton and J. Still. Manchester: Manchester UP, 1990.

Taylor, C. "The Politics of Recognition." In *Multiculturalism.* Ed. A. Gutman. Princeton: Princeton UP, 1992. 25–73.

Templeton, A. "Human Races: A Genetic and Evolutionary Perspective." *American Anthropologist* 100.3 (1998): 932–51.

Vernberg, E. M. "Psychological Adjustment and Experiences with Peers during Early Adolescence: Reciprocal, Incidental, or Unidirectional Relationships?" *Journal of Abnormal Child Psychology* 18 (1990): 187–98.

Whitlark, J. "Kipling's Scriptural Paradoxes for Imperial Children." *Children's Literature Association Quarterly* 24.1 (1999): 24–33.

Willis, P. *Learning to Labour: How Working Class Kids Get Working* Class *Jobs.* New York: Columbia UP, 1981.

Wojcik-Andrews, A. "Telling Tales to Children: The Pedagogy of Empire in MGM's *Kim* and Disney's *Aladdin.*" *Lion and the Unicorn* 20.1 (1996).

Wright, P. A. "Connected Knowing." *ReVision* 22 (2000): 2–6.

Chapter Fourteen

The Civic Leadership of *Harry Potter*: Agency, Ritual, and Schooling

Rebecca Skulnick and Jesse Goodman

Rorty (1989) makes an excellent insight where he notes that throughout Western history, and, in particular, during the age of mass communication, young people's values and their conceptions of a good society are strongly and perhaps primarily influenced by children's popular culture. All one has to do is view TV news to know that, in the United States, the influence of popular music, films, and TV shows on young people is a regular topic of commentators. Unfortunately, this popular culture is rarely studied within the context of schooling. As a result, teachers have few opportunities to explore this powerful aspect of our society with the young people they are educating. As teachers, we often pass up wonderful opportunities to use particular artifacts of popular culture as catalysts for thoughtful social inquiry and self-reflection. Although some children's popular culture is studied by curriculum scholars (e.g., Giroux, 1989, 1999; Steinberg & Kincheloe, 1997), most of it is not considered appropriate material for study in elementary or high schools. However, every once in a great while, a product of popular culture finds its way into the classrooms of our nation's schools. The books of *Harry Potter* represent the rare occurrence when a well-written and thought-provoking series of books has been welcomed into the school curriculum. As a result, it has provided many teachers with excellent opportunities to engage children in thoughtful study of children's popular culture.

Given the length of this series, Harry and his world provide educators and their students with a plethora of potential topics for study. In an effort to take advantage of this opportunity, we explore one of the many potential topics that could possibly be studied by teachers and their students. As the title of this chapter suggests, we focus our analysis on the subject of civic leadership. First, we briefly explore the portrayal of Harry as a literary hero. However, we are most interested in the role that rituals play in the illumination of a central concept of civic leadership, namely, the issue of agency and circumstance. Finally, we take the lessons learned from this series of books, and we apply them to a situation of civic leadership, or the lack thereof, in a specific school. We conclude with some final thoughts on popular culture and curriculum.

Harry is both a typical and atypical hero. Like most young heroes in Western literature throughout history, from David Copperfield to Huckelberry Finn to Luke Skywalker, Harry Potter is a white male. However, Harry is not physically a stereotypical hero. He is skinny and appears weak, has black hair that falls in his face and sticks up no matter how many haircuts he receives, wears broken glasses, and even gets bullied by other students. However, like Clark Kent, Harry has magical powers that make him a Superman. These characteristics, of course, are part of what is so alluring about Harry. Most children can easily identify with this somewhat awkward looking boy, and fantasize about having his powers. Similar to other literary heroes, Harry is brave, honest, smart, athletic, and, perhaps, most important, willing to take risks for the "greater good."

Throughout Harry's adventures we observe him questioning authority and even breaking rules; however, he does so always for the purpose of advancing traditional notions of goodness. In fact, like much of children's literature, Harry's world is devoid of much ambiguity: Dumbledore's Hogwarts is good whereas Voldemort and his followers are evil. Even when Harry and his friends break rules, we know as readers that, in fact, their efforts are morally righteous. For example, Harry, Hermione, and Ron use Harry's Invisibility Cloak to travel, while they are supposed to be sleeping, to the forbidden forest and other such prohibited places. Harry's intentions, and therefore the results of his actions, typically uphold the "goodness" of Hogwarts.

Harry is also similar to those previously mentioned Western heroes in that he comes from less than ideal circumstances. His parents are dead, and he is raised by relatives who do not care for or about him and is even victimized by them. In addition, he must tolerate being humiliated by his cousin. However, Harry does not become bitter over his circumstances. To the contrary, he rises above them, and one gets the impression that his past provides the foundation for his compassion toward others. Throughout Harry's many adventures he befriends and defends the weak, downtrodden, and marginalized, including Moaning Myrtle, a ghost who cries in the bathroom, and Hagrid, the half-giant gamekeeper who earns (with Harry's help) the title of Hogwarts teacher. However, like so many Western heroes, his sense of caring and willingness to side with the less fortunate are limited. He does not question the basic justice of his world or school. He lives in a society dominated by those who have either cultural or economic capital. As one might expect from a British setting, it is a world and school in which classes are clearly distinguished and many take it for granted that those with greater capital (money or knowledge) are better human beings than those without these assets. It is also a world in which European men of good breeding are expected to rule. For all of his compassion and identification with those characters from the lower rungs, he never questions the gender, class, or European hegemony of his world.

Given this brief overview of Harry as hero, we can see that this series of books provides an interesting portrayal of heroes, and thus an opportunity to explore the nature of heroes and heroism. In pursuing this idea more fully, we now turn our attention to the role that rituals can play in understanding the phenomenon of civic leadership. When analyzing Harry's engagement with rituals, we can better discern his "civic virtues of self-discipline, civility, honesty, trust, courage, compassion, tolerance, and respect for the worth and dignity of all individuals" (Patrick, 2000a, p. 35). In each ritual Harry performs, he carries a certain amount of agency, and within this agency, he constructs his own civic heroism.

We begin by questioning how schooling, as an institution, uses ritual in order to cultivate civic heroism in *Harry Potter*. Harry's ability to construct himself as a civic hero depends on the particular institutional settings in which he performs rituals. In the Sorting Hat ceremony in *Harry Potter and the Sorcerer's Stone*, Harry sits center stage in a ceremonial room within Hogwarts. By the end of the ceremony, the readers know that he will be sorted into a house. The ending is scripted and the entire Hogwarts staff and students monitor his behavior. The second ritual we examine is performed outside on a sports field: Quidditch. During Quidditch matches, Harry's performance is not directly monitored by the staff: he performs outdoors on a field rather than in a ceremonial room and the end of the match is unknown. What is more, because Harry's behavior is not as directly monitored by the staff and students, he is better able to perform with agency. However, this lack of social control also brings the risk of miscreant activities. Finally, we will explore a speech ritual, Harry's pronouncement of the name "Voldemort," in order to further recognize Harry's unique civic courage. In looking at how these rituals constrain, facilitate, and provide opportunities for Harry to manifest his civic courage, the reader of these texts can gain a deeper understanding of the relationship between the characteristics of civic leaders and the community in which they are embedded.

Rituals and Civic Leadership

The primary discourse we examine in this chapter is that of ritual, namely, those ceremonies that denote Harry's status as a potential civic leader. In particular, we explore how Harry's participation in various rituals reflects and constitutes his potential toward civic leadership. As we previously mentioned, we have a special interest in understanding the ways in which rituals enable Harry to develop and manifest his civil leadership. In the *Harry Potter* books, a civic hero is not the human who follows the institution's rules. Rather, such an individual is one who makes choices and understands rules as socially negotiated agreements. Harry's choices are guided by his sense of citizenship, his ability to make concerted choices, and his willingness to negate or promote the rules of his popular government, the Hogwarts institution. While Harry may not act as a hero in the Muggle world, he is able to perform as an activist within the narrative of his experience as a student at Hogwarts. If Harry is able to perform as a hero within his school system, then his performance can prompt the readers of this text to question "how do we use our schools and other venues of education to more adequately prepare the people to assume their responsibilities of citizenship?" (Patrick, 2000b, p. 54). Through the study of this series, teachers and students would be wise to focus their attention on two formal and one informal rituals, the Sorting Hat ceremony, the Quidditch match, and the naming of evil.

The Sorting Hat Ceremony

Perhaps the first ritual of significance in the text occurs shortly after the children arrive at Hogwarts. Upon entering school, freshman students across the world are asked to perform rites of passage in public events for their peers, their teachers, and their institution. *Harry Potter* and the adolescent experience is full of such rituals. La Fontaine (1985, p. 79) notes that "initiation is a patterned performance whose purpose is action to achieve transformed individuals but whose effect is to demonstrate the power of traditional knowledge and legitimize a continuing social order." Each of Harry's rituals transforms him from a student into a leader. The first ritual that we examine represents the common dynamic of integrating new members into the existing social world of Hogwarts.

The Sorting Hat ceremony, which takes place at the beginning of every Hogwarts school year, is symbolic of a newcomer's quest to mark their identity as individuals, and more important, as members of a larger group, in this case, the students' house at Hogwarts. Marking the beginning of each academic year, this ritual sorts students into four different houses, in which, "each house will be something like your family" (Rowling, 1998, p. 114). The students spend their time at Hogwarts earning points so that they may win the coveted House Cup at the end of each school year. What is particularly noteworthy is that this ritual has an audience: the entire Hogwarts population of teachers, students, groundkeepers, and even ghosts. This public performance underscores the importance of the monitoring of public events and issues that must be understood in order to locate the potential participatory skills of democratic citizenship (Patrick, 2000b, p. 51). The Sorting Hat, an old and tattered wizard's hat, acts as the primary monitor of the ceremony and presumes all agency over this first ritual.

The hat is placed on a new student's head, and the individual is told to which house he or she belongs. The students are clearly told that "there's nothing hidden in your head/ the Sorting Hat can't see,/ So try me on and I will tell you/ Where you ought to be" (Rowling, 1998, p. 117). Most Hogwarts students react with fear to the magical hat that can see inside the heads of children. On the surface, this ritual suggests little potential for a student's agency: the hat is the ultimate decision maker. For example, when the hat is placed on Malfoy's head, "the hat had barely touched his head when it screamed, 'SLYTHERIN'" (Rowling, 1998, p.120). Malfoy is unable to react in between the hat's positioning and its calling.

Harry's experience with the hat is strikingly different from that of Malfoy and the other students. The moment of rupture in this ritual performance takes place silently, in a head to head discussion between Harry and the Sorting Hat. Rather than immediately pronounce to which house Harry belonged, as it had for Malfoy and the other students, the hat asks Harry a question, suggesting that Harry has some control over his positioning: "Plenty of courage, I see. Not a bad mind either. There's talent, oh my goodness, yes—and a nice thirst to prove yourself, now that's interesting . . . so where shall I put you?" (Rowling, 1998, p. 117). Harry sits in the center of the Hogwarts community when he is asked the question and answers, "Not Slytherin, not Slytherin." As a civic hero, Harry actively participates in the Sorting Hat ritual in a way that the other students do not. The hat asks Harry if he is sure, "Slytherin will help you on the way to greatness . . . Well, if you're sure, better be GRYFFINDOR" (Rowling, 1998, p. 121).

Both Harry and Malfoy possess leadership qualities. Both are able to convince others to follow where they go and what they do. However, whereas Harry is the text's hero, Malfoy acts as the text's antihero.[1] This hero/antihero relationship relies on a dichotomous relationship: the antihero performs as the antithesis of the hero while both are protagonists in the text. While Harry is skinny and lives with his Muggle aunt and uncle who treat him poorly, Draco Malfoy is stout and lives with parents who are "pure-blood" wizards, members of the wizard power structure, and who treat Draco like a prince. In this ceremony, Harry's identity is pronounced not in relation to who he is but in opposition to who he is not. Echoing Butler's (1998) theory on identity formation, the "self is from the start radically implicated in the Other" (p. 727). Harry searches to define himself as not Slytherin and defines Hogwarts as not Voldemort's domain. Perhaps Rowling is also portraying, through the Sorting Hat ceremony, an important distinction between noncivic and civic heroes, namely, the agency the latter plays in the creation of his/her own identity. The Sorting Hat places Draco in the house to which he knew he belonged while the hat listened to Harry and allows him to have a voice in the decision.

Harry seems to recognize the uniqueness of his position when he asks his mentor, the great Dumbledore, if he was supposed to belong to Gryffindor rather than Slytherin. Dumbledore responds, "It is our choices, Harry, that show what we truly are, far more than our abilities" (Rowling, 1999a, p. 333). However, even though Harry is positioned to have choices that suggest his agency, the degree of this agency is questionable. Did Harry construct his own identity or did the hat trick him into believing in his own self-construction in order to manipulate him so that he would have more faith in the Hogwarts system? The Sorting Hat not only validates the power of Hogwarts but also demonstrates the dissonance between self-determination and predetermination: are civic identities comprised of choices or are they a birthright? Long after the ceremony is over, this question is dramatized when Harry has nightmares that "he must transfer to Slytherin at once, because it was his destiny" (Rowling, 1999a, p. 206). In cultures that are marked by democratic citizenship and in the world of Harry Potter, neither destiny nor an institution can create a hero. Rather, citizenship depends upon the "knowledge, skills, habit, and actions of committed citizens and the political and civic conditions they create, and not merely on . . . institutional structures" (Patrick, 2000a, p. 36). Harry's decision to participate in the Gryffindor house was based on his action as a committed citizen and the conditions he created for himself within the constraints of his environment.

The Sorting Hat ceremony not only introduces the readers to Harry's world—the students, professors, ghosts, villains, and the institution of Hogwarts itself (symbolically manifested in the Sorting Hat), but also to the central question of agency in the construction of the civic hero's identity. We now turn our attention toward understanding how Harry performs his civic leadership in front of his peers in order to gain deeper insight into how Rowling positions Harry as a civic hero. It is in this ceremony that readers might notice how a hero maintains agency even in constraining circumstances.

Quidditch

Stoeltje (1988) suggests that any narrative is comprised of rituals that respond to each other in order to create an institution that enables and disenables an individual's agency. When a ritual is conducted under the monitoring of the institution, the individual is less able to act as a subversive agent, and others are less able to undermine the institution by breaking the ritual's rules. During the Sorting Hat ceremony, all of Hogwarts gather in the Great Hall and watch each new student get sorted into a house. The ceremony is monitored and the students have little room to protest their placement. Quidditch matches, conversely, are played outdoors and performed more for the Hogwarts students than for the Hogwarts staff. Both environments allow for the participatory skills of interacting, monitoring, and influencing what a civic leader must possess (Patrick, 2000b). Additionally, both environments act as places where rites of passage are performed. While U.S. students represent their schools as sports players or musicians, Hogwarts students play Quidditch. A seemingly innocuous and inconspicuous ritual, Quidditch provides Harry with a place to demonstrate his agility and strength and augment his magical powers with athletic dexterity. When a ritual is not directly monitored by the administration of an institution, subversive activity becomes more frequent. While Quidditch's adult audience is present and involved in the game, they are not as directly in control of the field's performance space as they were in the Great Hall during the Sorting Hat ceremony. It is no coincidence that Quidditch matches allow for more subversive activity than the Sorting Hat ceremony.

While Harry did not break rules during the Sorting Hat ceremony, and, instead, negotiated with the hat to define his belonging, he did break rules when it came to flying. According to the second letter sent to Harry, "Parents are reminded that first years are not allowed their own broomsticks" (Rowling, 1998, p. 67). The first Hogwarts rule that the text pronounces concerns owning broomsticks and the regulation of magic. During a flying lesson, a Slytherin made fun of Harry and, in retaliation, he ignored the orders of Madam Hooch, "none of you is to move. You leave those brooms where they are or you'll all be out of Hogwarts before you can say Quidditch" (Rowling, 1998, p. 147). Even though Harry (unlike children who were born into wizard families) had never before flown, he picked up the broom and flew with agility and strength. Rather than punish Harry, however, Professor McGonagall led him to the captain of his house's Quidditch team, gave him his own broom, and allowed him to be the team Seeker, the most coveted position on the Quidditch team.

Harry's choice to fly underscores a major trait of civic heroism: rules may be broken when their rupture serves to uphold rather than subvert the cultural values embedded in the institution. The need for a talented Seeker was more important to the maintenance of Hogwarts's society than to the upholding of the broom-flying rule. The text does not confirm why McGonagall was willing to break the flying rules; perhaps this teacher wanted to support her team, the Gryffindors; she might have wanted to promote Harry Potter as a hero of Hogwarts. Both of these reasons may be interpreted as immoral. Even so, what is more important than McGonagall's immorality is her ability to choose with selfish intentions and remain a "good" character. Potter characters frequently act out of selfish intentions but they always remain "good" so long as their acts do not threaten the demise of Hogwarts. Once again, Harry prompts us to notice that rules are negotiable and the institution of Hogwarts is a moral place because it allows for the negotiation of it own socially constructed rules.

Whereas the Sorting Hat ceremony highlighted the importance of the institution's affirmation of Harry's heroic agency, the Quidditch match underscores the importance of peer affirmation of Harry's heroic agility. Conducted on an informal and public field, the Hogwarts students' gaze is an important monitoring device on the Quidditch field.[2] Harry earns praise from his peers as the boy who was able to break the school rules in order to play on the Quidditch field: "they had painted a large banner on one of the sheets . . . it said Potter for President, and Dean, who was good at drawing, had done a large Gryffindor lion underneath. Then Hermione had performed a tricky little charm so that the paint flashed different colors" (p. 184). Allowing Harry to be Seeker reaffirms his position as hero both to his peers at Hogwarts and to his readers. It is on the Quidditch field that readers notice the intense support Harry receives from his peer community and his friends Hermione and Ron.

If the Quidditch field is a place where Harry may find reward for breaking rules, a place where the rules of the institution can be negotiated, then the field is also a place that might undermine this same institution. It is also important to note that Quidditch is not performed inside the safe (and enchanted) haven of Hogwarts or monitored primarily by the Hogwarts faculty. Unlike the Great Hall, the Quidditch field is not enchanted and, although adults were present during the Quidditch games, they were unable to save Harry from the magical spell put on his broom. During one of the more important Quidditch matches, Harry's broom becomes entranced and behaves "as though the broom was trying to buck him off . . . zigzagging through the air, and every now and then making violent swishing movements that almost unseated him" (Rowling, 1998, p. 189). The broom was enchanted by the stuttering Professor Quirrell, a teacher who acted as the Defense Against the Dark Ages teacher at Hogwarts in order to work covertly for the evil Lord Voldemort and capture the famous Sorcerer's Stone that would ensure its owner eternal life. Hermione and Ron believed that the broom was jinxed by Snape, who "had his eyes fixed on Harry and was muttering nonstop under his breath" when, in reality, Snape was trying to save Harry. While trying to focus on Snape, the two friends "knocked Professor Quirrell headfirst into the front row" and unknowingly, the two friends rescue Harry (Rowling, 1998, p. 190).

The scene demonstrated two very important concepts. The first is related to the Quidditch field as an institution that is not formally monitored: Quirrell is able to abuse the rules of the institution in order to subvert the institution because of the informal position of the Quidditch ritual. Therefore, while the Quidditch field serves as a place for Harry to show off his ability to make choices and demonstrate civic agency, it also serves as a place where others may make nefarious choices and contradict the ideals of heroic citizenship. The place in which citizens may influence policy decisions is also the place in which the institution may be undermined.

The second concept the Quidditch field emphasizes is the importance of community support. When Hermione and Ron realized that the broom was hypnotized, they recalled and effectively enacted a charm to rescue their friend. Even though their immediate intention was to disarm Snape, their primary objective was to protect their friend. Harry would not have been able to succeed on the Quidditch field had it not been for the support of his friends. Unlike the Rambo hero who single-handedly fights as a representative of his country, Harry Potter is the hero who remains embedded in his community rather than separate from it; he utilizes the support of his friends and community in order to support his mission and deter his enemies. The most dramatic time in which Harry utilized the help of his friends was in *Harry Potter and the Goblet of Fire* during the Triwizard Tournament in which the only way Harry could effectively win the tournament was to completely depend upon his friends' particular skills. Like the Triwizard Tournament, a public game where Voldemort's followers were also were able to invade, the Quidditch field is the civic place where both danger and heroism are possible, where wizards may interact with other citizens in order to promote citizenship.

Pronouncing Evil

Civic heroes perform their strength in their institution not only through action but also through the act of speech and names. Most superheroes have both given and superhuman names, for example, Anakin Skywalker is called Darth Vader and Clark Kent is called Superman. Harry, however, is always known as Harry Potter. In *Harry Potter and the Chamber of Secrets*, Aragog, a fierce spider, feeds off humans but saves Harry because of his relation to Hagrid, Aragog's surrogate father. When Harry asks Aragog who it is that he fears (since this villain would lead Harry to defeat Voldemort), Aragog answers, "*(w)e do not speak of it* . . . we do not name it. I have not even told Hagrid the name of that dread creature, though he asked me, many times" (p. 279). Aragog proves to the readers that, even though he is physically dangerous, he does not have the strength to name evil.

Rowling distinguishes her hero, Harry, from others by emphasizing the heroic strength he has to call a thing by its given name rather than its pseudonym. Neither Harry's peers nor his teachers at Hogwarts will say the name Voldemort out loud; rather, they call him *he who must not be named*. Not speaking the name Voldemort becomes a de-facto ritual that all follow; all except Harry and Dumbledore. Individualizing himself from the rest of his peer community, Harry likens himself to his mentor, Dumbeldore, who also speaks the name Voldemort. As opposed to Aragog and his other peers, Harry names evil Voldemort and confirms the goodness of the institution. One of the key cognitive skills of democratic citizenship, according to Patrick (2000b), is the civic leader's ability to articulate phenomena or events of political and civic life. Neither Dumbledore nor Harry is physically strong, and neither destroys life; they do, however, continually exhibit courage and fortitude as a member of Hogwarts by articulating evil.

In explaining language as a ritual, Butler (1997) cites Toni Morrison's Nobel Prize speech on the agency in language. In this speech, Morrison explains that "we do things with language, produce effects with language, and we do things to language, but language is also the thing that we do, language is a name for our doing: both 'what' we do and that which we affect, the act and its consequence" (quoted in Bulter, 1997, p. 11). While the Sorting Hat ceremony and Quidditch facilitated the becoming of Harry's civic leadership, this ritual is the manifestation of his civic leadership: it is both what Harry does and what he affects.

We have already established that Harry breaks Hogwarts rules, often risking his life, in his quest to fight his evil villain, Lord Voldemort. He wears an Invisibility Cloak in *Sorcerer's Stone*, transfigures into Slytherins in *Chamber of Secrets*, saves a convicted felon in *Harry Potter and the Prisoner of Azkaban*, and breaks the rules of the Triwizard Tournament in order to save Hermione's life in *Goblet of Fire*. Why is naming evil any different a function than breaking these other rules? All of the aforementioned rules and Harry's disregard for those rules are pronounced and legitimized by both the magical and Hogwarts communities. While Harry's peers envy his Quidditch skills and his magical dexterity, they seem uncertain about his willingness to pronounce the name Voldemort.

It is Harry's inconspicuous speech act,[3] pronouncing the name Voldemort that firmly distinguishes his performance from that of his peers: this ritual act of speaking demonstrates Harry's willingness to act against the de-facto ritual of his friends and uphold his own civic heroism. Harry's ability to call Voldemort by his name is supported and explained by his mentor, Dumbledore. According to Dumbledore (Rowling, 1998), the reason why Harry should continue to call Voldemort by his name is because a hero should "always use the proper name for things. Fear of a name increases the fear of the thing itself" (p. 298). Therefore, Harry's pronouncement indicates his lack of fear of Voldemort's evil powers and his faith in Hogwarts's good powers. While during the Sorting Hat ceremony and the Quidditch match, Harry performed in congruence with the tradition of Hogwarts, Harry's pronouncement of Voldemort contradicts the "tradition" of Hogwarts. Rather than supporting Harry's growth as a civic leader, this inconspicuous speech ritual demonstrates Harry's heroic accomplishment. Even so, Harry's ability to contradict tradition relied on the support of his mentor.

Harry's speech act verifies that in the *Harry Potter* world, those who are evil are defined as those who work against the life of wizards and those who are good are defined as those who work for the institution. Like most of the Centaurs, Harry does not question the validity of his heavens, the Hogwarts institution, and the power of Albus Dumbledore (Rowling, 1999a). After successfully defeating his villain, Harry tells Voldemort that he is not the greatest sorcerer in the world because "the greatest wizard in the world is Albus Dumbledore." Harry's proof? "Everyone says so. Even when you were strong you didn't dare try and take over at Hogwarts. Dumbledore saw through you when you were at school and he still frightens you now, wherever you're hiding these days'" (p. 314). Harry pronounces both what is evil and what is good based on the institution in which he is lent the power of hero.

Additionally, Harry does not question whether he acts on behalf of good or evil. Perhaps this is why the *Harry Potter* series is a respite for so many people, both young and old: the magical Hogwarts community is one that does not question the integrity of the institution itself. What is called evil is evil and what is called good is good. As individuals working within our own hegemonic structures, *Harry Potter* readers may finish their novels feeling relieved that they do not have to destroy their institution(s) in order to fight against evil forces and retain some sense of agency, some ability to negotiate rules; that one can become a civic leader without having to reconstruct the institution's hegemonic structure. Even though at the end of *Goblet of Fire*, Dumbledore voices grave concerns about the

Ministry of Magic, the largest and most powerful institution of the magical world, no one (besides the evil Voldemort) questions Dumbledore.

Harry Potter and a Fifth-Grade Classroom: A Contemporary Folktale

The characters of *Harry Potter* are not only those who exist inside the actual narrative, the folktale, but also those who read the text and perform rituals of their own, those who participate in schooling rituals and are thus a part of the larger folklore. The folklore of *Harry Potter* is currently being performed throughout the world. The most stirring stories we have heard concerning the *Harry Potter* series were those performed in the public schools, where *Harry Potter* has been banned and lauded with equal force. As bell hooks (1990, p. 5) pronounces,

> We . . . identify and construct ourselves as social beings through the mediation of images. This is not simply a case of people being dominated by images, but of people seeking and obtaining pleasure through the experience of the consumption of those images. An understanding of contemporary culture involves a focus on both the phenomenology of watching and the cultural form of images.

The contemporary culture that consumes the *Harry Potter* series, as the volumes collect on the shelves, shares classroom (and cultural) space with those who protest the books' message as antireligious. If the *Harry Potter* series were to affirm that our institutions should not be completely and absolutely trusted, the fact that some school systems across the United States are banning these books would not run contrary to the message in *Harry Potter*. However, if Hogwarts is a noble institution and children-readers consume this image by having blind faith in their institutions, they will be severely disappointed. A hero is not just someone who upholds the value system of the institution in which she or he belongs but rather is someone whose consciousness of the changing needs of individuals who survive in a given institution allows them to change it.

Once upon a time, in a small town located between Kalamazoo and Grand Rapids in western Michigan, a young teacher wanted to read *Harry Potter* aloud to her fifth-grade classroom.[4] She knew that reading this contested novel might present a controversy and so she asked all parents at the annual Open House if they would object to their children reading the series in class. No parents objected, the teacher read, and the children were enamored with our civic leader, Harry Potter. The teacher was thrilled, the children wanted to read along with the teacher, everyone looked forward to silent reading time, and the parents seemed happy.

However, after two weeks, one mother, whom the teacher calls, "the smother mother," decided that her religious beliefs oppose the messages conveyed in *Harry Potter*, even though she had not yet read the books. This mother was very powerful in the community. She was the wife of a government official and a member of one of the only upper-middle-class families in the district. The teacher spoke to the mother at length and gave the parent an article that explains how *Harry Potter* upholds traditional Judeo-Christian values. Even so, the parent preferred to read the book to her child at home so that she could augment the reading with lessons on religious morality.

Not wanting to cause too much of a stir, the teacher asked the parent if it would be okay for the child to go to the library during reading time since she already was almost half-way through *Sorcerer's Stone*. The parent was happy, the teacher was happy, and the students were happy. After speaking with the smother mother's child about the situation while leading her to the library, the teacher felt certain that this situation was best for everyone and that this child was happy to have reading time separate from the class. She was always eager to go to the library and offered reading suggestions to the teacher upon her return to the classroom.

Two weeks later, the parent decided that taking the child out of class was humiliating. Rather than speak to the teacher about this humiliation, the parent went to the first-year principal and asked him to take the book out of all classrooms. That week, the principal held a meeting with all of the teachers and told them that they must ask him for permission to read any books aloud in their classrooms. The teachers were aware that this declaration was related to the *Sorcerer's Stone* scenario. In addition, none of the fifth-grade teachers, all of whom were reading the *Harry Potter* series to their classes, had tenure and none wanted the new principal to think they were unresponsive to his situation.

When the teacher returned to her classroom, she told her students that the principal didn't want them to read *Harry Potter*. The class had a one-hour discussion about how they felt; most children told this teacher that they felt mad or sad and didn't understand why they couldn't read this story. The teacher told her students that she too felt sad and mad and she told the children that they could bring in their own copies of *Harry Potter* and read them during silent sustained reading. And so they did. *Harry*

Potter became the most popular book of the class. Children read during lunch, they read during their playtime, and they happily read during silent sustained reading. All children, that is, except Henry.

Like the other children in the class, Henry turned the pages of *Sorcerer's Stone* with ferocity. But not because he was reading. He couldn't read. Henry had severe learning difficulties, he was emotionally impaired, and he could not read the *Harry Potter* series. Instead, he pretended to read until it all became too much for him to handle. After two weeks of silent sustained reading, Henry took his book to the bathroom, tore apart all of the pages, and cried until the teacher found him and held him and told him that everything would be okay—that she could get him *Sorcerer's Stone* on tape, and he could listen to the stories while he read.

Rather than end with a sense of closure, this folktale ends with a teacher's and student's frustration. The children were suffering because of the power inherent in her institution: because a mother with power who had never read the book objected to this curricular choice; because the principal was too concerned with his first-year position to contradict the sentiments of the commissioner's wife; because the teacher was too scared of losing her position to read *Harry Potter* and reject her principal's rule.

Harry Potter tells us that the institution is a place of goodness; if you only trust in the institution, or act as Harry and perform rites of heroism in favor of the institution, the institution will support the interests of the children. What happens, then, when principals make decisions based on the politics of their constituents, when teachers do not act out of fear of losing their jobs, when students rip up books because they cannot read? If *Harry Potter*, the folktale and folklore, is to teach us anything about heroism, it teaches us that "(i)t is our choices . . . that show what we truly are, far more than our abilities."

Conclusion

When determining how to make heroic choices, teachers and administrators would be wise to seek the advice of Harry Potter. While nontenured teachers must choose their battles wisely, they would be wise to follow the advice of our hero, Harry. First, Harry proves that it is necessary for institutions to allow for individual agency. While the Sorting Hat ceremony allowed Harry to compromise with the hat in order to find his place, the elementary school principal written about in the above passage was not able to compromise with the teacher. This principal's decision resulted in a banned book.

Second, the *Harry Potter* series suggests that where evil may usurp goodness, a hero relies on his friends. Likewise, the hallways of any school building links nontenured teachers to tenured teachers and become the inconspicuous places where new teachers receive mentoring and support. The mentor program is a schooling ritual that must link teachers together: the only way new teachers will be able to make effective decisions is if they work with other teachers and create a community of support. It is important for those teachers who are not on the "Quidditch field," those who are tenured and secure in their position, to be vocal about their support of nontenured teacher's choices. If the entire fifth-grade teaching staff would have supported the nontenured teacher, she may have been able to reach a successful compromise with her principal and the parent.

Finally, teachers pronounce their civic leadership every day before their student audience. Neither saying the name Voldemort nor reading *Harry Potter* was ever declared "against the rules." Rather, teachers and Harry were strongly discouraged from practicing these rituals. When the institution's de-facto rituals do not support the goodness of the institution, tenured teachers might consider not following such rituals and nontenured teachers might consider asking the tenured teachers, as Harry asked Dumbledore, to lend support as to why it is important to not follow such rituals.

In this chapter, we have emphasized the fact that educational civic leaders must be willing to pronounce the important goals of education, supporting the needs of the students and teachers' integrity. "Supporting student needs" is a much more ambiguous concept than "supporting Hogwarts" and therefore the tactics used to support its intention are more difficult to conceive. Even so, civic leadership must include the ability to either question or not question the institution itself as if it were always like the Quidditch field, a place that can house both good and evil. Students do not simply need a standardized curriculum of canon friendly material; they need a curriculum that can affect their lives as potential civic heroes. Rather than simply denounce efforts by teachers to find a place for popular culture in the lives of their classrooms, we would encourage administrators, teachers, and parents to look seriously at the lessons popular culture can teach classrooms, teachers, and students alike.

Notes

1. Additionally, Dumbledore may be characterized as another textual hero and Voldemort his antihero.

2. The term "gaze" is used in performance theory and cultural studies, to describe when looking is an active, rather than passive, monitoring device (DeLauretis, 1984).

3. The term "speech act" was coined by Judith Butler (1997) in order to emphasize that speech and language comprise an action as well as a method of communication.

4. This account was communicated to us by Ms. J. Rubin, the teacher at this school.

References

Butler, J. *Excitable Speech: a Politics of the Performative*. New York: Routledge, 1997.

———. "Imitation and Gender Subordination." In *Literary Theory: An Anthology*. Ed. M. Ryan. Malden: Blackwell Publishers, 1998.

de Lauretis, T. *Alice Doesn't: Feminism, Semiotics, Cinema*. Bloomington: Indiana UP, 1984.

Giroux, H. *Popular Culture, Schooling, and Everyday Life*. New York: Bergin and Garvey, 1989.

———. *The Mouse that Roared: Disney and the End of Innocence*. Lanham: Rowman and Littlefield, 1999.

hooks, b. *Yearning: Race, Gender, and Cultural Politics*. Boston: South End P, 1990.

La Fontaine, J. S. L. *Initiation: Ritual Drama and Secret Knowledge across the World*. New York: Viking Penguin, 1985.

Patrick, J. "Concepts at the core of education for democratic citizenship." In *Principles and Practices of Education for Democratic Citizenship: International Perspectives and Projects*. Ed. C. Bahmueller and J. Patrick. Bloomington: ERIC, 2000a. 1–40.

———. "Education for Constructive Engagement of Citizens." In *Principles and Practices of Education for Democratic Citizenship: International Perspectives and Projects*. Ed. C. Bahmueller and J. Patrick Bloomington: ERIC, 2000b. 40–60.

Rorty, R. *Contingency, Irony, and Solidarity*. Cambridge: Cambridge UP, 1989.

Rowling, J. K. *Harry Potter and the Sorcerer's Stone*. New York: Scholastic P, 1998.

———. *Harry Potter and the Chamber of Secrets*. New York: Scholastic P, 1999a.

———. *Harry Potter and the Prisoner of Azkaban*. New York: Scholastic P, 1999b.

———. *Harry Potter and the Goblet of Fire*. New York: Scholastic P, 2000.

Steinberg, S., and J. Kincheloe. *Kinderculture: The Corporate Construction of Childhood*. Boulder: Westview P, 1997.

Stoeltje, B. "Gender Representations in Performance: The Cowgirl and the Hostess." *Journal of Folklore Research* 25.3 (1988): 219–41.

Appendix

Authenticity in *Harry Potter—* The Movie and the Books

Alexander R. Wang

I have read various volumes of the *Harry Potter* books approximately fifteen times each and have reread the first book about twenty times. I enjoy the characters and their development, the complexity of the plot, and the creativity of the details. For these reasons, I am very much aware of the fine points of the books and have been disappointed when details within the texts seemed to be inconsistent. I disapproved of the books being made into a movie because I believed it would hurt the image of the books. I have seen many books made into films and I usually prefer the experience of the book. My judgment of the movie would have been more favorable if I hadn't read the books, but I was dissatisfied by both the mood and the details of the movie. The following lists reveal my concerns about authenticity. I know that there are many other details that could be added to such lists, but these were the ones that struck me as particularly significant.

I. How the Movie Portrays the Book

As I watched the movie, I really noticed that it didn't portray what Harry was thinking or feeling. This was my biggest concern. The presentation made you guess how he was feeling and that hurts the character in general because he is a very thoughtful boy and it develops the plot if you know what he is thinking. There were also many details that could have easily been more authentic. The following list refers to a comparison of the book (Rowling, 1997) and movie (Heyman, 2001) each with the same title, *Harry Potter and the Sorcerer's Stone.*

1.) The "Put-Outer" was suppose to look like an ordinary cigarette lighter, which it did not. In the movie they had it look like some magical device (p. 9).

2.) McGongall was too old in the beginning of the movie. She was not an old woman thirteen years before Harry went to school because it was thirteen years before.

3.) Dudley was supposed to be enormous. I, personally, pictured him as a great fat boy. In *Harry Potter and the Chamber of Secrets*, he was described as wider than he was tall. He couldn't have changed so much from the first book.

4.) Dudley was also supposed to be blonde as was Aunt Petunia (p. 21).

5.) They didn't take Dudley's friend with them to the zoo, so it didn't seem as big of a deal when Harry went (p. 27).

6.) When the glass to the snake cage disappeared it never reappeared and trapped Dudley inside (pp. 28–29).

7.) When the Hogwarts letters started to come owls did not bring them. They came in so many numbers because Dumbledore let Hagrid use his magic (p. 63).

8.) The Dursleys just left after the Sunday and drove for a day before stopping on the hut on the rock (p. 41–44).

9.) Hagrid came and Uncle Vernon threatened him with a gun. Hagrid then twisted the gun. Not stating that Hagrid could twist the iron makes Hagrid seem less intimidating in my opinion (p. 47).

10.) Harry was supposed to have wild black hair and green eyes (it said so throughout the book), but his hair was brown and reasonably neat and his eyes looked blue.

11.) The broomsticks were not crooked and rough. The nimbus was described as sleek. Why would someone want a crooked broom? "Sleek and shiny, with a mahogany handle, it had a long tail of neat straight twigs and Nimbus Two Thousand written in gold near the top" (p. 166).

12.) The Vault 713 did not open but "simply melted away"(p. 75).

13.) Harry does not meet Malfoy on the train, but in the robe shop that he never went to in the movie (p. 77).

14.) Harry tries a lot more wands before getting the right one (pp. 82–84).

15.) When Hagrid tells Harry about Voldemort they are at the hut on a rock, not at a restaurant (pp. 54–55).

16.) Hagrid sees Harry off to go back to the Dursleys, not to Hogwarts. And the Dursleys bring Harry to the station on their way to get his cousin Dudley's pig tail removed (p. 90).

17.) The candy, Chocolate Frogs, were not actual frogs that bounce around. They are eaten like chocolate bunnies for Easter. At least that is how I thought of them when I was reading about them.

18.) Harry never reads the back of the Chocolate Frog so he never found out about the Sorcerer's Stone (pp. 102–3).

19.) Hermione was not the first to be sorted (p. 119).

20.) Hermione, when she was sorted, "almost ran to the stool" (p. 120) but in the movie she looked nervous.

21.) The third corridor was not found because the staircase moved. It was because of the midnight duel, which they neglected to put in (chapter 9).

22.) In the Quidditch match, no one ever fell off their brooms. That was just an easy way to put some action in the story, when they left out a lot of the real action.

23.) Harry never surfs on the broom. That was probably the worst thing that they could have done, in my opinion, because, in the book, Quidditch is a very serious sport, but in the movie, it seems like some little kids' game half the time.

24.) When Hagrid gets the dragon, Dumbledore never found out.

25.) The plant that is under the trap door does not hate sunlight. It hates fire (p. 278).

26.) They skipped the dead troll under the trap door in the movie (p. 284).

27.) They skipped Snape's challenge with the potions and logic (p. 286).

28.) The keys that were bewitched never attacked Harry (p. 280).

29.) I did not think that the stone would be a shining ruby but more of a rock-like stone.

30.) At the end of the book, when Harry touches Quirrell, Quirrell does not turn to dust. He gets boiled.

32.) Voldemort never went though Harry's body. Harry's scar was giving him too much pain to handle because it gets painful when Voldemort is near or when Voldemort is feeling murderous.

II. Inconsistencies within the Books

Although I enjoy many of the details of the books and find the fantasy enjoyable, there are inconsistencies within the books that are hard to ignore. These inconsistencies create doubts that interfere with the integrity of the fantasy world. It is harder to get lost in a world when that world doesn't hold together. A reader should worry about the characters and not the author's use of details. The following list includes details from each of the first four books.

1.) If the ghosts are present and can chat with students, why aren't Harry Potter's parents ghosts? Who is allowed to be a ghost and why? If murder victims (like Nearly Headless Nick) are allowed or forced to stay in a ghost form, then Harry's parents would be there. If they only let people with unfinished business become ghosts Harry's parents would be ghosts since his parents still had to raise him.

2.) Why do these kids absolutely never miss their parents when they are at school? Do all of these kids come from a situation like Harry's? Obviously not because Ron has nice parents.

3.) If Harry Potter was raised with such severe child abuse, why isn't he weird?

4.) Why don't the students ever take regular classes such as Math or English?

5.) Why do so many things have to be purchased instead of conjured up?

6.) Why would decent quality wizards live in poverty? Couldn't they perform basic magic to gain material goods?

7.) Wouldn't it be a simple spell for Ron to make his old robes new looking? Wouldn't this be pretty easy magic for his parents?

8.) Why don't the Weasleys have a house elf since elves don't get any money or reward for working?

9.) Why do Ginny and Ron have secondhand wands when there is supposed to be a special one for each person and wizards "will never get quite as good results with another wizard's wand"? Is Ron actually a super good wizard since he gets pretty good results from his used wand? And then, why does he get the same results when he finally gets a new wand?

10.) How could the Marauder's Map really be useful? It is described as a regular map that can fold, yet Hogwarts is a complicated three-dimensional place.

11.) Why couldn't Lupin turn into a werewolf any time there was a full moon? If there were clouds, he couldn't change.

12.) How did Mrs. Weasley get money from Harry's vault?

13.) Why aren't any flying lessons described after the first one? Do students only get one lesson? What does Madame Hooch do besides give one lesson?

14.) Why would there be a sign at the first Quidditch match saying "Potter for President" in Britain?

15.) Why do the Hogwarts's toilets empty into the lake? This is disgusting, especially since Merpeople live there. Why wouldn't magic or modern plumbing be used to solve this problem?

16.) If there is a French school for wizards, is there an American one? Asian or African schools?

17.) Why wouldn't all the other kids keep on playing Quidditch during a Tournament year?

18.) If Moody just wanted to make something into a portkey and get

Harry to touch it so that he could be delivered to Voldemort, why didn't he use an ordinary object that he was sure Harry would touch? Why did it have to be the tournament cup, which Harry might not have gotten to first?

References

Harry Potter and the Sorcerer's Stone. Dir. C. Columbus. Prod. D. Heyman. Warner Brothers, 2001.

Rowling, J. K. *Harry Potter and the Sorcerer's Stone.* New York: Scholastic P, 1997.

———. *Harry Potter and the Chamber of Secrets.* New York: Scholastic P, 1998.

———. *Harry Potter and the Prisoner of Azkaban.* New York: Scholastic P, 1999.

———. *Harry Potter and the Goblet of Fire.* New York: Scholastic P, 2000.

Contributors

Anne Hiebert Alton is an associate professor of English at Central Michigan University, where she teaches courses in children's and Victorian literature. Her recent publications include articles on P.L. Travers and Diane Duane, along with a scholarly edition of *Little Women* (2001).

Hollie Anderson teaches fifth grade at Window Rock Elementary School within the Navajo Nation. She has a master's degree from Purdue University, where she taught multicultural education. She did her undergraduate work at Northern Arizona University. She is interested in Navajo education, multiculturalism, and ethnic identity.

Peter Appelbaum is an associate professor of curriculum theory and math/science/technology education at Arcadia University. He is the author of *Popular Culture, Educational Discourse and Mathematics* (1995) and co-editor of *(Post) Modern Science (Education)* (2000). His research interrogates the liminal terrain of curriculum theorizing, technoculture, and children's experiences of consumer culture.

Ernest Bond is an associate professor of education at Salisbury State University in Maryland. Among other writings, he has entries in the *Cambridge Guide to Children's Literature* and manages the U.S. Board on Books for Young People's website (http://www.usbby.org) and Children's Literature Links (http://home.earthlink.net/~elbond/home.htm) and is authoring young adult literaure textbooks for Merril/Prentice Hall.

Deborah De Rosa is an assistant professor of English at Northern Illinois University. Her recent publications include book chapters on womanist approaches in Toni Morrison's novels and the book, *Into the Mouths of Babes: Nineteenth-Century Domestic Abolitionists' Literary Subversions* (2002).

Charles Elster is an associate professor of literacy education at Purdue University. He conducts research and teaches courses in early literacy acquisition, influences of textual and contextual variables on reading processes, and classroom uses of children's literature.

Jesse Goodman is a professor at Indiana University. His scholarly interests include the relationship between education and democracy, issues of school reform, teacher education/socialization, and research methodology. He has had over thirty manuscripts on these topics published in a wide variety of scholarly journals and books, and has received five national awards for distinguished research. He is the author of *Elementary Schooling for Critical Democracy* (1992), and he is currently working on two books.

Anne E. Gregory is an assistant professor of reading education at Boise State University. She researches and teaches courses in early literacy acquisition, examining specifically the role of intersubjectivity, cultural learning, and intertextuality in this complex process.

Elizabeth E. Heilman is an assistant professor in the College of Education at Michigan State University. Her research on ideology, gender, culture, and social class appears in journals such as *Youth and Society, The High School Journal,* and *Theory and Research in Social Education.*

John Kornfeld is an associate professor and director of graduate studies in the School of Education at Sonoma State University. His research in curriculum, children's literature, and school/university collaboration has been published in such journals as *Theory into Practice, The Teacher Educator, Social Education,* and *Theory and Research in Social Education.*

Kathleen F. Malu is an assistant professor of education at William Paterson University of New Jersey where she teaches in the Graduate Reading Program. She has taught language and literacy at the K-12 level for many years in a wide variety of settings including the Congo, Rwanda, Washington, DC, and the United Nations International School in New York City. Her research interests include multicultural education, teaching rhetoric and practice, and education reform at the middle level. She is the mother of two boys who attended New York City public schools.

Nancy Michelson is an associate professor of reading in the Education Department at Salisbury University, where she is director of the John & Florence Simonds Literacy Lab. She is a coauthor of "Literature-based Curricula in High Poverty Schools," in *The First R: Every Child's Right to Read,* and a contributing writer for *Tapestry: A Multicultural Anthology,* among other works.

Maria Nikolajeva is a professor of comparative literature at Stockholm University, Sweden. She is the author and editor of several books on children's literature, among them *Children's Literature Comes of Age: Toward the New Aesthetic* (1996) and *From Mythic to Linear: Time in Children's Literature* (2000).

Laurie Prothro is a school library consultant and children's librarian in Sonoma County, California. She specializes in collection development and young adult literature. Her most recent publication, *Shared Stories: Exploring Cultural Diversity,* accompanied a traveling art exhibit of multicultural children's picture books.

Heather L. Servaty is an assistant professor at Purdue University. She is the current book review editor of *Omega: Journal of Death and Dying.* Her principal interests include issues of death and dying with particular emphases on the developmental aspects of grief, death-related attitudes and beliefs, and loss as a broad conceptual model.

Rebecca Skulnick is pursuing a Ph.D. in curriculum studies and American studies as a Dean's Fellow at Indiana University where she teaches in the secondary education program. She is currently writing her dissertation on the relationship between adolescent development, visual rhetoric, peer group cultures, activism, and schooling.

Deborah J. Taub is associate professor of educational studies and coordinator of the graduate program in College Student Personnel at Purdue University. Her M.A. and Ph.D. are from the University of Maryland, College Park. She has a B.A. in English from Oberlin College. A longtime reader of fantasy, she is the mother of two.

Tammy Turner-Vorbeck is pursuing a Ph.D. in curriculum studies at Purdue University. Her focus includes multiculturalism/diversity, curriculum theory, and sociology of education. Her research explores relationships among schooling, culture, and identity, particularly family structure diversity and equity issues.

Alexander R. Wang, "Alex," born in 1988, wrote this as a student at West Lafayette Jr. / Sr. High School in Indiana. He coauthored a paper for the American Educational Research Association conference on Harry Potter in 2001. His favorite authors besides J. K. Rowling include Orson Scott Card, S. E. Hinton, and John Grisham.

Index